Exam Guide with Key points and Workbook

Chemistry

For the Pearson Edexcel Level 1/Level 2 GCSE (9-1)

GCSE in Combined Science and GCSE in Chemistry

First Edition

Mahesh Selvaraj

Exam guide with key points and workbook

Chemistry 2019 edition

For the Pearson Edexcel Level 1/Level 2 GCSE (9-1)

ISBN: 978-1-9996443-4-5

First Published 2019

© Mr. Chem Education Limited

The moral rights of the author have been asserted with the Copyright,

Design and Patents Act 1988.

All rights reserved. No part of this publication may be copied, reproduced or reworked, stored in an electronic device or transmitted in any form or by any means including photocopying, without prior written permission of the author and publisher.

Permission can be obtained in writing from the publisher.

Any person who commits any unauthorised act in relation to this publication may be liable to criminal prosecution and civil claims for damages.

A catalogue record of this book is available from British Library.

ISBN: 978-1-9996443-4-5

Cover page and artwork Illustrations are designed by **Borsos Agnes Zsuzsanna**

Table of content

Acknowledgement..6

How to use this text book?..7

Common Topics..8

Topic 1 - Key Concepts in Chemistry......................................16

Topic 2 - States of matter & Methods of Purifying Substances......52

Topic 3 - Chemical Changes..64

Topic 4 - Extracting metals and Equilibria...............................80

Topic 5 - Separate Chemistry 1 (GCSE in Chemistry only).........94

Topic 6 - Groups in the periodic table...................................111

Topic 7 - Rate of reactions and energy changes......................119

Topic 8 - Fuels & earth science..135

Topic 9 - Separate chemistry 2 (GCSE in Chemistry only).......146

Workbook - Exam style questions...168

Workbook - Six mark questions..187

Acknowledgements

I would like to express my sincere gratitude towards all my chemistry teachers, who have inspired me to pursue a teaching career in this field. I would like to extend my thanks to everyone from my previous schools who I have worked with for the last 19 years, for their continuous support.

I am privileged to be part of teaching community which has provided me with the opportunity to share my knowledge and expertise to help students develop their knowledge further in chemistry and to provide students with invaluable application skills, making them life-long learners.

My sincere thanks to my lifetime mentor, Mr Mohamed Baba, who inspired and supported me tremendously all throughout my teaching journey. I would like to reiterate my thanks to all my students who have motivated and encouraged me to write books to help them with their revision. Special thanks to my family and friends who have been a tremendous support for my career and aspirations.

I would also like to thank Dr. Brotati Veraitch, for her contribution in proof reading in great detail with valuable suggestions.

Every effort has been made to contact copyright holders of material reproduced in this book. Any omissions will be rectified in forthcoming edition if notice is given to the publisher.

How to use this text book?

Key definition: Isotopes are atoms of the same element with the same number of protons but different number of neutrons.

→ Definition need to be learnt as per specification

Keynote: Together protons and neutrons are called nucleons.

→ With Keynote, give extra attention to make your understanding much clearer

1.19 understand how to deduce the electronic configurations of the first 20 elements from their positions in the Periodic Table

→ Learning objectives for GCSE in *combined science*

1.12 Calculate the relative atomic mass of an element from the relative masses and abundances of its isotopes (H)

→ Learning objectives for GCSE in *combined science* – Higher ONLY

9.21C Explain how the uses of polymers are related to their properties and vice versa: including poly(ethene), poly(propene), poly(chloroethene) (PVC) and poly(tetrafluoroethene) (PTFE)

→ Learning objectives with a C for *GCSE in chemistry*

9.22C Explain: a) why polyesters are condensation polymers (HC)

→ Learning objectives with a C for *GCSE in chemistry ONLY* – Higher ONLY

Note:

- Core practical objectives are *not* covered in this text book.
- Space is given to write answers in the work book for both exam style and six-mark questions.
- Some of the following common topics are covered within the topic itself
    - Recall the formulae of elements, simple compounds and ions
    - Write word equations
    - Write balanced ionic equations
- All objectives from the chemistry syllabus have been included in the revision guide. The objectives may not be in the same order as the syllabus to ensure that the topic flows well to facilitate concept formation and understanding.

7

Common topics (paper 1 and 2)

Safety in Science laboratory

Hazards and risks

Key Points: Hazards and risks

- It is important to create a safe environment in the science classroom especially while conducting practicals.
- To keep the safe environment the concept of hazards and risks needs to be clear for understanding and implementation.
- A **hazard** is any source of potential damage or harm to an individual's health or life under certain conditions, irrespective of places.
  Example: Broken glasses – It can harm by a cut
- **Risk** is the chance or possibility of a person being harmed or experiencing a health effect if exposed to a hazard.
  Example: a wet floor is a hazard, and there is a possibility (risk) that someone might be harmed by slipping and falling.
- Risks can be avoided or reduced by taking precautionary measures to control the hazard.
  Example: the risk of falling could be reduced by placing warning signs of the wet floor or blocking access to the area where the hazard exists.
- **Hazard symbols** in chemical containers are essential and useful as they:
  - Indicate the danger associated with the contents present in the container.
  - Allow people around to recognise them easily and take precautions to avoid hazardous situation.

Hazard Name	Symbol	Risk	Precaution
Caution	!	May irritate the skin.	Avoid skin and eye contact.
Corrosive		May cause burns to skin and destroys living tissues, such as skin and eyes.	Avoid skin and eye contact, and do not breathe its vapour.
Dangerous to the environment		Harmful to environment, toxic to aquatic life with long lasting effects.	Materials should be disposed responsibly.
Explosive		Explodes due to fire, shock, friction or heat. Catches fire easily.	Materials should be kept away from potential sources.
Harmful	X	Harmful to health.	Wear appropriate work wear, googles and gloves.
Flammable		Catches fire easily.	Ignition sources should be avoided.
Long term health issue		Causes serious long-term health effects when the substances are exposed for short or long term.	Skin contact or ingestion should be avoided with this material.
Oxidising		Burns in the absences of air by providing oxygen to make other substances burn more fiercely.	Materials should be kept away from potential sources.
Toxic		Can cause death, e.g. if swallowed, breathed in or absorbed by skin.	Skin contact or ingestion should be avoided with this material.

Hazard symbols

8

Key Table: Common apparatus and its uses

Equipment name	Image	Uses
Beaker		To hold, mix, and heat liquids
Bunsen burner		Heat source
Burette		To dispense an accurate volume of a liquid
Crucible		To hold chemicals during heating to very high temperatures
Dropper		To add liquid drop by drop
Erlenmeyer flask (or) Conical flask		To hold and mix chemicals.
Evaporating dish		To heat liquids for evaporation
Funnel		To transfer liquid from one container into other containers with small openings. Also, can be used with filter paper to separate solid from liquid in filtration.

Equipment name	Image	Uses
Measuring cylinder		To measure a precise volume of liquid
Mortar and pestle		To crush and grind materials
Stirring rod		To stir and mix
Test tube		To hold and mix liquids
Thermometer		To measure temperature in celsius
Tongs		To pick up beakers
Tripod		To hold and support glassware while heating on top with wire gauze
Volumetric flask		To prepare solutions to an accurate volume
Volumetric pipette		To measure small amounts of liquid accurately.

Equipment name	Image	Uses
Watch glass		To hold solids while they are being weighed.
Weighing balance		Measuring mass
Wire gauze		To support a container, while it is being heated.

Key Diagram: Collection of gases

- **Upward delivery tube**
    - Less dense than air
    - Examples: hydrogen, **H_2** and ammonia, **NH_3**
- **Downward delivery tube**
    - Dense than air
    - Examples: hydrogen chloride, **HCl** and carbon dioxide, **CO_2**
- **Over water − Displacement**
    - Insoluble gases over water
    - Examples: methane, **CH_4** and hydrogen, **H_2**

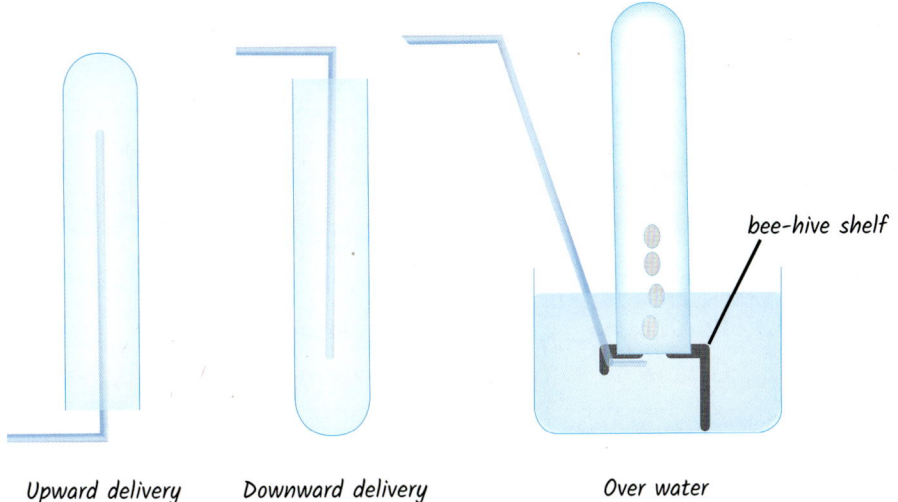

Upward delivery   Downward delivery   Over water

Collection of gases

Key Steps: To balance a chemical equation

Step 1: Divide the reactants and products by drawing a line in between them.
Step 2: List down all the atoms on each side in the following order.

- Metal
- Non-metal (exclude H and O)
- Hydrogen
- Oxygen (most of the time oxygen automatically gets balanced)

Step 3: Count the atoms on each side and list them below.
Step 4: Change the coefficient ONLY. Do not change the subscripts.
Step 5: Balance the number as per the list of order mentioned in step 2. Keep the loop going and cross check the coefficients every time an atom or polyatomic ion is balanced.
Step 6: Cross check the number of atoms on each side to confirm that all the atoms are balanced.

Note:

- If there is more than one polyatomic ion, keep them as it is which makes balancing much easier.
- Do not forget subscript outside the bracket and the atoms inside the bracket must be multiplied by the subscript number.

Worked example 1: Balance the following equation:

$$Mg + H_2O \longrightarrow Mg(OH)_2 + H_2$$

Solution:

Step 1: Divide the reactants and products by drawing a line in between them.

Reactants	Products
$Mg + H_2O$	$Mg(OH)_2 + H_2$

Step 2: List down all the atoms on each side in the following order.

- Metal
- Non-metal (exclude H and O)
- Hydrogen
- Oxygen (most of the time oxygen automatically gets balanced)

Reactants	Products
$Mg + H_2O$	$Mg(OH)_2 + H_2$
Mg	Mg
H	H
O	O

Step 3: Count the atoms on each side and list them below.

Reactants	Products
Mg + H$_2$O	Mg(OH)$_2$ + H$_2$
Mg = 1 H = 2 O = 1	Mg = 1 H = 4 O = 2

Step 4: Change the coefficient ONLY. Do not change the subscripts.

Reactants	Products
Mg + **2**H$_2$O	Mg(OH)$_2$ + H$_2$
Mg = 1, self balanced H = **2**, in water add **2** as a coefficient to make hydrogen 4 O = 1	Mg = 1, self balanced H = 4 O = 2

Step 5: Balance the number as per the list of order mentioned in step 2. Keep the loop going and cross check the coefficients every time an atom or polyatomic ion is balanced.

Reactants	Products
Mg + **2**H$_2$O	Mg(OH)$_2$ + H$_2$
Mg = 1 H = 4 O = 1, adding coefficient of **2** to water makes oxygen automatically **2**	Mg = 1 H = 4 O = 2

Step 6: Cross check the number of atoms on each side to confirm that all the atoms are balanced.

Reactants	Products
Mg + **2**H$_2$O	Mg(OH)$_2$ + H$_2$
Mg = 1 H = 4 O = 2	Mg = 1 H = 4 O = 2

Balanced equation is: Mg + **2**H$_2$O $\longrightarrow$ Mg(OH)$_2$ + H$_2$

Worked example 2: Balance the following equation:

$$Cu(NO_3)_2 + NaOH \longrightarrow Cu(OH)_2 + NaNO_3$$

<u>Solution:</u>

Step 1: Divide the reactants and products by drawing a line in between them.

Reactants	Products
$Cu(NO_3)_2 + NaOH$	$Cu(OH)_2 + NaNO_3$

Step 2: List down all the atoms on each side in the following order.

- Metal
- Non-metal (exclude H and O)
- Hydrogen
- Oxygen (most of the time oxygen automatically gets balanced)

<u>Note:</u>
- If there is more than one polyatomic ion, keep them as it is which makes balancing much easier.
- Do not forget subscript outside the bracket and the atoms inside the bracket must be multiplied by the subscript number

Reactants	Products
$Cu(NO_3)_2 + NaOH$	$Cu(OH)_2 + NaNO_3$
Cu	Cu
Na	Na
NO_3	NO_3
OH	OH

Step 3: Count the atoms on each side and list them below.

Reactants	Products
$Cu(NO_3)_2 + NaOH$	$Cu(OH)_2 + NaNO_3$
Cu = 1	Cu = 1
Na = 1	Na = 1
NO_3 = 2	NO_3 = 1
OH = 1	OH = 2

Step 4: Change the coefficient ONLY. Do not change the subscripts.

Reactants	Products
$Cu(NO_3)_2 + NaOH$	$Cu(OH)_2 + 2NaNO_3$
Cu = 1, self balanced	Cu = 1, self balanced
Na = 1, self balanced	Na = 1, self balanced
NO_3 = 2	NO_3 = 1, add coefficient of 2 to $NaNO_3$ which makes NO_3 and Na 2. So NO_3 is balanced **but not** Na
OH = 1	OH = 2

Step 5: Balance the number as per the list of order mentioned in step 2. Keep the loop going and cross check the coefficients every time an atom or polyatomic ion is balanced.

Reactants	Products
$Cu(NO_3)_2$ + **2**$NaOH$	$Cu(OH)_2$ + **2**$NaNO_3$
Cu = 1 Na = **1** in NaOH, add **2** as a coefficient to NaOH to make sodium **2**. Now OH becomes 2 **and** is balanced NO_3 = 2 OH = **2**	Cu = 1 Na = **2** NO_3 = 2 OH = **2**

Step 6: Cross check the number of atoms on each side to confirm that all the atoms are balanced.

Reactants	Products
$Cu(NO_3)_2$ + **2**$NaOH$	$Cu(OH)_2$ + **2**$NaNO_3$
Cu = 1 Na = 2 NO_3 = 2 OH = **2**	Cu = 1 Na = **2** NO_3 = 2 OH = **2**

Balanced equation is: $Cu(NO_3)_2$ + **2**$NaOH \longrightarrow Cu(OH)_2$ + **2**$NaNO_3$

Atomic structure

Early days about atoms

1.1 Describe how the Dalton model of an atom has changed over time because of the discovery of subatomic particles.

Key Points: John Dalton and J J Thomson

- John Dalton published his ideas about atoms in 1803.
- Atoms are tiny spheres which cannot be divided.
- All matter is made up of tiny particles known as atoms.
- Several years later J J Thomson discovered the electron.
- His model of atom suggest that the atom is a ball of positive charge surrounded by negative charge inside it (Fig 1.1 (a)).

Fig 1.1 (a) - J J Thomson's plum-pudding model

J J Thomson's model of atom is known as plum pudding model.

Positively charged particles are known as alpha particles.

Key Points: Ernest Rutherford and Niel Bohr

- In 1909, plum pudding model was tested by Ernest Rutherford.
- In the experiment, positively charged alpha particles were bombarded at a thin gold foil.
- Some particles were scattered in different directions and the other particles went straight through the foil (Fig 1.1 (b)).
- This evidence shapes up a new model for the atom called the nuclear model.
- Nuclear model states that the mass of the atom is concentrated at its centre called the nucleus and it is positively charged.

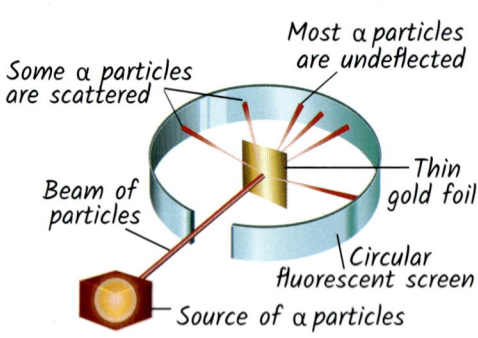

Fig 1.1 (b) - Alpha particle scattering experiment

Key Points: Niel Bohr and James Chadwick

- Using Rutherford's nuclear model, with mathematical evidence Bohr suggested that electrons orbit the nucleus in shells.
- Further experimental evidence proved that the nucleus contains small particles called protons with a small amount of positive charge.
- In 1932, James Chadwick found the particles in the nucleus with mass but no charge. These particles are called neutrons.
- Refer Fig 1.1 (c) which led to the atomic model with subatomic particles.

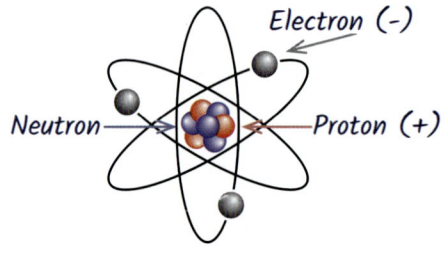

Fig 1.1 (c) - Nuclear model of the atom

The structure of an atom

1.2 Describe the structure of an atom as a nucleus containing protons and neutrons, surrounded by electrons in shells
1.3 Recall the relative charge and relative mass of a proton, neutron and an electron

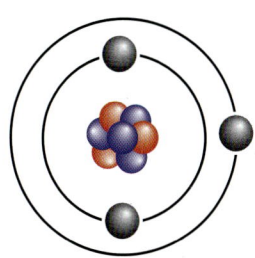

Electrons 4 Neutrons  3 Protons

Fig 1.2 – The structure of a lithium atom

Subatomic Particle	Location in the atom	Relative mass	Relative charge
Proton	Nucleus	1	+1 (positive)
Neutron	Nucleus	1	0 (no charge, zero)
Electron	Orbit around nucleus in the shell	$\frac{1}{1850}$	-1 (negative)

Table 1.1 – A summary of an atom's subatomic particles

1.4 Explain why atoms contain equal numbers of protons and electrons
1.5 Describe the nucleus of an atom as very small compared to the overall size of the atom
1.6 Recall that most of the mass of an atom is concentrated in the nucleus

Key Points: The structure of an atom

- The atom consists of subatomic particles called protons, neutrons and electrons.
- Protons and neutrons are located inside the nucleus, whereas electrons orbit around the nucleus in the shell (Fig 1.2).
- Each subatomic particle has a relative charge (Table 1.1).
- Atoms are electrically neutral, so they contain equal number of protons and electrons to **cancel out** the **charge**.
- Since the nucleus contains protons and neutrons, most of the mass of an atom is concentrated in its nucleus.
- The nucleus of an atom is very small compared to the overall size of the atom. The radius of an atom ranges from 1×10^{-8} to 5×10^{-8} cm, whereas the diameter of a nucleus is around 10^{-12} cm.

Together protons and neutrons are called nucleons.

An atom is a million times smaller than the thickest human hair.

1.7 Recall the meaning of the term mass number of an atom
1.8 Describe atoms of a given element as having the same number of protons in the nucleus and that this number is unique to that element

Key Points: Atomic number and mass number

- The **atomic number**, Z, which is the total number of protons in the nucleus of an atom.
- The mass number (or) Atomic Mass, A, which is the total number of protons **AND** neutrons in the nucleus of an atom.
- All atoms of a given element have the same number of protons, so all the atoms of a particular element have the same atomic number.

Key definition: The mass number of an atom is its total number of protons and neutrons in the nucleus.

1.10 Calculate the numbers of protons, neutrons and electrons in atoms given the atomic number and mass number

Key Points: Calculating number of subatomic particles of an atom

- The symbol for an atom comes from the periodic table with its mass number and its atomic number.
- The highest number among the two numbers is the mass number, generally mass number is shown at the top.
- The lowest number among the two numbers is the atomic number, generally atomic number is shown at the bottom.
- Number of protons = Atomic number
- Number of electrons = Number of protons
- Number of electrons = Number of protons = Atomic number
- Mass number = Number of protons + Number of neutrons
  (Total number of particles inside the nucleus)
- Number of neutrons = Mass number − Number of protons
  OR
  Number of neutrons = Mass number − Atomic number

Number of neutrons can be calculated by taking away the lowest number from the highest number among the numbers in the element in the periodic table.

Worked example 1: Calculate the subatomic particles of lithium atom.

Solution:

Number of protons = Atomic number = 3
Number of electrons = Atomic number = 3
Number of neutrons = Mass number − Atomic number
         = 7 − 3 = 4

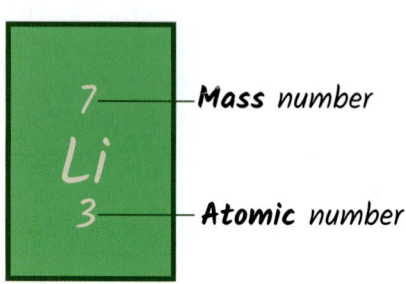

7 — **Mass** number
Li
3 — **Atomic** number

18

Worked example 2: Calculate the subatomic particles of potassium atom.

Solution:

Number of protons = 19
Number of electrons = 19
Number of neutrons = 39 - 19 = 20

Isotopes

1.9 Describe isotopes as different atoms of the same element containing the same number of protons but different numbers of neutrons in their nuclei

Key definition: Isotopes are atoms of the same element with the same number of protons but different number of neutrons.

Isotopes are also defined as the atoms of the same elements with the same atomic number but different mass number.
Example: Common isotopes of chlorine:
$^{35}_{17}Cl$ and $^{37}_{17}Cl$

Isotopes of hydrogen is common to be assessed in the exam.
$^{1}_{1}H$ $^{2}_{1}H$ $^{3}_{1}H$
H – 1: Protium
H – 2: Deuterium
H – 3: Tritium

Key Points: Isotopes

- As isotopes have similar number of electrons, their chemical properties are the same.
- As isotopes have the same atomic number, sometimes an isotope is shown with only mass number.
For example, bromine-79 is an isotope of bromine with a mass number of 79.

Key Points: Calculating subatomic particles of isotopes

- Use the same method used in calculating the subatomic particles of the atom.
- Number that comes with the symbol is the isotopic mass number.
Example of bromine: Br - 79 and Br - 81. 79 and 81 are the isotopic mass number, not the atomic number.
- Use the periodic table to find the atomic number of the given element.

Worked example 3: Calculate the subatomic particles of isotopes C-12, C-13 and C-14.

Solution:

Note: Atomic number of carbon is **6** which is taken from the Periodic table (atomic number = number of protons = number of electrons) and mass number is picked along with the symbol given in the question (number of neutrons = mass number – atomic number).

Isotopes	Atomic number	Mass Number	Number of protons	Number of electrons	Number of neutrons
C – 12	6	12	6	6	12 – 6 = 6
C – 13	6	13	6	6	13 – 6 = 7
C – 14	6	14	6	6	14 – 6 = 8

1.11 Explain how the existence of isotopes results in relative atomic masses of some elements not being whole numbers

Key Points: Relative atomic mass (Ar)

- The relative atomic mass of an element is a weighted average of the masses of the atoms of the isotopes.
- Relative atomic masses are not whole number due to the average taken from the abundance of each of the isotopes of the element. However, it is often rounded to the nearest whole number.

Key definition: The **relative atomic mass** of an element is the weighted average of the masses of the isotopes in the naturally occurring element relative to the mass of an atom of the carbon-12 isotope, which is taken to be exactly 12.

1.12 Calculate the relative atomic mass of an element from the relative masses and abundances of its isotopes

Worked example: 4 Calculate the relative atomic mass of chlorine, given that it has two naturally occurring isotopes:

Cl-35 with percentage abundance 75.0%
Cl-37 with percentage abundance 25.0%

The relative atomic mass is the average mass of all isotopes of an element. It is calculated as shown below for two naturally occuring isotopes:

$$A_r = \frac{(\text{relative isotopic mass 1} \times \text{\% abundance}) + (\text{relative isotopic mass 2} \times \text{\% abundance})}{100}$$

Solution:
Average mass of chlorine atoms is:

$$\frac{(35 \times 70.0) + (37 \times 25.0)}{100} = 35.5$$

Worked example: 5 Calculate the relative atomic mass of magnesium, given that it has three naturally occurring isotopes:

Mg-24 with percentage abundance 79.0%
Mg-25 with percentage abundance 10.0%
Mg-26 with percentage abundance 11.0%

Solution:
Average mass of magesium atoms is:

$$\frac{(24 \times 79.0) + (25 \times 10.0) + (26 \times 11.0)}{100} = 24.32$$

It is the relative atomic mass of magnesium which can be found in the Periodic Table as a whole number 24.

The Periodic Table

Early days of the periodic table

1.13 Describe how Mendeleev arranged the elements, known at that time, in a periodic table by using properties of these elements and their compounds.
1.14 Describe how Mendeleev used his table to predict the existence and properties of some elements not then discovered.
1.15 Explain that Mendeleev thought he had arranged elements in order of increasing relative atomic mass but this was not always true because of the relative abundance of isotopes of some pairs of elements in the periodic table

Key Points: Starting point of the periodic table

- Discovery of elements are a result of continuous discovery from early days.
- Many elements were unknown.
- Elements were classified by arranging them in order of their atomic weight.
- Elements were placed in groups with inconsistent properties of elements

Atomic weight is known as relative atomic mass now.

Key Points: Mendeleev's periodic table

- Russian chemist Dmitri Mendeleev published his first periodic table of the elements in 1869.
- He arranged the elements in order of increasing atomic weight.
- With increasing atomic weight, he also considered arranging the elements and their compounds with their properties, which led to gaps in the periodic table.
- Also, he lined up the elements with similar chemical properties in groups.
- Overall, some pairs of elements were shown in the wrong order from their atomic weights, due to the relative abundance of isotopes.
- Gaps left in his periodic table were very useful to predict the properties of undiscovered elements.
- For example, he predicted the element that should fit below aluminum in his periodic table. When the new element, gallium, was discovered, its properties were found to be close to his predictions.

The modern periodic table

1.16 Explain the meaning of atomic number of an element in terms of position in the periodic table and number of protons in the nucleus
1.17 Describe that in the periodic table
   a. elements are arranged in order of increasing atomic number, in rows called periods
   b. elements with similar properties are placed in the same vertical columns called groups
1.18 Identify elements as metals or non-metals according to their position in the periodic table, explaining this division in terms of the atomic structures of the elements

Key Points: Groups and Periods in the periodic table

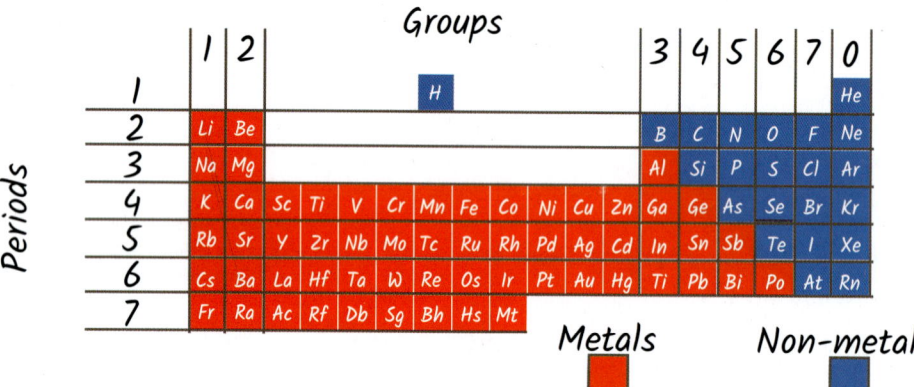

Fig 1.3 - Groups and Periods in the periodic table

- The elements are **arranged in increasing order of atomic number** which is the number of protons in the nucleus.
- The elements with similar properties are placed in vertical columns in the periodic table, known as **groups** (Fig 1.3).
- The horizontal rows in the periodic table are known as **periods** (Fig 1.3).
- There are 8 groups in total, which starts from left to right group 1 to 7, and the last group is known as **Group 0**.
- There are 7 periods in the periodic table from top to bottom.
- The metals are on the left and the non-metals are on the right side of the periodic table (Fig 1.4).
- Zigzag line in the periodic table indicates the division of metals and non-metals (Fig 1.4).
- The elements on the zigzag line are known as metalloids.

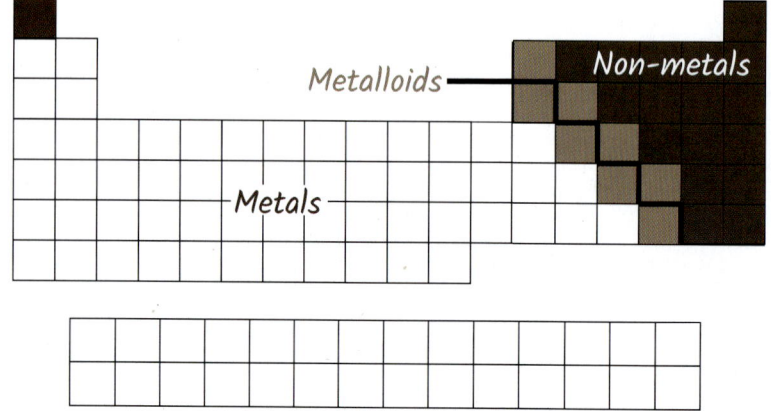

Fig 1.4 - Zigzag line to separate metals and non-metals

The elements which share the properties of both metals and nonmetals are known as **Metalloids**

22

Electronic configuration

1.19 Predict the electronic configurations of the first 20 elements in the periodic table as diagrams and in the form, for example 2.8.1
1.20 Explain how the electronic configuration of an element is related to its position in the periodic table

Key Points: Electronic configuration of the first 20 elements and its position in the periodic table

- Electrons occupy different shells or energy levels.
- The way in which electrons are arranged in an atom among the various electron shells is known as electron configuration.
- Each electron shell can hold a maximum number of electrons (Fig. 1.5).
- Total number of electrons can be determined from the atomic number of the given element.
- Each electron shell must be completely filled with electrons before the next level is filled.
  <u>Exception</u> – For the first 20 element in the periodic table, in 3rd electron shell, only 8 electrons can be occupied.
- Group and period number are helpful in working out the electronic configuration of an element.

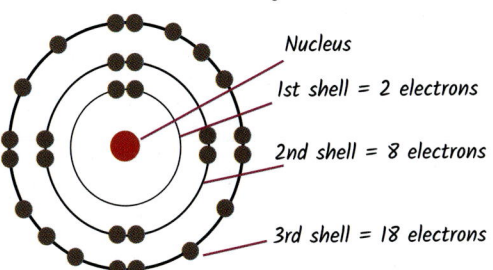

Fig 1.5 - Electron occupancy

a) Number of electrons in the outermost electron shell is equal to the group number
b) Number of electron shell in an atom is equal to the period number

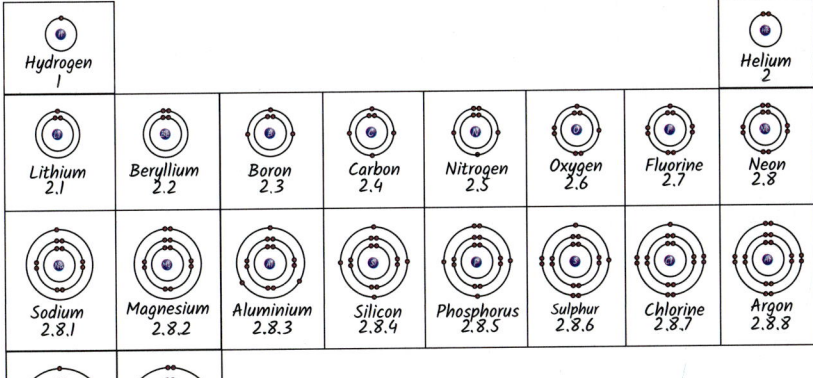

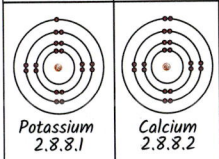

Fig 1.6 - Electronic configuration and atomic structure of first 20 elements

Worked example: 6 *Write the electronic configuration of potassium, K.*

<u>Solution:</u> Electronic configuration of potassium, K is 2. 8. 8. 1
Explanation:
- Atomic number of potassium is 19, total number of electrons is 19
- Maximum 2 electrons can occupy first electron shell (19 − 2 = 17 left)
- Out of 17 electrons maximum of 8 electrons can occupy second electron shell (17 − 8 = 9 left)
- Out of 9 electrons maximum of 8 electrons can occupy third electron shell (9 − 8 = 1 left)
- Remaining 1 electron moves to outer electron shell
- So, electronic configuration of K is 2. 8. 8. 1
- Dot (.), separates an electron shell from the next electron shell.

Ionic Bonding

Formation of Ionic Bonds

1.21 Explain how ionic bonds are formed by the transfer of electrons between atoms to produce cations and anions, including the use of dot and cross diagrams
1.22 Recall that an ion is an atom or group of atoms with a positive or negative charge
1.23 Calculate the numbers of protons, neutrons and electrons in simple ions given the atomic number and mass number
1.24 Explain the formation of ions in ionic compounds from their atoms, limited to compounds of elements in groups 1, 2, 6 and 7

Key Points: Formation of Ionic Bonds

- The metal atom loses electrons, to become a positively charged ion (a cation).
- The non-metal atom accepts/gains electrons, to become a negatively charged ion (an anion).
- The positive and negative ions are attracted to each other by electrostatic force of attraction, producing a neutral compound with a bond called IONIC BOND.

Transfer of outer electrons enables both atoms to achieve the stable noble gas configuration.

Key definition: Ionic bonding occurs as a result of a metal atom transferring its outer electron(s) to a non-metal atom.

Key Points: Formation of sodium chloride

- Sodium atom becomes a sodium ion by losing it outer electron and chlorine atom becomes a chloride ion by gaining an electron to its outer shell or energy level.

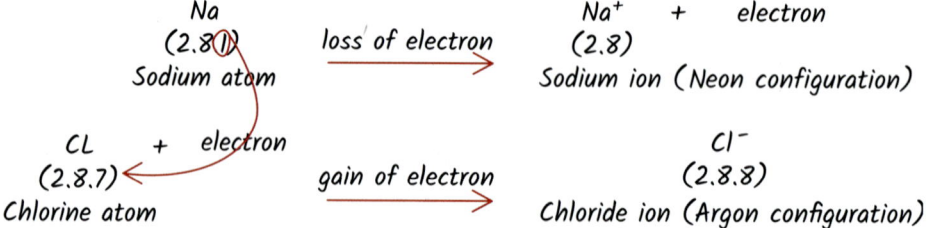

Fig 1.7 – Movement of electrons between sodium and chlorine atoms

- Oppositely charged ions are attracted through strong electrostatic forces of attraction, forming the ionic bond.
- In the formation of an ionic compound, metal atoms in groups 1, 2 and 3 will lose electrons to form ions with a +1, +2 and +3 charge respectively, and elements in groups 5, 6 and 7 will gain electrons to form ions with a -3, -2 and -1 charge, respectively.

Ionic compounds can be formed by any combination of positive and negative ions.

Key Diagrams: Dot and cross structure of ionic bonding

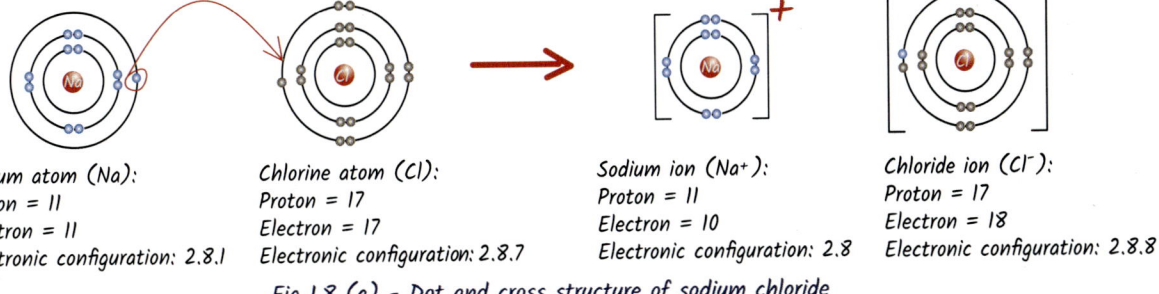

Sodium atom (Na):
Proton = 11
Electron = 11
Electronic configuration: 2.8.1

Chlorine atom (Cl):
Proton = 17
Electron = 17
Electronic configuration: 2.8.7

Sodium ion (Na+):
Proton = 11
Electron = 10
Electronic configuration: 2.8

Chloride ion (Cl-):
Proton = 17
Electron = 18
Electronic configuration: 2.8.8

Fig 1.8 (a) - Dot and cross structure of sodium chloride

Key Points: Ions and its subatomic particles

- Calculating subatomic particles of ions is different from atoms.
- Ions are formed by losing (or) gaining electrons
- Refer Fig 1.8 (a) – Sodium atom loses its outer electron (11e⁻ - 1e⁻ = 10 e⁻) to become sodium ion and becomes stable, forming Na⁺¹, whereas chlorine atom gains an electron to become chloride ion (17e⁻ + 1e⁻ = 18e⁻), forming Cl⁻.
- Movement of electron (or) electrons never affects the particles present in the nucleus, so the number of protons and neutrons remains unchanged.
- Fig 1.8 (b) – Magnesium atom loses two electrons and oxygen atom gains two electrons and becomes stable respectively, forming Mg^{2+} and O^{2-} ions.
- Refer Table 1.2 to understand the comparison of parent atom and its ions.

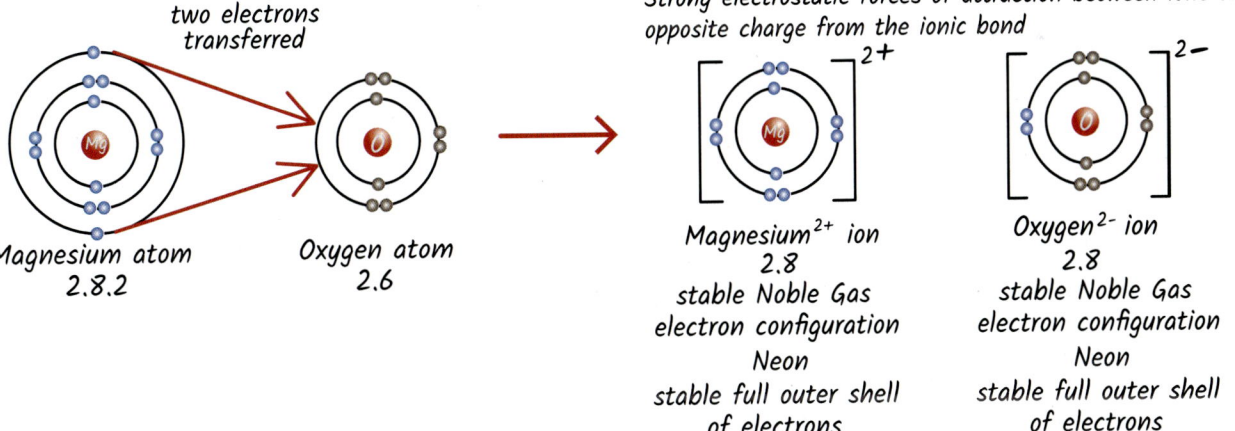

Fig 1.8 (b) - Dot and cross structure of magnesium oxide

	$^{24}_{12}Mg$	Mg^{2+}	$^{16}_{8}O$	O^{2-}
# Protons	12	12	8	8
# Electrons	12	10	8	10
# Neutron	12	12	8	8

Table 1.2 – Subatomic particles of parent atoms and its ions

Naming and deducing the formulae of compounds

1.25 Explain the use of the endings –ide and –ate in the names of Compounds

Key Points: Difference between suffix 'ide' and 'ate' in the names of compounds

- The suffix 'ide' is used for compounds containing two elements such as magnesium sulph**ide** (MgS) and silver chlor**ide** (AgCl).
- The suffix 'ate' is used for compounds which contains 2 elements in anions, one of which must be oxygen, such as magnesium sulph**ate** (MgSO$_4$) or copper(II) nitr**ate** (Cu(NO$_3$)$_2$).

1.26 Deduce the formulae of ionic compounds (including oxides, hydroxides, halides, nitrates, carbonates and sulfates) given the formulae of the constituent ions.

Key Points: Things to remember before deducing the formulae of compounds

To deduce the correct chemical formula, the key points required are:
- Know the charges of the ions **(Table 1.3 and Fig 1.9)**.
- Determine how many cations and anions are needed to reach a zero charge using basic maths.
- Write the chemical formula always with the cation first, followed by the anion
- Finally, write the formula with the lowest ratio of cations and anions to create a net neutral compound.

Group 4 element can be either +4 (or) -4 depends upon the bonding.

Transition elements comes with variable charge of oxidation state as a result charges are given in Roman letters in a bracket.
E.g 1 Iron(III) chloride – Charge of Iron is +3
E.g 2 Iron(II) chloride – Charge of Iron is +2

Anions	Ionic charge	Symbol
hydroxides	1-	OH$^-$
halides	1-	X$^-$
nitrates	1-	NO$_3^-$
oxides	2-	O^{2-}
carbonates	2-	CO$_3^{2-}$
sulphates	2-	SO$_4^{2-}$

Table 1.3 – Ionic charge of anions

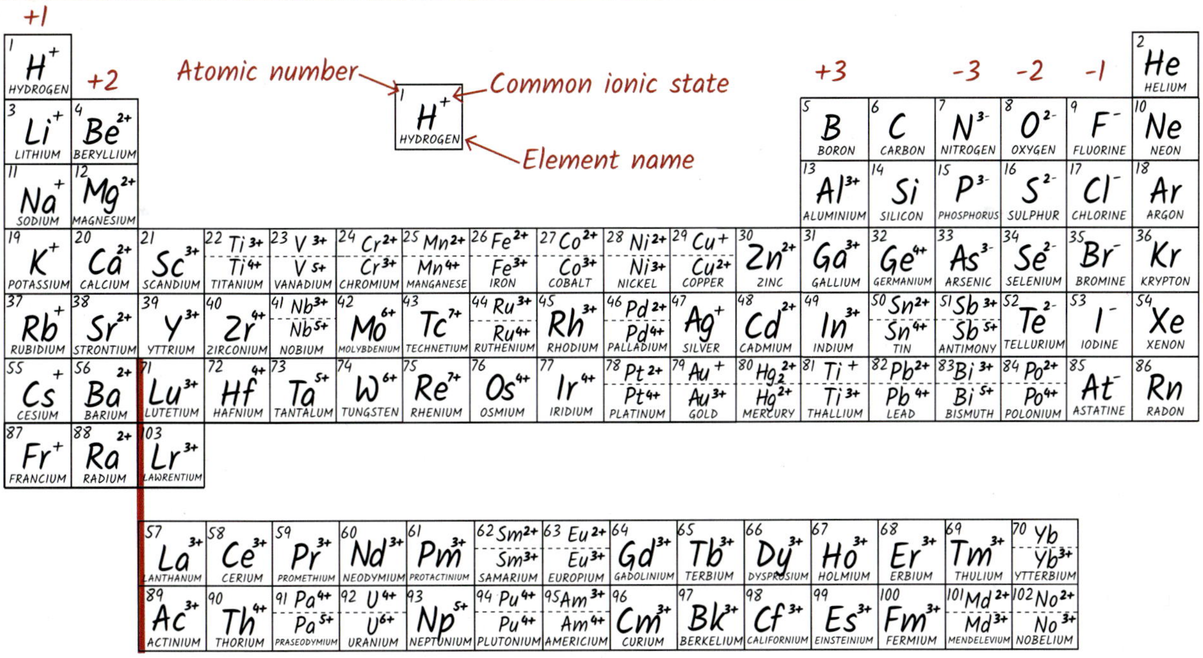

Fig 1.9 - Common ionic states of the elements

Key Steps: To deduce the formulae of the ionic compounds

Step 1: Write the symbol of elements in the compound
Step 2: Write the charge of the element
Step 3: If the charge numbers are different then swap the number between the element and go to step 5
Step 4: If the charge numbers are same then cancel out the charge and go to step 5
Step 5: Write the formulae of the compound by keeping number as subscript.

Note 1: While swapping the numbers, if anion has a subscript number then use a bracket to distinguish the numbers
Note 2: Net charge can be proved as Zero by multiplying step 2 and 3 (or) 4 and add the charges together.

Worked example: 7 Deduce the formula of calcium chloride

Solution

Step 1: Write the symbol of elements in the compound	Ca	Cl
Step 2: Write the charge of the element	2+	1-
Step 3: If the charge numbers are different then swap the number between the element and go to step 5	1	2
Step 4: If the charge numbers are same then cancel out the charge and go to step 5	step skipped	
Step 5: Write the formulae of the compound by keeping number as subscript.	$CaCl_2$	
Net charge can be proved as Zero by multiplying step 2 and 3 (or) 4 and add the charges together.	Ca (2+ × 1) = 2+ Cl (1- × 2) = 2- = 0	

Topic 1 - Key Concepts in Chemistry

27

Worked example: 8 *Deduce the formula of magnesium oxide*

<u>Solution</u>

Step 1: Write the symbol of elements in the compound	Mg	O
Step 2: Write the charge of the element	2+	2-
Step 3: If the charge numbers are different then swap the number between the element and go to step 5	step skipped	
Step 4: If the charge numbers are <u>same</u> then cancel out the charge and go to step 5	~~2+~~ =1	~~2-~~ =1
Step 5: Write the formulae of the compound by keeping number as subscript.	MgO	
Net charge can be proved as Zero by multiplying step 2 and 3 (or) 4 and add the charges together.	Mg (2+ × 1) = 2+ O (1- × 2) = 2- = 0	

Worked example: 9 *Deduce the formula of copper(II) nitrate*

<u>Solution</u>

Step 1: Write the symbol of elements in the compound	Cu	NO$_3$
Step 2: Write the charge of the element	2+	1-
Step 3: If the charge numbers are <u>different</u> then swap the number between the element and go to step 5	1	2
Step 4: If the charge numbers are same then cancel out the charge and go to step 5	step skipped	
Step 5: Write the formulae of the compound by keeping number as subscript.	Cu(NO$_3$)$_2$	
<u>Note 1:</u> While swapping the numbers, if anion has a subscript number then use a bracket to distinguish the numbers		
Net charge can be proved as Zero by multiplying step 2 and 3 (or) 4 and add the charges together.	Cu (2+ × 1) = 2+ NO$_3$ (1- × 2) = 2- = 0	

Lattice structure of ionic compounds

> 1.27 Explain the structure of an ionic compound as a lattice structure
> a) consisting of a regular arrangement of ions
> b) held together by strong electrostatic forces (ionic bonds) between oppositely-charged ions

Key Points: The lattice structure of ionic compounds

- The ions that make up ionic compounds arrange themselves into a regular pattern, a lattice structure **(Fig 1.10)**.
- No fixed number of ions are involved, but the ratio of cations to anions is constant for a given compound.
- The positively charged ions are packed as closely as possible to the negatively charged ions, and the ions with the same charge are as far apart as possible.
- This arrangement serves to maximise the electrostatic attraction between the positive and negative ions and minimise the repulsion between similar charged ions, thus lowering the overall chemical potential energy of the lattice.
- Sodium chloride provides a good example of a **giant ionic lattice**.
- Each positive sodium ion is surrounded by six chloride ions, and each chloride ion is surrounded by six sodium ions.

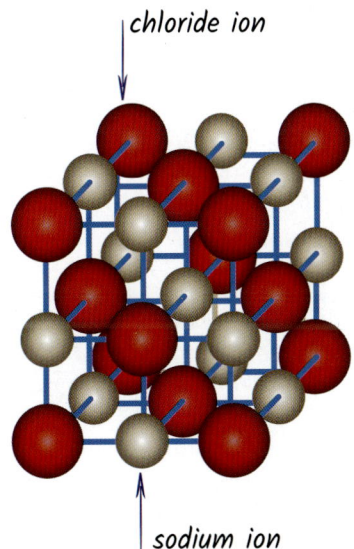

Fig 1.10 - The lattice structure of ionic compound

Covalent Bonding

Formation of covalent bonds

1.28 Explain how a covalent bond is formed when a pair of electrons is shared between two atoms
1.29 Recall that covalent bonding results in the formation of molecules

Key Points: Formation of covalent bond

"The electrostatic attraction between the shared pair of electrons and the nuclei of the atoms"

- Electrons are shared between two non-metal atoms.
- The electrons of the bond make up a bonding pair.
- As only one pair of electrons is occupying the space between the two nuclei, a single covalent bond forms.
- Any other pairs of outer-shell electrons that do not actually take part in the bond are known as LONE PAIRS (**non-bonding pairs**) of electrons.

Single bond – 1 shared pair of electrons.
Double bond – 2 shared pairs of electrons.
Triple bond – 3 shared pairs of electrons.

Key definition: Covalent bonding occurs when a pair of electrons is **shared** between two non-metal atoms and a covalent bond is formed.

1.30 Recall the typical size (order of magnitude) of atoms and small molecules

Key Points: Size of atoms and molecules

- Atoms are so small that their size are written using standard form.
- An atom has the order of magnitude of 10^{-10} m.
- A molecule has the order of magnitude of 10^{-9} m.

1.31 Explain the formation of simple molecular, covalent substances, using dot and cross diagrams, including: a) hydrogen b) hydrogen chloride c) water d) methane e) oxygen f) carbon dioxide

Key Steps: To draw dot and cross diagram of covalent bonding

Step 1: Find the total number of outer electrons in each atom.
Step 2: Place the least electronegative atom in the centre **except** hydrogen and draw the dot and cross notation for each type of atom (only outer electrons).
Step 3: Make electron pairs to form bonds between all atoms

Electronegativity: is a measure of the ability of an atom to attract a pair of electrons in a bond. Apart from noble gases, the electronegative values increases across the periodic table from left to right. For example the most electronegative atom is fluorine

Most least electronegative elements are found:
Period: In the left side of the periodic table
Group: In the bottom of the group of the periodic table

Step 4: Draw the circle around electrons and make sure shared electrons are shown in between the circles.
Step 5: Check the octet rule (eight electrons) on the outer atoms, **except** hydrogen.
Step 6: If the central atom does not have an octet, move electrons from outer atoms to form double or triple bonds.
Step 7: Confirm the octet rule using dot and cross structure from step 6. If step 6 is not applicable, then go to step 4 and confirm the diagram.
Step 8: Check the total number of electrons in the final diagram is equal to the number of electrons calculated in step 1.

> **Octet rule:** Eight outer electrons in its outermost electron shell of every atom.
> Note: Hydrogen is an exception as it has only two outer electrons.

Worked example: 10 Draw the dot and cross diagram of hydrogen chloride, HCl.

Solution

Step 1	Find the total number of outer electrons in each atom.	H = 1	Cl = 7
		Total number of outer electrons = 8	
Step 2	Place the least electronegative atom in the centre except hydrogen and draw the dot and cross diagram for each type of atom (only outer electrons).	Only two atoms are involved, so no difference in terms of placing central atom	
Step 3	Make electron pairs to form bonds between all atoms.		
Step 4	Draw the circle around electrons and make sure shared electrons are shown in between the circles.		
Step 5	Check the octet rule (eight electrons) on the outer atoms, except hydrogen.	Due to exception, hydrogen is surrounded by two electrons	Chlorine satisfies the octet rule by holding eight electrons
Step 6	If the central atom does not have an octet, move electrons from outer atoms to form double or triple bonds.	Not applicable	
Step 7	Confirm the octet rule using dot and cross structure from step 6. If step 6 is not applicable, then go to step 4 and confirm the diagram.		
Step 8	Check the total number of electrons in the final diagram is equal to the number of electrons calculated in step 1.	Yes, 8 electrons in step 1 and step 7, now each atom has a complete octet.	

Worked example: 11   Draw the dot and cross diagram of oxygen, O_2

Solution

Step 1	Find the total number of outer electrons in each atom.	O = 6	O = 6
		Total number of outer electrons = 12	
Step 2	Place the least electronegative atom in the centre except hydrogen and draw the dot and cross diagram for each type of atom (only outer electrons)	Only two atoms are involved, so no difference in terms of placing central atom. Atoms are same type, so only dot notation is used. However, dot and cross can also be used.	
Step 3	Make electron pairs to form bonds between all atoms.		
Step 4	Draw the circle around electrons and make sure shared electrons are shown in between the circles.		
Step 5	Check the octet rule (eight electrons) on the outside atoms, except hydrogen.	O = 7, octet is not satisfied	O = 7, octet is not satisfied
Step 6	If the central atom does not have an octet, move electrons from outer atoms to form double or triple bonds.	Move the unpaired electron from each oxygen atom to form double bond.	
Step 7	Confirm the octet rule using dot and cross structure from step 6. If step 6 is not applicable, then go to step 4 and confirm the diagram.	Each oxygen atom contains 8 electrons which satisfy the octet rule	
Step 8	Check the total number of electrons in the final diagram is equal to the number of electrons calculated in step 1.	Yes, 12 electrons in step 1 and step 7, now each atom has a complete octet.	

Key Diagrams: Dot and cross structures of simple molecular covalent substances.

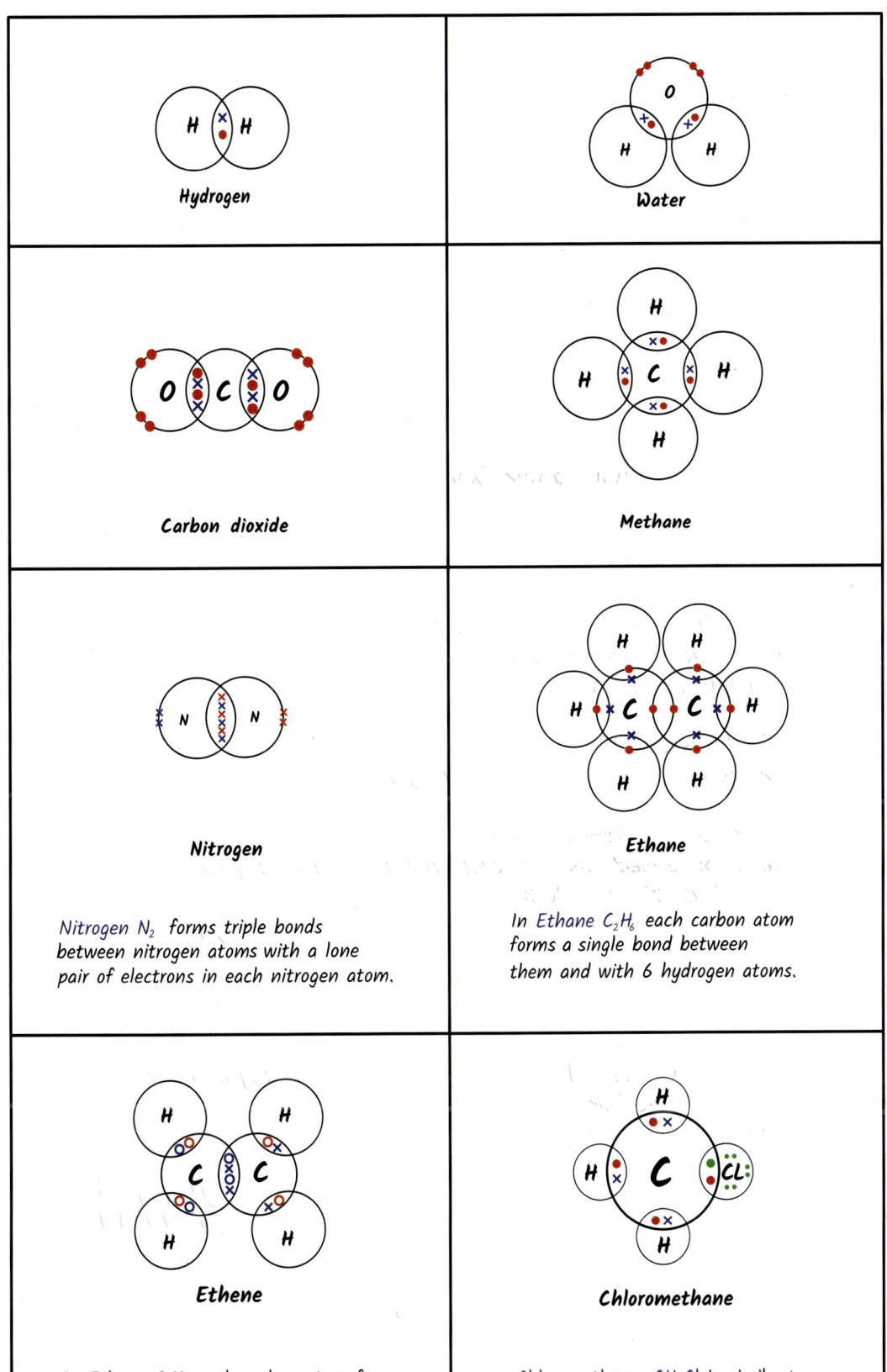

Table 1.4 - Dot and cross structures of simple covalent compounds

Topic 1 - Key Concepts in Chemistry

2D & 3D representations of covalent substances

1.41 Describe the limitations of representations and models, to include dot and cross, ball and stick models and two- and three-dimensional representations

Key Points: Dot & cross, 2D & 3D representations of covalent substances

- A dot and cross diagram show the pairs of outer electrons of each atom involve in the compound.
- 2D diagram show the bonds between the atoms present.
- 3D ball and stick model show how the atoms and bonds are arranged in space.

Key Diagrams: 2D & 3D representations of covalent substances

Name	2D	3D
Methane	H—C—H (with H above and below)	
Ethane	H—C—C—H (with 2H above and 2H below)	
Ethene	H₂C=CH₂	
Chloromethane	H—C—Cl (with H above and below)	

Table 1.5 - 2D and 3D representations of covalent compounds

Types of substance

Classifications of compounds and its structuret

1.32 – 1.34 Classification of types of substances and the physical properties of ionic and covalent compounds

Key Summary: Classifications of different types of compounds and its structure

Type of bonding / Physical properties	Ionic structure	Simple molecular covalent structure	Giant covalent lattice structure	Metallic structure
Melting and boiling points	**Very high** requires large amounts of energy to break the bonds as electrostatic force of attraction is strong	**Low** requires little energy to break as bonding between molecules is weak	**Very high** requires great amount of energy to break the strong covalent bonds. Hence, they are solids with high melting and boiling points	**Increases from low to high** size and the charge on the cation determines the melting point
Solubility	**Soluble** If a substance dissolves, it is due to the attraction of the ions to the water molecules, which are greater than the attraction of the ions to each other.	Most of the simple molecular covalent substances are **insoluble in water.** The soluble simple molecular covalent substances form hydrogen bonds with water molecules. However, most of the substances are **soluble in organic solvents**	these substances do not dissolve in any solvents (The covalent bonds are too strong)	Some metals will react with water to form alkaline solutions (Generally the bonds within a metal are too strobg to be broken by water).
Electrical conductivity	Ionic substances conduct in molten and aqueous state. (Ions are free to move and conduct electricity when dissolved in water or when molten).	Do not conduct electricity All unpaired electrons form covalent bonds so unable to move around.	Carbon in graphite is the element that conducts electricity in network lattice. (The delocalized electrons between the layers of carbon atoms in graphite can conduct electricity There are no free electrons or other charged particles in the network lattice).	All metals conduct electricity in the solid state. (The sea of delocalized electrons conducts the electricity

Table 1.6 – Physical properties of different substances

Giant Molecular Substances

1.35 Recall that graphite and diamond are different forms of carbon and that they are examples of giant covalent substances
1.36 Describe the structures of graphite and diamond

Key Points: Giant Molecular Substances

- Some substances consist of large molecules which are known as giant molecules or macromolecules.
- These macromolecules contain billions of atoms per molecule.
- Diamond, graphite, silica (or) silicon(IV) oxide are the common examples of giant molecules.

Key Summary: Classifications of different types of compounds and its structure

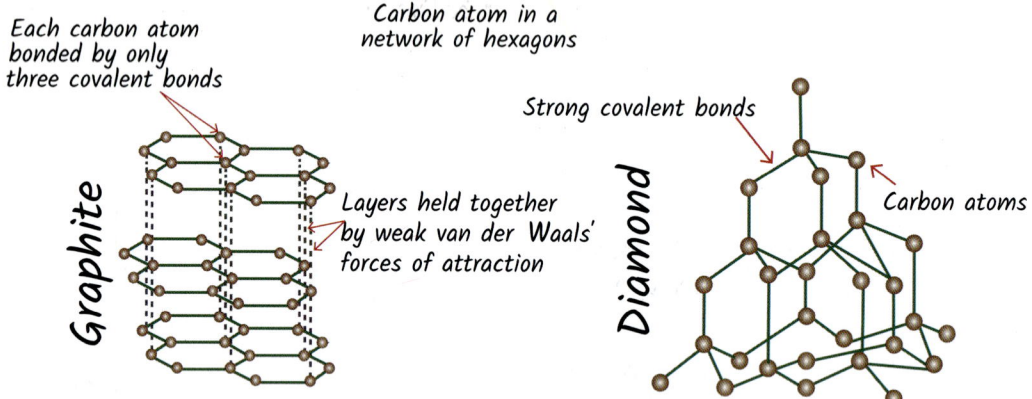

Fig 1.11 - Structure of graphite and diamond

1.37 Explain, in terms of structure and bonding, why graphite is used to make electrodes and as a lubricant, whereas diamond is used in cutting tools
1.38 Explain the properties of fullerenes including C_{60} and graphene in terms of their structures and bonding

Key Points: Graphite is used as electrodes

- Graphite is used to make electrodes as it is a good conductor of electricity.
- In graphite each carbon atom in the layer is only bonded to three other carbon atoms
- Therefore, there are delocalised (free) electrons in graphite, which can move and carry a charge. Hence, graphite conducts electricity.

Key Points: Graphite is used as lubricants

- Graphite consists of layers of bonded carbon atoms.
- Each carbon atom is bonded to 3 other carbon atoms in a hexagonal arrangement.
- The different layers are held together by weak van der Waals' forces of attraction.
- The different layers slide over each other and thus graphite acts as a lubricant.

Key Points: Diamond is used in cutting tools

- Diamond is very hard.
- Atoms of carbon cannot slide over each other due to strong covalent bonds in the structure, making it hard and suitable to cut tools.

> Diamonds are not the only substance that are capable of cutting glass. Topaz and quartz can be used to cut glass.

Key Points: Diamond has very high melting and boiling point

- Diamond has strong covalent bonds.
- A lot of energy is required to break the strong covalent bonds between the carbon atoms.
- Hence diamond is hard with very high melting and boiling point.

Key Points: C_{60} fullerene has poor electrical conductivity

- In C_{60} each carbon atom is bonded to only three other atoms (Fig 1.12).
- The material consists of individual molecules, there can be little or no flow of electrons through the bulk material unless other substances are present.
- Therefore, these delocalized electrons can move around with electric charge, so C_{60} conducts electricity.

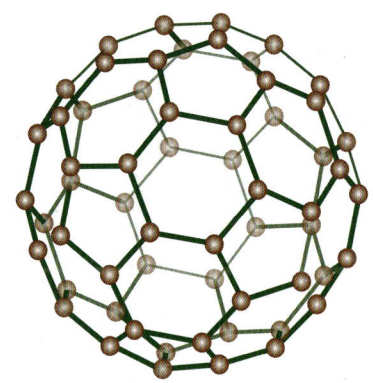

Fig 1.12 - Structure of C_{60} fullerene

Key Points: C_{60} fullerene have low melting and boiling point

- C_{60} fullerene is made up of 60 carbon atoms joined together by strong covalent bonds.
- Individual molecules are held together by weak intermolecular forces.
- Very little energy is needed to overcome these forces
- Hence, C_{60} have low melting point and boiling point.

> - C_{60} fullerene is also known as "buckyball".
> - Structure of C_{60} fullerene is a combination of 12 pentagonal and 20 hexagonal rings, forming a sphere shape with 60 vertices for the 60 carbons

Key Points: Graphene is a layer of graphite

- Graphene is a single layer taken from graphite.
- It is very strong with high melting point due to its strong covalent bonds between the carbon atoms.
- Graphene conducts electricity due to its delocalised electrons that are free to move around the layer which is similar as graphite.

> Graphene is a giant covalent substance.

1.39 Describe, using poly(ethene) as the example, that simple polymers consist of large molecules containing chains of carbon atoms

Key Points: Poly(ethene) – A polymer

- Poly(ethene) is a polymer made by a process called polymerization.
- Polymer is a long chain molecule which is joined by repeating units of monomer.
- Single unit of polymer is a monomer.
- In poly(ethene), ethene is the monomer (Fig 1.13)
- Due to strong covalent bonds between monomers of ethene, it has a high melting point.

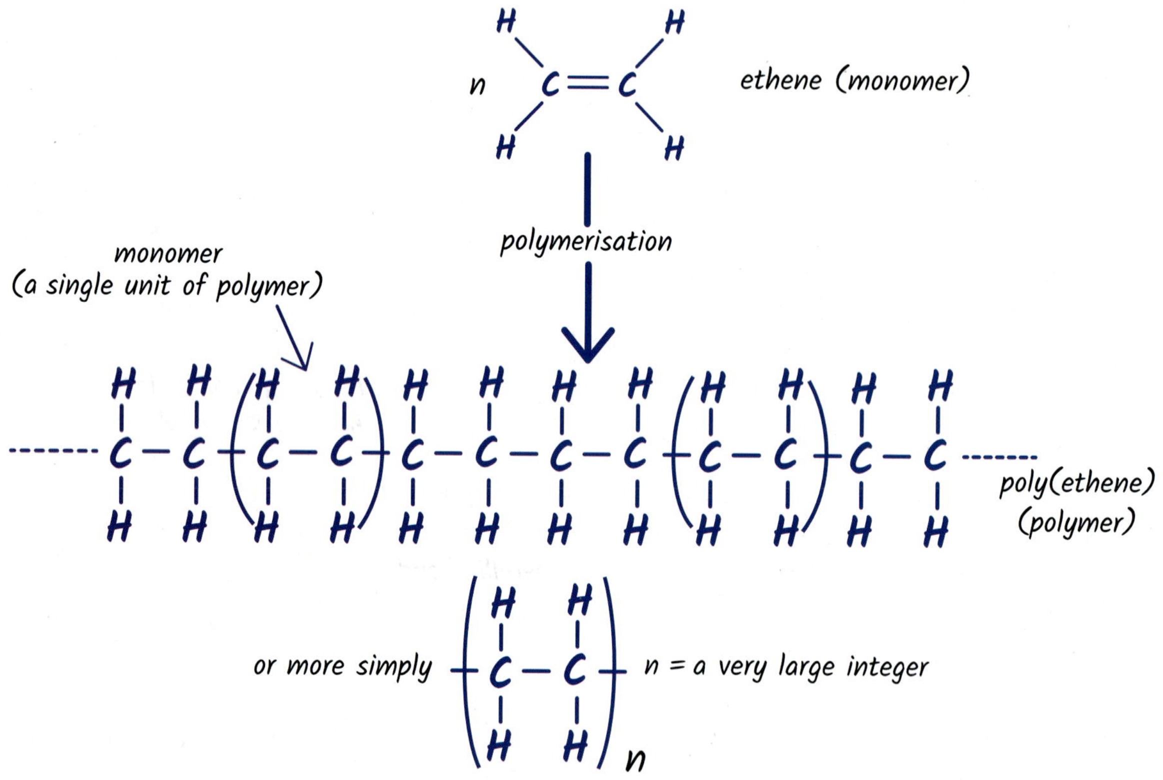

Fig 1.13 - Structure of poly(ethene)

Metallic Bonding

Structure of metal

1.40 Explain the properties of metals, including malleability and the ability to conduct electricity

1.42 Describe most metals as shiny solids which have high melting points, high density and are good conductors of electricity whereas most non-metals have low boiling points and are poor conductors of electricity

Key Points: Metallic bonding

- Metallic lattice consists of positive ions surrounded by delocalised electrons (Fig 1.14).
- The electrostatic force of attraction between positive ions and delocalised electrons creates a bonding called metallic bonds.

Key Points: Metals are good conductors of electricity. Why?

- In metals, positive ions are surround by delocalised electrons which are mobile.
- If a charge is applied at the surface of the metal, the electrons will move with electrical current throughout the structure and conduct electricity.

Physical properties of metals and non-metals

Key Points: Physical properties of metals

- **Good conductor of electricity and heat:** Delocalised electrons carries electricity and heat throughout the structure.
- **High melting and boiling points:** Due to the presence of strong forces of attraction between the positive ions and delocalised electrons, a lot of energy is required to overcome the forces of attraction to break the metallic bond.
- **Malleable and ductile:** Same size of atoms can slide over each other into new positions without breaking the metallic bond.
- **Shiny:** In the presence of light, delocalised electrons vibrates. When the electrons vibrate, light is produced and the metal looks shiny.
- **High density:** Oppositely charged electrons and positive ions are held together by strong forces of attraction with no air gaps.

Positively charged ions i.e. nuclei and inner electrons.

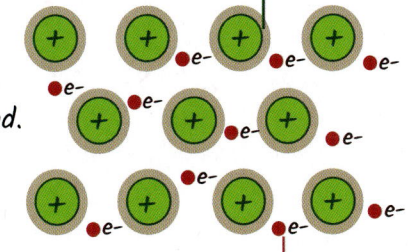

Sea of delocalised outer electrons.

Fig 1.14 Metallic bonding

Malleable: Can be hammered into sheets.
Ductile: Can be drawn out into wires.

Key Points: Physical properties of non-metals

- **Poor conductor of electricity and heat:** Non-metals have fewer free electrons which are held tightly bond and are not allowed to move freely.

Metal: Good conductor of electricity and heat.
Noon-metal: Poor conductor of electricity and heat (some exceptions – E.g. graphite).

- **Low melting and boiling points:** Molecules are held together by weak intermolecular forces, so it takes less time to change from a solid to a liquid or a liquid to a gas.

Topic 1 – Key Concepts in Chemistry

Calculations involving masses

Relative formula mass

1.43 Calculate relative formula mass given relative atomic masses

Key Points: To calculate the relative formula mass

- Using the periodic table to find the relative atomic mass for each element
- Multiply the number of each atom with the relative atomic mass
- Add up the relative atomic masses

Worked example: 12   a) Calculate the relative formula mass of **$CaCO_3$**

Solution

Relative formula masses:

$$Ca = 40; \; C = 12; \; O = 16$$
$$= (1 \times 40) + (1 \times 12) + (3 \times 16)$$
$$= 40 + 12 + 48$$
$$= 100$$

Calculating relative molecular mass is very straightforward. All you need to do: add up the relative atomic masses from the Periodic table.

Remember: Highest number of an element in the periodic table is relative atomic mass (Mass number)

b) Calculate the relative formula mass of **$CuSO_4.5H_2O$**

Solution

Relative formula masses:

$$Cu = 63.5; \; S = 32; \; O = 16; \; H = 1$$
$$= (1 \times 63.5) + (1 \times 32) + (16 \times 4) + \mathbf{5\,((2 \times 1) + 16.00)}$$
$$= 159.5 + 90$$
$$= \mathbf{249.5}$$

Sometimes 'H_2O' in hydrated compounds may be confusing. $5H_2O$ means there are 5 molecules of water present in the water of crystallisation. All you need to do: calculate the relative formula mass of H_2O and multiply by 5 AND add with relative formula mass of $CuSO_4$.

Empirical formulae

1.44 Calculate the formulae of simple compounds from reacting masses or percentage composition and understand that these are empirical formulae

1.45 Deduce: a) the empirical formula of a compound from the formula of its molecule
b) the molecular formula of a compound from its empirical formula and its relative molecular mass

1.46 Describe an experiment to determine the empirical formula of a simple compound such as magnesium oxide

Key definition: Empirical formula is the simplest ratio of atoms in a compound.
Molecular formula is the actual formula of a compound.

Key Table: To calculate the empirical formula

Steps	Method	A Element 1	B Element 2
1	Mass (or) Percentage given		
2	Relative atomic mass		
3	Using values above to calculate the $$\text{Moles} = \frac{\text{Mass}}{\text{Relative atomic mass}}$$		
4	Divide by the least number from above in both sides		
5	Simplest ratio		
	Empirical formula	A$_{ratio\ 1}$	B$_{ratio\ 2}$

Keep adding the element in the table as per the question.

In step 4, you may get decimal of 0.5 (E.g: 0.5, 1.5, 2.5 etc.).
In that case you must multiply the value of all the elements by 2 to get the simplest ratio.

Worked example: 13 A compound contains 25.3g of magnesium and 74.7g of chlorine. Calculate the empirical formula for this compound.

Solution

Steps	Method	Mg	Cl
1	Mass (or) Percentage given	25.3	74.7
2	Relative atomic mass	24.0	35.5
3	Using values above to calculate the $\text{Moles} = \dfrac{\text{Mass}}{\text{Relative atomic mass}}$	$\dfrac{25.3}{24.0} = 1.05$	$\dfrac{74.7}{35.5} = 2.10$
4	Divide by the least number from above in both sides	$\dfrac{1.05}{1.05} = 1$	$\dfrac{2.10}{1.05} = 2$
5	Simplest ratio	1	2
	Empirical formula	\multicolumn{2}{c}{$Mg_1Cl_2 = \mathbf{MgCl_2}$}

Worked example: 14 A compound has the composition by mass of 43.4% sodium, 11.3% carbon and oxygen. Find the empirical formula.

Solution

Consider mass and percentage of substance are same. Total percentage of all elements present in a compound is equal to 100

Steps	Method	Na	C	O
1	Mass (or) Percentage given	43.4	11.3	100 − (43.4+11.3) = 45.3
2	Relative atomic mass	23.0	12.0	16.0
3	Using values above to calculate the $\text{Moles} = \dfrac{\text{Mass}}{\text{Relative atomic mass}}$	$\dfrac{43.4}{23.0} = 1.89$	$\dfrac{11.3}{12.0} = 0.94$	$\dfrac{45.3}{16.0} = 2.83$
4	Divide by the least number from above in both sides.	$\dfrac{1.88}{0.94} = 2.00$	$\dfrac{0.94}{0.94} = 1.00$	$\dfrac{2.83}{0.94} = 3.01$
5	Simplest ratio	2	1	3
	Empirical formula	\multicolumn{3}{c}{$Na_2C_1O_3 = \mathbf{Na_2CO_3}$}

Worked example: 15   A compound contains by mass of 68.4g chromium and 31.6g oxygen. Find the empirical formula.

Solution

Steps	Method	Cr	O
1	Mass (or) Percentage given	68.4	31.6
2	Relative atomic mass	52.0	16.0
3	Using values above to calculate the Moles = $\frac{Mass}{Relative\ atomic\ mass}$	$\frac{68.4}{52.0} = 1.32$	$\frac{31.6}{16.0} = 1.98$
4	Divide by the least number from above in both sides	$\frac{1.32}{1.32} = 1$ $= 1 \times 2 = 2$	$\frac{1.98}{1.32} = 1.5$ $= 1.5 \times 2 = 3$
5	Simplest ratio	2	3
	Empirical formula	Cr_2O_3 =	**Cr_2O_3**

1.49 is a close to 1.5, so it must be converted into a whole number to get simplest ratio by multiplying entire number by 2

Converting Empirical formulae into molecular formulae

> molecular formula = x (Empirical formula)
>
> x = An integer

Worked example 16:   A compound has the empirical formula of CH_2O and a relative molecular mass of 180. What is the molecular formula of the compound?

Solution

Ar = Relative atomic mass (Mass number)

$$x\ [\ (1 \times Ar\ (C)) + (2 \times Ar\ (H)) + (1 \times Ar\ (O))\ ] = 180$$
$$x\ [\ (1 \times 12) + (2 \times 1) + (1 \times 16)] = 180$$
$$x\ [30] = 180$$
$$x = \frac{180}{30} = 6$$

Molecular formula = 6 (CH_2O) = **$C_6H_{12}O_6$**

43

Worked example: 17 A compound has the composition by mass of 30.8% carbon, 7.7% hydrogen and 61.5% oxygen. What is the molecular formula if the molecular mass is 234?

Solution

> Consider mass and percentage of substance are same. Total percentage of all elements present in a compound is equal to 100

Steps	Method	C	H	O
1	Mass (or) Percentage given	30.8	7.7	61.5
2	Relative atomic mass	12.0	1.0	16.0
3	Using values above to calculate the Moles = $\frac{Mass}{Relative\ atomic\ mass}$	$\frac{30.8}{12.0} = 2.57$	$\frac{7.7}{1.0} = 7.70$	$\frac{61.5}{16.0} = 3.84$
4	Divide by the least number from above in both sides.	$\frac{2.56}{2.56} = 1.00$ = 1 x 2 = 2	$\frac{7.70}{2.56} = 3.01$ = 3 x 2 = 6	$\frac{3.84}{2.56} = 1.50$ = 1.5 x 2 = 3
5	Simplest ratio	2	6	3
	Empirical formula		$C_2H_6O_3 = C_2H_6O_3$	

Now, using the empirical formula from the table calculate the molecular formula:

x [(2 x Ar (C)) + (6 x Ar (H)) + (3 x Ar (O))] = 234
x [(2 x 12) + (6 x 1) + (3 x 16)] = 234
x [78] = 234
x = $\frac{234}{78}$ = 3

Molecular formula = $3(C_2H_6O_3)$ = $C_6H_{18}O_9$

Worked example 18: A group of students investigated the relationship between the mass of magnesium burned and the mass of magnesium oxide formed, in order to calculate the empirical of magnesium oxide. The reaction can be represented by the chemical equation below:

$$2Mg + O_2 \rightarrow 2MgO$$

Magnesium was allowed to burn in oxygen in a crucible covered by a lid, over a Bunsen burner. The students carried out the following measurements:

Mass of crucible and lid: 32.35g
Mass of crucible, lid and magnesium ribbon: 33.02g
Mass of crucible, lid and magnesium ribbon (after heating): 33.46g.

Calculate the following: (a) Mass of magnesium
(b) Mass of magnesium oxide
(c) Empirical formula of Magnesium oxide

Solution

(a) Mass of magnesium = Mass of crucible, lid and magnesium ribbon - Mass of crucible and lid = 33.02 - 32.35 = 0.67g

(b) Mass of magnesium oxide = Mass of crucible, lid and magnesium ribbon (after heating) - Mass of crucible and lid = 33.46 - 32.35 = 1.11g
Empirical formula of magnesium oxide can be calculated by:
Mass of oxygen = Mass of magnesium oxide - Mass of magnesium = 1.11 - 0.67 = 0.44g

Steps	Method	Mg	O
1	Mass (or) Percentage given	0.67	0.44
2	Relative atomic mass	24.0	16.0
3	Using values above to calculate the Moles = $\frac{Mass}{Relative\ atomic\ mass}$	$\frac{0.67}{24}$ = 0.0279	$\frac{0.44}{16}$ = 0.0275
4	Divide by the least number from above in both sides	$\frac{0.0279}{0.0275}$ = 1.01	$\frac{0.0275}{0.0275}$ = 1
5	Simplest ratio	1	1
	Empirical formula	Mg_1O_1 = **MgO**	

Worked example 19: A sample of hydrated calcium sulphate, $CaSO_4.xH_2O$, has a relative formula mass of 172. What is the value of x?

Solution:
Relative formula mass of $CaSO_4.xH_2O$
= (1×40) + (1×32) + (4 × 16) + x [(1×2) + 16] = 172
= 136 + 18x = 172
18x = 172 - 136
18x = 36
x = $\frac{36}{18}$ = **2**
= $CaSO_4.2H_2O$

Worked example 20: A sample of 13.2g of hydrated zinc sulphate, $ZnSO_4.xH_2O$, was strongly heated until no further change in mass was recorded. On heating, all the water of crystallisation evaporated:
$$ZnSO_4.xH_2O \rightarrow ZnSO_4 + xH_2O$$
Calculate the number of moles of water of crystallisation in the zinc sulphate sample given that 7.4g of the solid remained after strong heating.

Solution:
- Firstly, workout the relative formula mass of $ZnSO_4$ and H_2O:
$ZnSO_4$ = (1 × 65) + (1 × 32) + (4 × 16) = **161**
H_2O = (2 × 1) + (1 × 16) = **18**

- secondly, workout the mass of $ZnSO_4$ and H_2O to find out the moles using the data given in the question:

Total mass of $ZnSO_4.xH_2O$ = 13.2g
Mass of $ZnSO_4$ = 7.4g [after heating = water evaporated, left out with $ZnSO_4$]
Mass of water (a - b) = 13.2 - 7.4 = 5.8g

Steps	Method	$ZnSO_4$	xH_2O
1	Mass (or) Percentage given	7.4	5.8
2	Relative formula mass	161	18
3	Using values above to calculate the $Moles = \dfrac{Mass}{Relative\ atomic\ mass}$	$\dfrac{7.4}{161} = 0.046$	$\dfrac{5.8}{18} = 0.322$
4	Divide by the least number from above in both sides.	$\dfrac{0.046}{0.046} = 1$	$\dfrac{0.322}{0.046} = 7$
5	Simplest ratio of number of moles	1	7
	Empirical formula	\multicolumn{2}{c}{$= ZnSO_4.7H_2O$}

Law of conservation of mass in reaction

1.47 Explain the law of conservation of mass applied to:
   a) a closed system including a precipitation reaction in a closed flask
   b) a non-enclosed system including a reaction in an open flask that takes in or gives out a gas

Key Points: Conservation of mass in a closed system

- Closed system is the system where no new substances are added or removed in a chemical reaction, so the overall mass of the substance remains same.
- Precipitation reaction in a closed flask can be considered as a closed system reaction.
- Aqueous silver nitrate reacts with aqueous sodium bromide to form a solid **cream precipitate** of bromide ion (sodium bromide) and a colourless solution of sodium nitrate. See the chemical equation below:

$$AgNO_3(aq) + NaBr(aq) \longrightarrow AgBr(s) + NaNO_3(aq)$$

- The balanced chemical equation shows that there is no change in the mass, as the number atoms remains in the system in a closed environment.

Key Points: Conservation of mass in a non-enclosed system

- Non-enclosed system is the system where substances can be added or removed in a chemical reaction, so the overall mass of the substance can either increase or decrease.
- Thermal decomposition in a non-enclosed environment can be considered as a non-enclosed system reaction.
- Thermal decomposition of solid limestone (Calcium carbonate, $CaCO_3$) forms solid lime (Calcium oxide, CaO) and carbon dioxide gas. See the chemical equation below:

$$CaCO_3(s) \longrightarrow CaO(s) + CO_2(g)$$

- The balanced chemical equation shows that with reaction progression, the overall mass of the system decreases, as the carbon dioxide gas escapes into the air

Calculating the masses of reactants and products from balanced equations

1.48 Calculate masses of reactants and products from balanced equations, given the mass of one substance
1.49 Calculate the concentration of solutions in gdm^{-3}

Key Points: To calculate the mass of reactants and products from balanced equations

1) Construct the balanced chemical equation.
2) Find out the number of moles of the known substance.
3) Figure out the molar ratio of the substance involved in the question.
4) Calculate the number of moles of the substance to be found.
5) Use the above step to work out the mass.

Worked example 21: Calculate the mass of magnesium sulphate ($MgSO_4$) produced when magnesium, Mg reacts with 294g of sulphuric acid, H_2SO_4.

Solution:

Balanced chemical equation	$Mg + H_2SO_4 \longrightarrow MgSO_4 + H_2$
Number of moles of the known substance	Value of H_2SO_4 is given in grams, use the moles formula related to solid: H_2SO_4 = (1×2) + (1×32) + (4×16) = **98** Moles = $\dfrac{Mass}{Relative\ formula\ Mass}$ = $\dfrac{294}{98}$ = 3 moles
Mole ratio of the substance involved in the question from *balanced equation*	1 mole H_2SO_4 : 1 moles $MgSO_4$
Calculate the number of moles of the substance to be found	1 mole of H_2SO_4 gives 1 mole of $MgSO_4$ Therefore, 3 moles of H_2SO_4 must give 1 = 1 3 = x x = $\dfrac{3 \times 1}{1}$ = 3 3 moles of magnesium sulphate
Mass of $MgSO_4$ produced	Mass = Moles × Relative formula Mass Molecular Mass of $MgSO_4$ = 120 = 3 × 120 = **360g**

Formula to calculate number of moles of SOLID (g,kg) is
Moles = $\dfrac{Mass}{Relative\ formula\ mass}$

Formula to calculate number of moles of SOLUTION (mol dm^{-3}, cm^3) is Moles = $\dfrac{Concentration \times Volume}{1000}$

Formula to calculate number of moles of GAS (dm^3) is
Moles = $\dfrac{Volume\ (dm^3)}{22.4}$

Worked example 22: Sodium is burnt in air in the presence of excess oxygen. Calculate the mass of sodium, Na, burnt in air when 496g of sodium oxide, Na_2O, is produced.

Solution:

Balanced chemical equation	$4Na + O_2 \longrightarrow 2Na_2O$
Number of moles of the known substance	Value of Na_2O is given in grams, use the moles formula related to solid. Relative formula mass of Na_2O: $(23 \times 2) + 16 = 62$ Moles = $\dfrac{Mass}{Relative\ formula\ Mass} = \dfrac{496}{62} = 8$ moles
Mole ratio of the substance involved in the question from *balanced equation*	4 moles Na : 2 moles Na_2O
Calculate the number of moles of the substance to be found	2 moles of Na_2O is produced from 4 moles of Na burnt Therefore, 8 moles of Na_2O must be formed from $\dfrac{2}{8} = \dfrac{4}{x}$ $x = \dfrac{4 \times 8}{2} = 16$ 16 moles of Na
Mass of Na burnt	Mass = Moles × Relative formula Mass Relative formula Mass of Na = 23 = 16 × 23 = **368g**

Moles of particles

1.50 Recall that one mole of particles of a substance is defined as:
a) the Avogadro constant number of particles (6.02×10^{23} atoms, molecules, formulae or ions) of that substance
b) a mass of 'relative particle mass' g

1.51 Calculate the number of:
a) moles of particles of a substance in a given mass of that substance and vice versa
b) particles of a substance in a given number of moles of that substance and vice versa
c) particles of a substance in a given mass of that substance and vice versa (H)

Key Points: Particles in terms of moles

- 1 mole of substance has 6.02×10^{23} particles of the substance.
- The mass of 1 mole of the substance is always equal to its relative atomic mass in grams.

M_r = g/mol
Avogadro constant = 6.02×10^{23}

Example: 1 mole of nitrogen (N_2) has a mass of
$14 \times 2 = 28g$

Worked example 23: Calculate the number of moles of Sulphur, S in 0.125 mole of Sulphur trioxide, SO_3.

Solution:
There is 1 S atom in 1 SO_3 molecule.
So 0.125 mole of SO_3 contains 0.125 mole of S atoms.

Worked example 24: Calculate the number of moles of atoms in 0.100 mole of aluminium oxide, Al_2O_3.

Solution:
There are 5 atoms present in 1 Al_2O_3 molecule
So 0.100 mole of Al_2O_3 contains
$5 \times 0.100 = 0.500$ mole of atoms

Number of particles = number of moles × Avogadro constant

Worked example 25: Calculate the number of particles present in atoms of O in 2.00 mol.

Solution:
Number of particles = $2.00 \times 6.02 \times 10^{23} = 1.20 \times 10^{24}$

Worked example 26: Calculate the number of particles present in oxygen atoms in 0.0711 mol of copper sulphate, $CuSO_4$.

Solution:
Number of particles present in copper sulphate ($CuSO_4$) = $0.0711 \times 6.02 \times 10^{23}$
= 4.28×10^{22}
Therefore, number of particles present in oxygen atoms = $4 \times 4.28 \times 10^{22}$
= 1.71×10^{23}

Limiting reactant and Excess reactant

1.52 Explain why, in a reaction, the mass of product formed is controlled by the mass of the reactant which is not in excess. (H)

Key Points: Limiting reactant

- The reactant in a chemical reaction that limits the amount of product that can be formed.
- The reaction will stop when all the limiting reactant is used up.
- The amount of product formed is determined by the amount of reactant that *is not in excess.*

Key Points: Excess reactant

- The reactant in a chemical reaction that remains when a reaction stops, when the limiting reactant is completely used up.
- The excess reactant remains because *nothing is there* with which it can react with.

Worked example 27: How much of the excess reagent remains if 14.3grams of carbon monoxide, CO reacted with 1.58grams of oxygen, O_2?

$$2CO + O_2 \longrightarrow 2CO_2$$

M_r of CO is 28
M_r of O_2 is 32

Solution:

a) Moles of CO = $14.3 \times \dfrac{1 \text{ mole}}{28}$ = 0.510moles of CO

b) Moles of O_2 = $1.58 \times \dfrac{1 \text{ mole}}{32}$ = 0.049moles of O_2

If all the oxygen is used up, $0.049 \times \dfrac{2}{1}$ or 0.098moles of CO are required.

Because there are 0.510moles of CO, CO is in **excess** and thus O_2 is the **limiting reactant.**

c) 0.510moles − 0.098moles = **0.412**moles left in excess.

Stoichiometry of the reaction

1.53 Deduce the stoichiometry of a reaction from the masses of the reactants and products (H)

Key Points: Deducing the stoichiometry of a reaction

- **Step 1:** Calculate the moles of each substance using the mass given.
- **Step 2:** Deduce the simplest ratio (refer to the examples of empirical formula for step 1 & 2).

    Note: The ratio of the moles of each substance is the stoichiometry of the reaction.
- **Step 3:** Write the balanced equation.

Worked example 28: Deduce the balanced chemical equation for the reaction when 2.3g of sodium reacts with 0.8g of oxygen to produce sodium oxide.

Solution:

- **Step 1:** Calculate the moles of each substance using the mass given.

    Moles of sodium = $\frac{2.3}{23}$ = 0.1

    Moles of oxygen = $\frac{0.8}{16}$ = 0.05

- **Step 2:** Deduce the simplest ratio

    Sodium = $\frac{0.1}{0.05}$ = 2

    Oxygen = $\frac{0.05}{0.05}$ = 1

    $Na_2O_1 = Na_2O$

- **Step 3:** Write the balanced equation.

    $4Na + O_2 \longrightarrow 2Na_2O$

States of matter

Kinetic particle theory

2.1 Describe the arrangement, movement and the relative energy of particles in each of the three states of matter: solid, liquid and gas

Key Points: Kinetic particle theory

- Matter is anything that occupies space with mass
- Matter consists of tiny particles; these particles can be atoms, molecules or ions.
- When matter is heated its particles gain more kinetic energy and move faster or vibrate more.
- When matter is heated it expands as its particles move further apart;
- All substances can be classified into three states of matter as solid, liquid and gas (Table 2.1)

Plasma is the fourth state of matter.

Property	Solid	Liquid	Gas
Fixed volume	Yes	Yes	No
Fixed shape	Yes	No fixed shape. Takes up the shape of the container.	No fixed shape. Takes up the shape of the container.
Compressible	No	No	Yes
Forces of attraction between particles	Very strong forces of attraction	Strong forces of attraction between particles	Very weak forces of attraction between particles
Motion of particles	Vibrate about a fixed position.	Vibrate, rotate and translate.	Vibrate, rotate and translate in random motion.
Particles in physical state	solid	liquid	gas

Table 2.1 - Three states of matter

52

Phase changes of matter

2.2 Recall the names used for the interconversions between the three states of matter, recognising that these are physical changes: contrasted with chemical reactions that result in chemical changes

2.3 Explain the changes in arrangement, movement and energy of particles during these interconversions

2.4 Predict the physical state of a substance under specified conditions, given suitable data

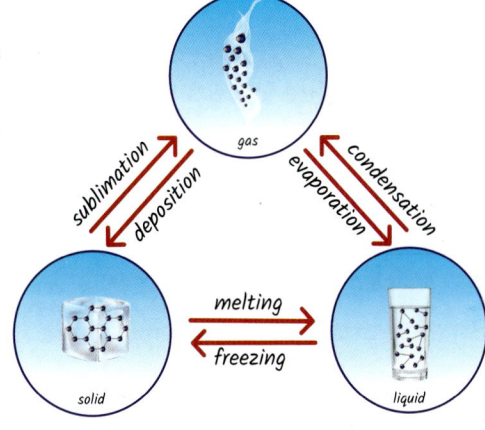

Key Points: Interconversion of states of matter

- Matter can change from one state to another (Fig 2.1).
- **Interconversion of the states of matter** is the phenomenon of the change of matter from one state to another and back to its original states.
- Matter can be changed from one state to another by changing **temperature or pressure**.
  - **Example:** converting ice into water

The heat is used to increase the kinetic energy of the particles of ice so that particles break away from original solid form, ice, and move around freely to form the liquid, water.

Fig 2.1 - Interconversion of states of matter

Key Points: Melting, Boiling and Freezing

- **Melting:** Melting is the process where solid changes into a liquid at a particular temperature.
- During melting, the particles of the solid gain sufficient energy and vibrate till they overcome the forces of attraction between them, moving faster and further apart.
- The temperature at which solid melts to become a liquid at the atmospheric pressure is called its **melting point**.
- **Freezing:** The process, where a liquid converts into a solid, is called freezing or solidification.
- During freezing, the particles lose energy and move closer together at a constant temperature from a liquid state to a solid state.
- The temperature at which liquid turns into solid is known as **freezing point**.
- **Boiling:** The process where liquid changes into a vapour at a particular temperature.
- During boiling, the particles of the liquid gain sufficient energy and slide over each other till they overcome the forces of attraction between them, moving randomly and very far apart.
- The temperature at which a liquid starts boiling at the atmospheric pressure is known as its boiling point.

The temperature remains constant until the entire solid melts into a liquid.

The temperature remains constant until the entire liquid boils into a gas.

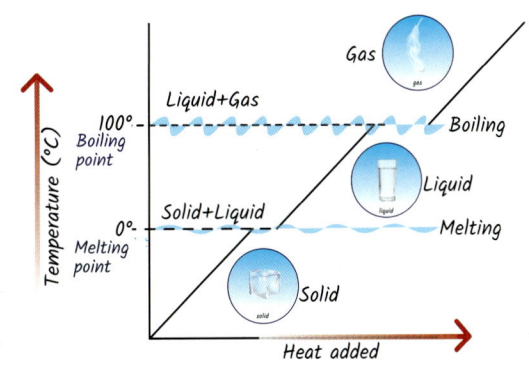

Fig 2.2 - Heating curve

Topic 2 – States of matter & Methods of Purifying Substances

53

Key Points: Condensation and Sublimation

- **Condensation:** The process where vapour changes to a liquid is called condensation.

  Example: Condensation of water vapour - Formation of water droplets on the outer surface of the glass with cold water.

  > The process where liquid changes into vapour at any temperature below its boiling point is evaporation.

- **Sublimation:** The process, where a solid on heating, directly changes into gas, without changing into liquid and a gas; and when cooled, directly changes to solid without changing into liquid is called **deposition**.

  Example: Solid ammonium chloride, on heating directly converts into vapours without changing to the liquid state.

  > The sublimation of Naphthalene and camphor can take place without heating them.
  > They sublime at room temperature.

Key Points: Predicting the physical state of a substance at a given temperature

- Melting point and boiling point of a substance is key to predict its physical state.
- It is SOLID, if given temperature **is less than** (<) melting point
- It is LIQUID, if given temperature **is between** melting and boiling points
- It is GAS, if given temperature **is greater than** (>) boiling point

Worked example 1: Predict the state of ammonia at -40°C using the data given below.

Ammonia, NH_3	
Boiling point	-33°C
Melting point	-78°C

Table 2.2 - Ammonia

Solution:

Liquid, because -40°C is between its melting and boiling points.

Methods of purifying substances

Pure substance and mixture

2.5 Explain the difference between the use of 'pure' in chemistry compared with its everyday use and the differences in chemistry between a pure substance and a mixture

2.6 Interpret melting point data to distinguish between pure substances which have a sharp melting point and mixtures which melt over a range of temperatures

Key Flowchart: Pure substance and mixture with everyday use

MATTER
Matter is anything that occupies space with mass.

PURE SUBSTANCE
A pure substance has a definite and constant composition. They are made up of only one matter.
Examples: gold, pure water, oxygen molecule etc.

MIXTURE
Mixtures are made up of several substances that are not chemically bonded.
Examples: air, mixture of alcohol AND water, blood, soil, alloys etc.

ELEMENT
An element is composed of a single kind of atom.
Gold is an example of an element.

COMPOUND
A compound is composed of two or more elements in a specific ratio.
Water is an example of a compound

HETEROGENEOUS MIXTURE
A heterogeneous mixture is a mixture where the components of the mixture are not uniform with different properties.
Different samples from the mixture are not identical to each other. There are always two or more phases in a heterogeneous mixture.
Examples: Cereal in milk, salad dressing, mixed nuts etc.

HOMOGENEOUS MIXTURE
A homogeneous mixture is a mixture where the components that make up the mixture are uniformly distributed throughout the mixture. The composition of the mixture is the same throughout. There is only one phase of matter observed in a homogeneous mixture.
Examples: Air, ethanol, rain water

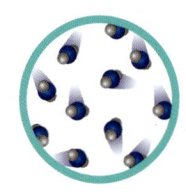

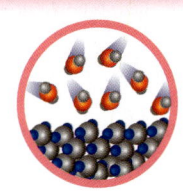

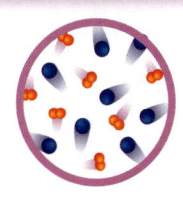

Flowchart 2.1 - Interconversion of states of matter

Topic 2 - States of matter & Methods of Purifying Substances

55

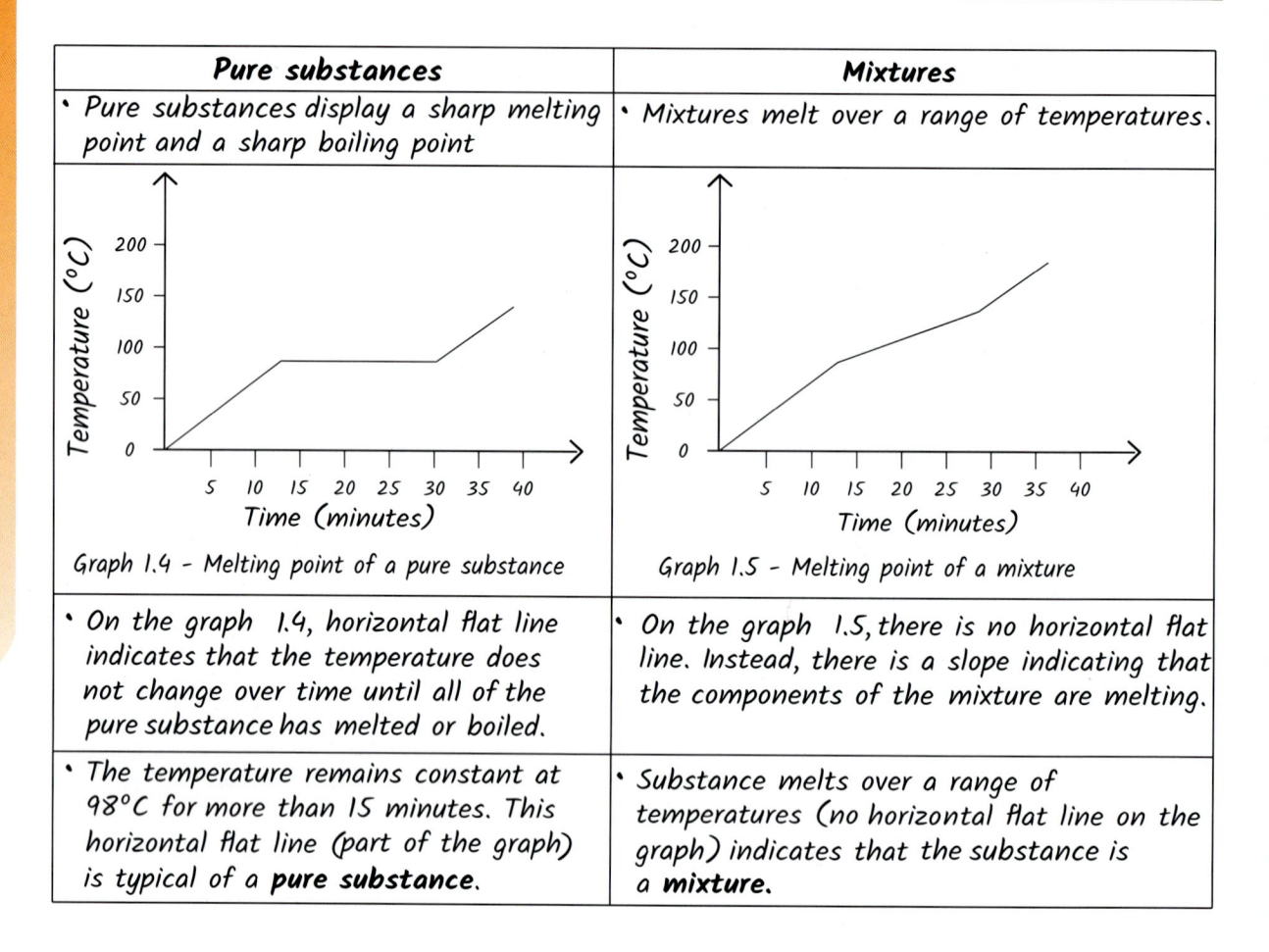

Key Table: Distinguish between pure substances and mixtures using melting point

> Sharpness of the melting point is often used to determine whether a substance is pure or impure.

Pure substances	Mixtures
• Pure substances display a sharp melting point and a sharp boiling point Graph 1.4 - Melting point of a pure substance	• Mixtures melt over a range of temperatures. Graph 1.5 - Melting point of a mixture
• On the graph 1.4, horizontal flat line indicates that the temperature does not change over time until all of the pure substance has melted or boiled.	• On the graph 1.5, there is no horizontal flat line. Instead, there is a slope indicating that the components of the mixture are melting.
• The temperature remains constant at 98°C for more than 15 minutes. This horizontal flat line (part of the graph) is typical of a **pure substance**.	• Substance melts over a range of temperatures (no horizontal flat line on the graph) indicates that the substance is a **mixture**.

Table 2.3 - Distinguish between pure substances and mixtures using melting point

Separation techniques and analysis

2.7 Explain the types of mixtures that can be separated by using the following experimental techniques:
   a) simple distillation
   b) fractional distillation
   c) filtration
   d) crystallization
   e) paper chromatography
2.8 Describe an appropriate experimental technique to separate a mixture, knowing the properties of the components of the mixture

Key Points: Filtration

- Filtration technique is used to separate **insoluble solid** from a **liquid**. Refer to Fig 2.9.
- Fold the filter paper in the shape of a cone and place it into a filter funnel.
- Wet the filter paper slightly.
- Pour the mixture into the filter funnel by sliding against the glass rod.
- Allow the solution to get filtered.
- The liquid (water) collected at the bottom in a beaker is known as the **FILTRATE**.
- The insoluble solid (sand) which remains on the filter paper is known as **RESIDUE**.
- Filtration technique is used to separate precipitate (insoluble solid) from the solution.

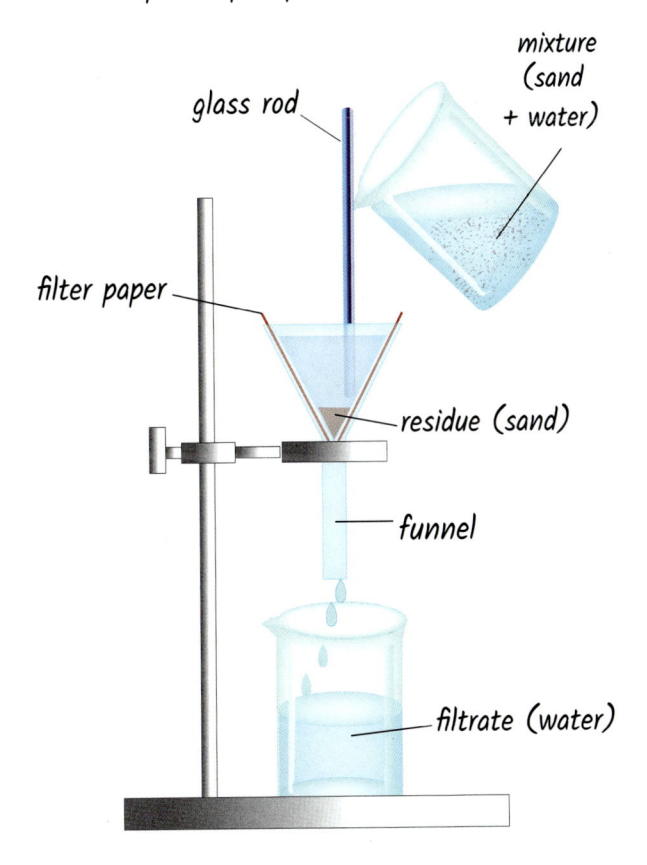

Fig 2.9 - Filtration

Key Points: Crystallisation

- Crystallisation is used to separate the pure solids (**solute**) in the form of crystals from the **solution**. Refer to Fig 2.10.
- Dissolve the impure solid in the solvent to make salt solution (**step 1**).
- The salt solution is filtered (**step 2**) by following the process of filtration.
- The salt solution is heated in an evaporating basin until a saturated solution is formed. (**step 3**).
- The saturated solution is cooled to form crystals that can be dried by pressing them between sheets of filter paper (**step 4**).
- Crystallisation is used to obtain pure sugar and purify the antibiotics.

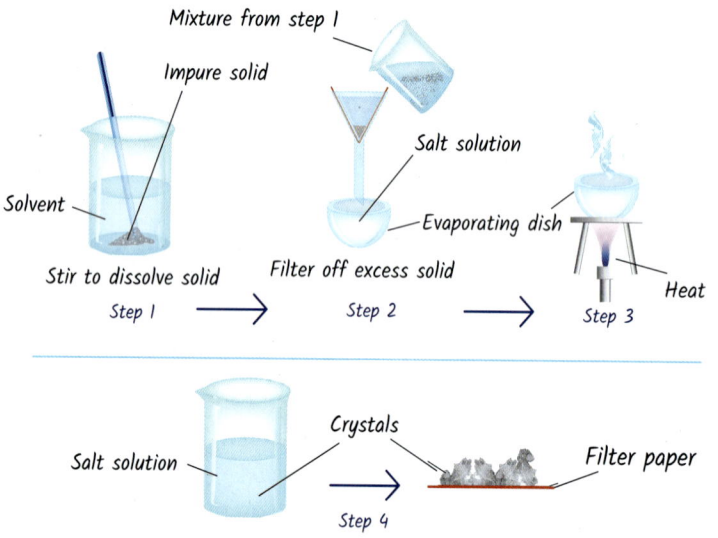

Crystals can be re-crystallised in order to obtain pure crystals.

Fig 2.10 - Crystallisation

Key Points: Simple Distillation

- Simple distillation is used to obtain **solvent** (**liquid**) from a solution of a solid (**solute**). Refer to Fig 2.11.
- Turn on the water tap to ensure circulation of water around the condenser.
- When the solution is heated and boiled, water is vapourised from the solution.
- At this stage the thermometer reads a constant temperature.
- The vapour moves up and is cooled and condensed as droplets of liquid.
- Collect the liquid (**distillate**) in the beaker until the temperature starts to rise.
- Simple distillation is used to obtain pure water from sea water.

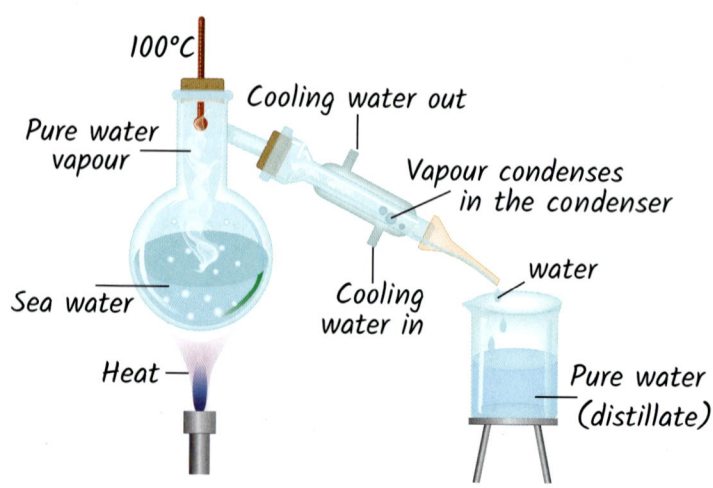

Fig 2.11 - Simple Distillation

Only particles that have reached boiling point would get vapourised.

Key Points: Fractional Distillation

- Fractional distillation is used to separate mixture of different liquids with different boiling points. Refer to Fig 2.12.
- Turn on the water tap to ensure a circulation of water around the condenser.
- When the solution is heated, **first liquid** is boiled, vapourised from the solution
- At this stage the thermometer reads a constant temperature.
- The vapour moves up and is cooled and condensed as droplets of liquid.
- Collect the liquid (**distillate**) in the beaker until the temperature starts to rise.
- Repeat the above process to collect the **second liquid** when the next constant temperature reading is reached.
- Repeat the process until the desired distillates have been collected.
- Fractional distillation is used to separate gases from liquid air and separation of hydrocarbon from crude oil.

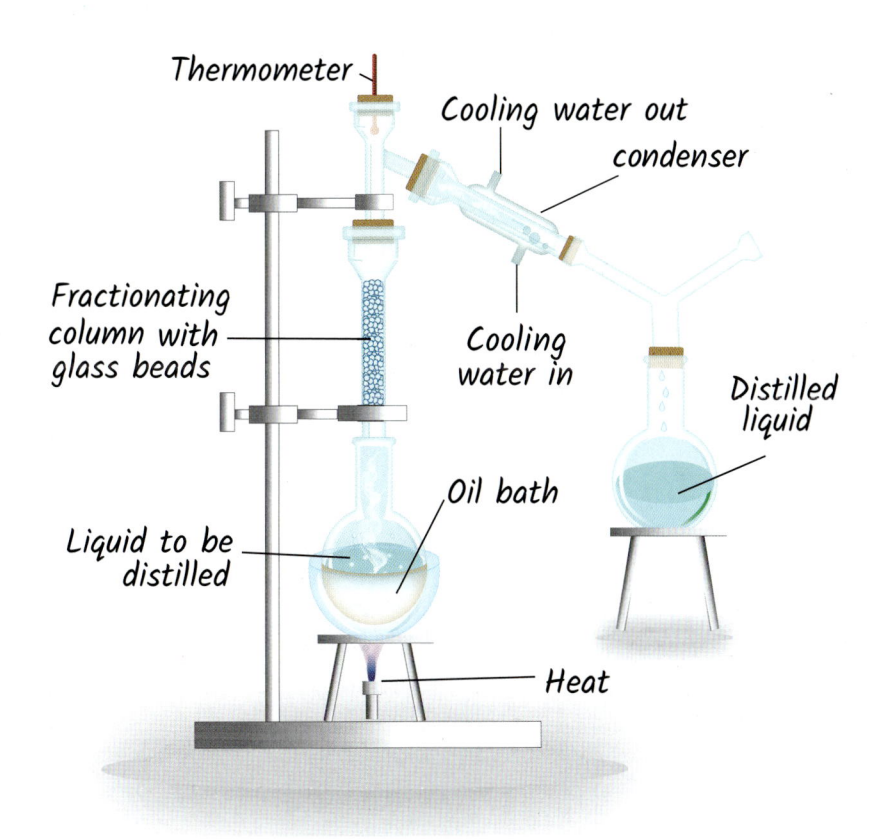

Fig 2.12 - Fractioal distillation

> Glass beads in the fractionating column is used to increase the surface area to allow both evaporation and condensation to take place.

Key Points: Chromatography

- Chromatography technique is used to
  - Separate two or more substances with different solubilities in the same solvent.
  Examples:
    - Separating mixtures of coloured inks (different colour have different solubility)
    - Separating mixtures of food colouring
    - Determine the purity of a substance.
    - Identify the unknown substance.

Different colours have different solubility.

- Principles of Chromatography
  - Different substances have different solubilities in the same solvent.
  - The more soluble the substance is, the faster it will dissolve in the solvent. This means that the more soluble substance will get carried further by the solvent ahead compared to the less soluble ones.

Key Points: Types of paper chromatography

- Types of paper chromatography (Fig 2.13)
  - Ascending paper chromatography
  - Descending paper chromatography

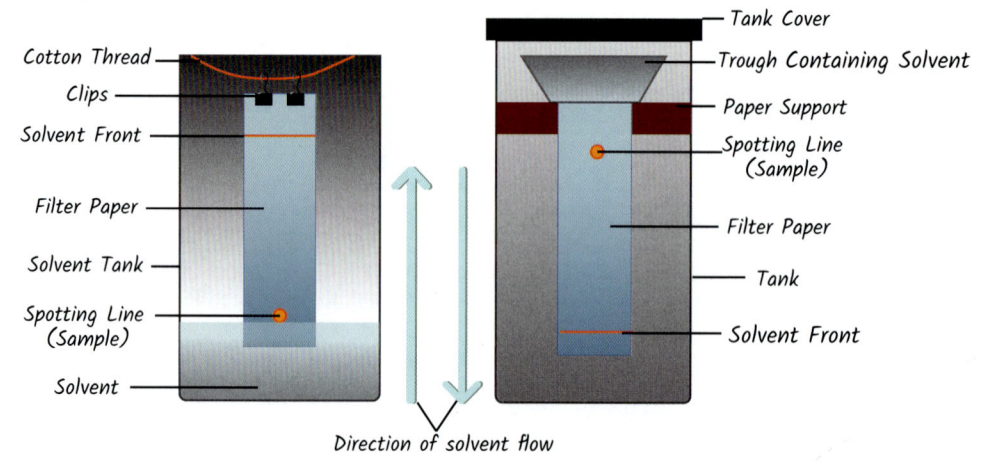

(a) - Ascending paper chromatography
(b) - Descending paper chromatography

Fig 2.13 - (a) & (b) Types of paper chromatography

Paper chromatography

2.9 Describe paper chromatography as the separation of mixtures of soluble substances by running a solvent (mobile phase) through the mixture on the paper (the paper contains the stationary phase), which causes the substances to move at different rates over the paper

Key Points: Paper chromatography

- An example of paper chromatography is shown in Fig 2.14. Dyes from an ink are separated by paper chromatography and a chromatogram is developed.

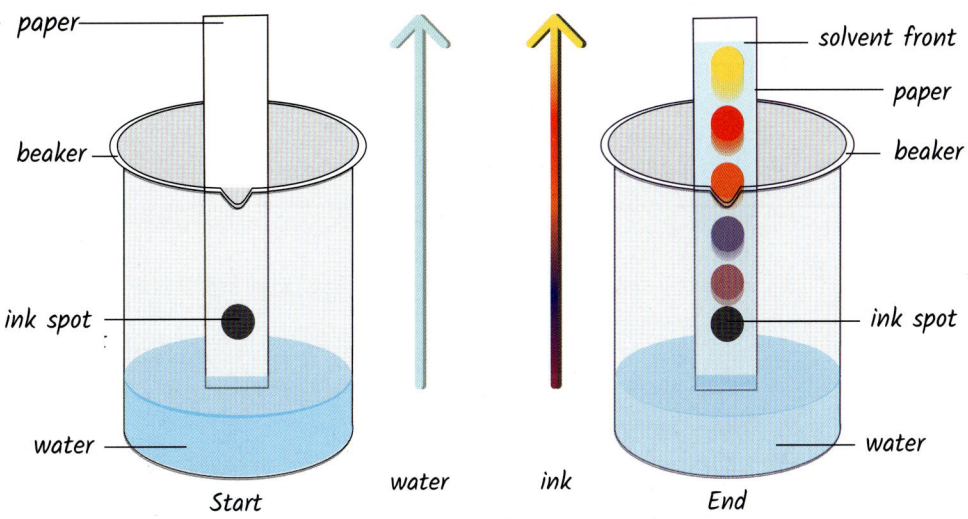

Fig 2.14 - Example of chromatography

- **Solvent front** is the furthest distance travelled by the solvent
- If no spots appear on the chromatogram, this could mean either of the substances are **insoluble in the solvent**.
- In this case, if the sample is insoluble with the solvent then it can be replaced. In most cases, ethanol can be a better solvent than water.
- R_f values (Retention factor) are fixed for each substance in a given solvent and can be obtained from reference books.
- R_f value must be always smaller than 1

Stationary phase is paper
Mobile phase is a liquid, commonly water, but could be ethanol or a non-polar solvent.

$$R_f = \frac{\text{distance moved by the solute (sample)}}{\text{distance moved by the solvent}}$$

- Pencil must be used to draw the start line (base line) because pen or marker itself made of mixture of different soluble dyes, will dissolve in the solvent and will move along the solvent, interfering with the result or gives incorrect data.
- Solvent level must be below the start line so that sample does not dissolve in the solvent.

2.10 Interpret a paper chromatogram:
   a) to distinguish between pure and impure substances
   b) to identify substances by comparison with known substances
   c) to identify substances by calculation and use of R_f values

Worked example 3: The diagram below shows the results of an experiment to identify the soluble substances of samples A and B

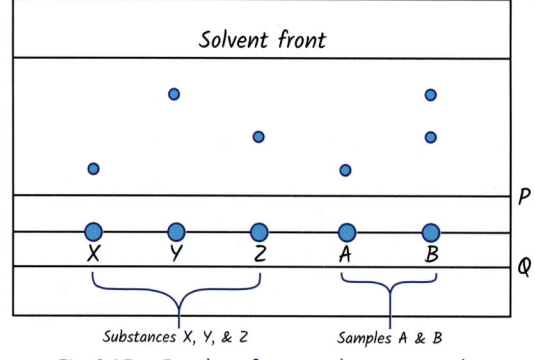

Fig 2.15 - Results of paper chromatography

a) Identify the spot (P or Q) to show the solvent level at the beginning of the experiment. Explain your answer.

Solution: Q, because solvent level should be below the start line so that sample does not dissolve in the solvent.

b) Start line is drawn using pencil. Explain why a pen was not used to draw the start line?

Solution: Pen contains ink which itself is a mixture of dyes. During the experiment dyes from the ink will also move along the solvent which may interfere with the result.

c) Use the results from the above diagram to identity which of the substances X, Y and Z were present in.
   1) sample A

Key steps: To find the answer for sample A (Refer to Fig 2.15 (a)

Step 1 Identify the **sample A and circle it**.
Step 2 Look for any dot (green dot) on the top and draw a **vertical line** (red dotted line) from sample A.
Step 3 Place a ruler **horizontally** on the dot and draw a line (Red dotted line) to any PARALLEL dot found.
Step 5 In this case we could find a dot on X (Red dot).
Step 6 Therefore, sample A contains the **substance X**.

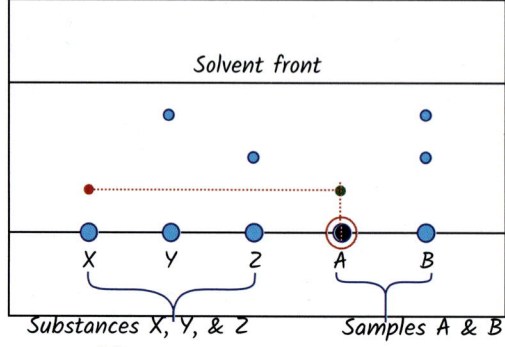

Fig 2.15 (a) - Interpreting paper chromatography

Solution: X

II) sample B

Key steps: To find the answer for sample B (Refer fig 2.15 (b))

Step 1 Identify the **sample B and circle it.**
Step 2 Look for any dot (green dot) on the top and draw a **vertical line** (red dotted line) from sample B. There are two dots found on the axis (green dots).
Step 3 Place a ruler **horizontally** on the dot and draw a line (Red dotted line) to any PARALLEL dot found.
Step 4 In this case we could find a dot on Z (Red dot)
Step 5 Repeat step 4 with the next green dot.
Step 6 In this case we could find a dot on Y (Red dot)
Step 7 Therefore, sample B contains the **substance Z and Y**

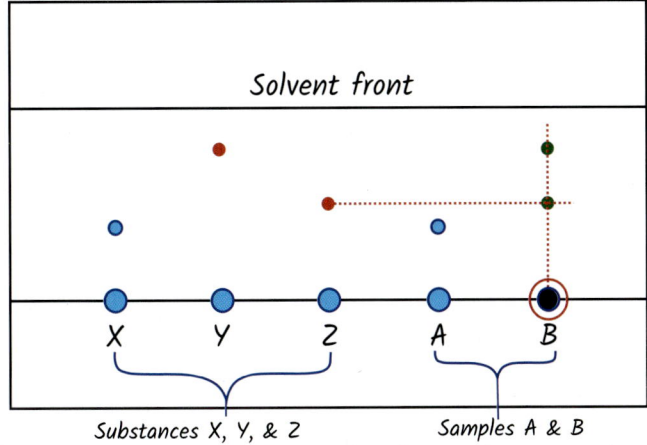

Fig 2.15 (b) - Results of paper chromatography

Substances X, Y, & Z   Samples A & B

Solution Z and Y

d) Using a ruler, calculate the R_f value of substance Z in cm.

Key steps: To calculate the R_f value of Z

Step 1 Identify the substance Z and circle it.
Step 2 Use your ruler to find the distance travelled by the solvent from start line in cm. In this case it is 8cm.
Step 3 Now, repeat the same procedure of measurement but this time from start line to the point of solute Z. In this case it is 5cm.
Step 4 Substitute the above values in the R_f formula.

$$R_f = \frac{\text{distance moved by the solute}}{\text{distance moved by the solvent}} = \frac{5}{8} = 0.625$$

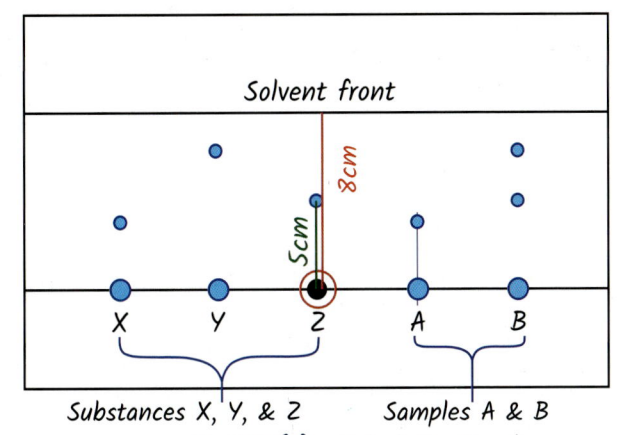

Fig 2.15 (c) - Calculating R_f value

Substances X, Y, & Z   Samples A & B

Solution: 0.625

Purification of water

2.12 Describe how:
   a) waste and ground water can be made potable, including the need for sedimentation, filtration and chlorination
   b) sea water can be made potable by using distillation
   c) water used in analysis must not contain any dissolved salts

Key steps: Purification of raw water

- Water from natural resources contains dissolved and undissolved impurities.
- Impurities including magnesium and calcium ions, microorganisms like bacteria, pollutants like washed fertilisers and chemicals and insoluble materials like dust, leaves, gravels and sludge in the form of sand.
- Water with these impurities cannot be supplied to public without purification.
- Water purification can be done in different stages (Fig 2.16).

Coagulation – The coagulation process involves adding iron or aluminum salts to the water. These chemicals are called coagulants and have a positive charge. When positive charged coagulants react with negative charged particles it binds as a heavy particle which is known as Coagulation.

Coagulation process is sometimes also called flocculation.

Sedimentation – During sedimentation, large heavily insoluble impurities settles to the bottom of the water supply, due to its weight. This settling process is called sedimentation.

Filtration – Once the heavy particles have settled to the bottom of the water supply, the clear water on top will pass through filters of varying compositions like sand and gravel and wash through porous media in order to remove dissolved particles, such as dust, bacteria, viruses, and chemicals.

The filter beds are cleaned periodically by pumping clean water backwards through the filter.

Chlorination (Disinfection) – Once water has been filtered, chlorine is added to water in order to kill any remaining microorganisms like bacteria and virus to protect the water and then it is sent to homes.

Keynote: Chlorine is used to sterilize water.

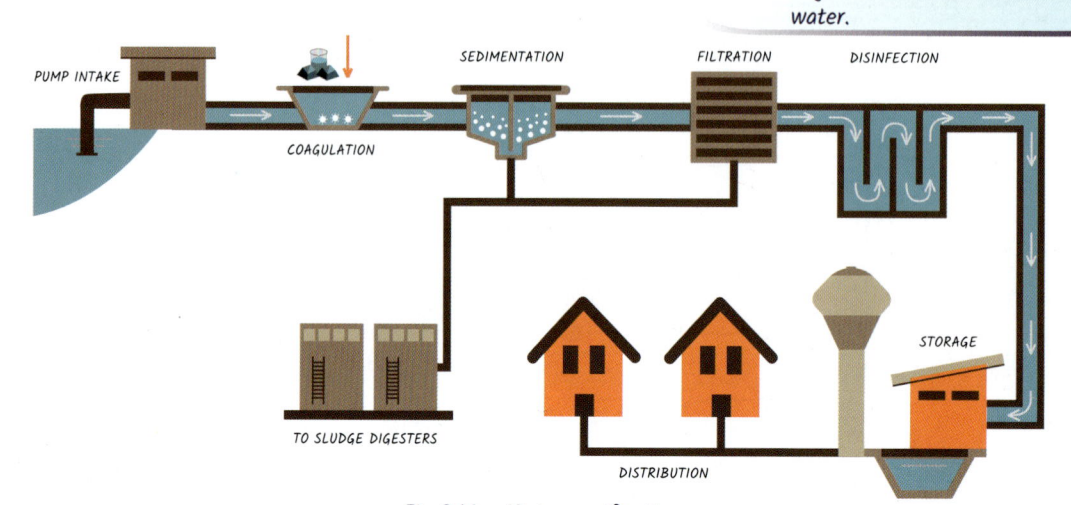

Fig 2.16 - Water purification process

Key steps: Purification of sea water

- Purifying seawater into freshwater is very useful in small scale using distillation process.
- This can be done by removing the dissolved salt in seawater.
- Boil some seawater in a pan, capturing the steam and condensing it back into drinkable water.
- This process involves lots of energy, to be done on a large scale where energy available is cheap and in excess.

Key steps: Chemical analysis of water

- Chemical analysis of water is carried out to check the quality of water by identifying and measuring the substance present in a water sample.
- Water sample must be free from dissolved salts so that it does not affect the process of analysis.

Acids and Bases

Acids & Indicators

> 3.1 Recall that acids in solution are sources of hydrogen ions and alkalis in solution are sources of hydroxide ions
> 3.2 Recall that a neutral solution has a pH of 7 and that acidic solutions have lower pH values and alkaline solutions higher pH values
> 3.3 Recall the effect of acids and alkalis on indicators, including litmus, methyl orange and phenolphthalein

Key Points: Acids and alkalis

- **An acid** is a substance which dissolves in water, dissociates to produce hydrogen ions, H^+.
- H^+ are the main constituent of an acid.
- In water:

$$\text{Hydrogen chloride gas} \longrightarrow \text{hydrogen ions} + \text{chloride ions}$$
$$HCl(g) \longrightarrow H^+(aq) + Cl^-(aq)$$

$$\text{Ethanoic acid} \rightleftharpoons \text{ethanoate ions} + \text{hydrogen ions}$$
$$CH_3COOH(aq) \rightleftharpoons CH_3COO^-(aq) + H^+(aq)$$

- **An alkali** is a substance which dissolves in water, dissociates to produce hydroxide ions, OH^-.
- Hydroxide ions, OH^- are the main constituent of alkali.
- In water:

$$\text{Sodium hydroxide} \longrightarrow \text{sodium ions} + \text{hydroxide ions}$$
$$NaOH(aq) \longrightarrow Na^+(aq) + OH^-(aq)$$

$$\text{Ammonia gas} \longrightarrow \text{ammonium ions} + \text{hydroxide ions}$$
$$NH_3(g) \rightleftharpoons NH_4^+(aq) + OH^-(aq)$$

Key Points: Indicators and pH

- **Indicators** are substances that have different colours in acidic and in alkaline solutions.
- **Litmus** is a common indicator that is red in acidic solutions and blue in alkaline solutions.
- More indicators are shown in table 3.1.

Indicator	Colour in acidic solutions	Colour in alkaline solutions
Litmus	Red	Blue
Methyl orange	Red	Yellow
Phenolphthalein	Colourless	Pink

Table 3.1 - The colours of common indicators

- Nature of the substance, whether it is acidic or alkaline in water can be measured used **pH scale**.
- pH scale has a measuring range from **0 to 14**. The universal indicator is used to measure the approximate pH value of an aqueous solution with a range of colours (Fig 3.1).

pH stands for potential of hydrogen or power of hydrogen.

- pH of 7 is neutral
- pH lower than 7 is acidic. The lower the pH, the solution is more acidic.
- pH greater than 7 is alkaline. The higher the pH, the solution is more alkaline.

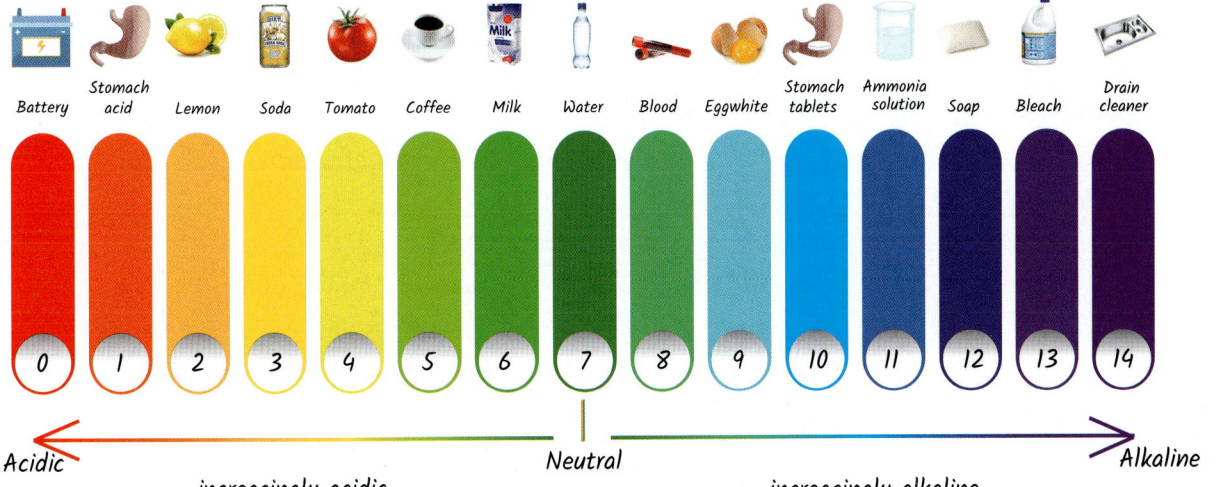

Fig 3.1 - pH scale with universal indicator in solution, showing the colour range

> **3.4** Recall that the higher the concentration of hydrogen ions in an acidic solution, the lower the pH; and the higher the concentration of hydroxide ions in an alkaline solution, the higher the pH
>
> **3.5** Recall that as hydrogen ion concentration in a solution increases by a factor of 10, the pH of the solution decreases by 1 (H)

Key Points: pH scale and its concentration

- If the H^+ ions concentration in a solution increases by a factor of 10, the pH of the solution decreases by 1 unit
- Or, if the pH decreases by 1 unit then the concentration of H^+ ions in a solution increases by ten-fold (Fig 3.2).

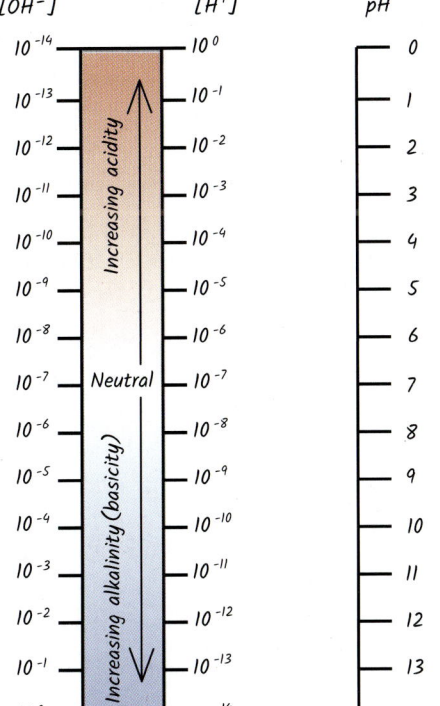

Fig 3.2 - The logarithm expression of pH scale

> The more **acidic** the solution is the greater the percentage of H^+ ions.

> The more **alkaline** the solution is the greater the percentage of OH^- ions.

> [ ] is used to represent the concentration of solution **mol/dm³**.

Topic 3 - Chemical Changes

67

3.7 Explain the terms dilute and concentrated, with respect to amount of substances in solution (H)

Key Points: Dilute and concentrated solution

- **Dilute** solution contains small amount of solute per litre of solution.
  Example: 25g of sugar in 1 litre of water.
- **Concentrated** solution contains more amount of solute per litre of solution.
  Example: 75g of sugar in 1 litre of water.
- Note in the above examples volume of water remains same.

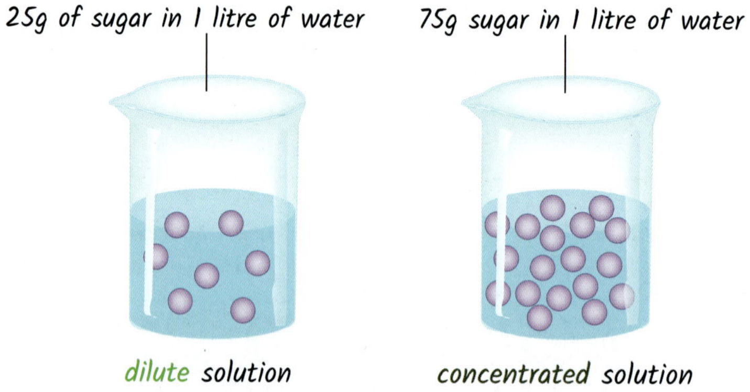

25g of sugar in 1 litre of water — dilute solution
75g sugar in 1 litre of water — concentrated solution

Fig 3.3 - Dilute solution vs concentrated solution

3.8 Explain the terms weak and strong acids, with respect to the degree of dissociation into ions (H)

Key Points: Strong and weak acids

- **STRONG ACIDS** dissociate H^+ **completely** in aqueous solution.
- The equation is given with a forward arrow.

$$HCl(aq) \longrightarrow H^+(aq) + Cl^-(aq)$$

STRONG ACIDS – HCl [Hydrochloric acid], H_2SO_4 [Sulphuric acid] and HNO_3 [Nitric acid].

- **WEAK ACIDS** dissociate H^+ **partially** in aqueous solution.
- The equilibrium arrow $\rightleftharpoons$ is very much essential as all weak acids dissociation is reversible and does not go to completion.

$$CH_3COOH(aq) \rightleftharpoons CH_3COO^-(aq) + H^+(aq)$$

WEAK ACIDS – CH_3COOH [Ethanoic acid] and H_2CO_3 [Carbonic acid].

3.9 Recall that a base is any substance that reacts with an acid to form a salt and water only
3.10 Recall that alkalis are soluble bases
3.11 Explain the general reactions of aqueous solutions of acids with the following substances to produce salts:
   a) metals   b) metal oxides   c) metal hydroxides   d) metal carbonates
3.13 Describe a neutralisation reaction as a reaction between an acid and a base
3.14 Explain an acid-alkali neutralisation as a reaction in which hydrogen ions (H^+) from the acid react with hydroxide ions

Key Points: Base and alkali

- Metal oxides and metal hydroxides are bases.
- **SOLUBLE bases are called alkalis.**
- **Alkaline solutions are formed when bases dissolve in water.**
- Since alkalis are soluble bases, the insoluble bases are not considered as alkalis. Therefore, all alkalis are bases, but not all bases are alkalis

Key Points: Neutralisation reaction

- **Neutralisation** is a chemical reaction in which acid reacts with a base to form salt and water only. $HCl(aq) + NaOH(aq) \rightarrow NaCl(aq) + H_2O(l)$
   acid   base   a salt   water

- In neutralisation reaction, H^+ ions from acid react with OH^- from the alkaline to form water, H_2O. $H^+(aq) + OH^-(aq) \rightarrow H_2O(l)$

- **A Salt** is formed when the H^+ of an acid are replaced by metal ions or the ammonium ion (NH_4^+). In the above example, **hydrogen ion** from hydrochloric acid is replaced by **sodium ions** from sodium hydroxide to form **sodium chloride salt**. Refer table 3.2.

- **Examples of neutralisation reactions:**
  $HCl(aq) + KOH(aq) \rightarrow KCl(aq) + H_2O(l)$
  $H_2SO_4(aq) + 2NaOH(aq) \rightarrow Na_2SO_4(aq) + 2H_2O(l)$
  $2HNO_3(aq) + MgO(aq) \rightarrow Mg(NO_3)_2(aq) + H_2O(l)$

Name of acid	Formula of acid	Name of salt ion	Formula of salt ion
Hydrochloric acid	HCl	chloride	Cl^-
Sulphuric acid	H_2SO_4	sulphate	SO_4^{2-}
Nitric acid	HNO_3	nitrate	NO_3^-
Carbonic acid	H_2CO_3	carbonate	CO_3^{2-}
Ethanoic acid	CH_3COOH	ethanoate	CH_3COO^-

Table 3.2 - Some common acids and its salts

Key Points: Chemical reactions of acids

- React with **most metals** (not below hydrogen in reactivity series) to produce **a salt and hydrogen gas.**   E.g: $2Li(s) + 2HCl(aq) \rightarrow 2LiCl(aq) + H_2(g)$

- React with **metal oxide** to produce **a salt and water.**
   E.g: $MgO(s) + H_2SO_4(aq) \rightarrow MgSO_4(aq) + H_2O(l)$

- React with **metal hydroxide** to produce **a salt and water.**
   E.g: $KOH(aq) + HNO_3(aq) \rightarrow KNO_3(aq) + H_2O(l)$

- React with **metal carbonates** to produce **a salt, water and carbon dioxide.**
   E.g: $CaCO_3(s) + 2HCl(aq) \rightarrow CaCl_2(aq) + H_2O(l) + CO_2(g)$

3.12 Describe the chemical test for: a) hydrogen
                                       b) carbon dioxide (using limewater)

Key Points: Test of hydrogen gas, H_2

- **Test:** Collect the gas in a test tube and hold the lighted splint to the mouth of the test tube.
- **Result:** Gas burns with a squeaky pop sound (Fig 3.4)
- Result confirms the presence of **hydrogen gas**

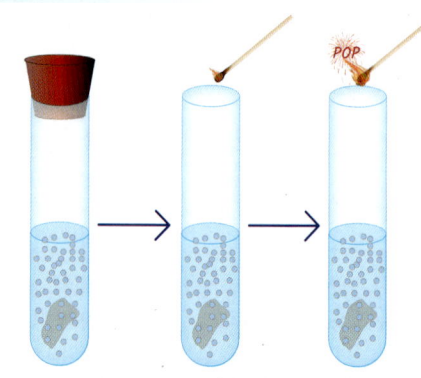

Fig 3.4 - Test of hydrogen gas

Key Points: Test of carbon dioxide gas, CO_2

- **Test:** Pass the gas in to a tube contains lime water.
- **Result:** Lime water turns cloudy and then milky white (Fig 3.5).
- Result confirms the presence of **carbon dioxide gas**

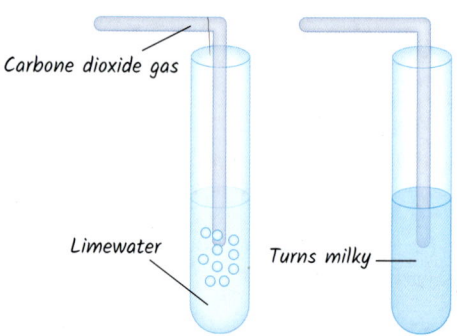

Fig 3.5 - Test of carbon dioxide gas

Solubility rules

3.19 Recall the general rules which describe the solubility of common types of substances in water

3.20 Predict, using solubility rules, whether or not a precipitate will be formed when named solutions are mixed together, naming the precipitate if any

Key Table: Solubility rules

Soluble salts	Insoluble salts
All common sodium, potassium and ammonium salts	All common carbonates (except sodium, potassium and ammonium carbonates)
All nitrates	All common hydroxides (except sodium, potassium and ammonium hydroxides)
All common chlorides except silver chloride and lead(II) chloride	
All common sulphates except calcium sulphate, barium sulphate and lead(II) sulphate	

Table 3.3 - Solubility rules

Key Flowchart: Soluble and insoluble salts

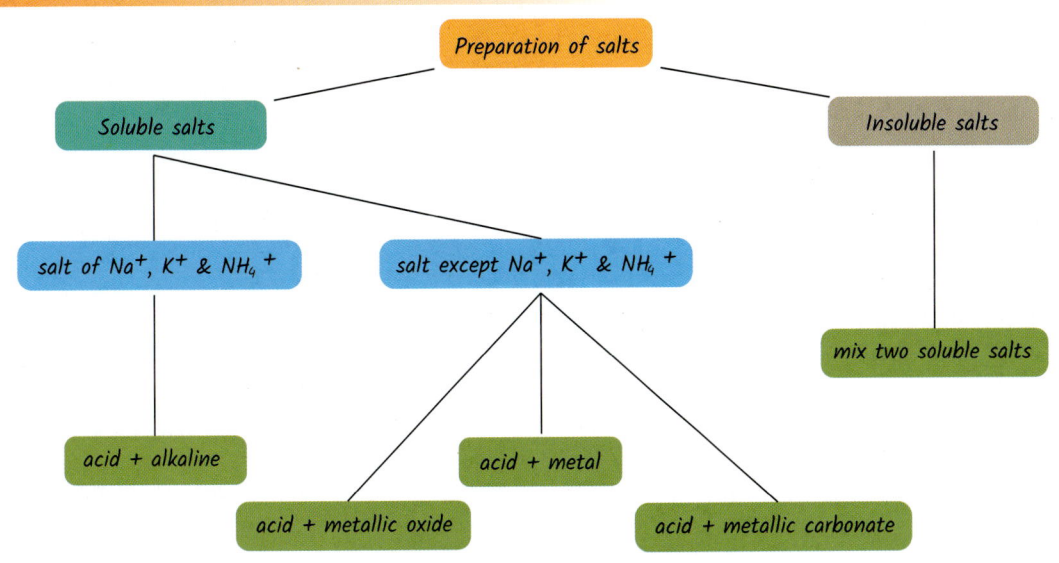

```
                          Preparation of salts
                         /                    \
                Soluble salts              Insoluble salts
               /            \                    |
    salt of Na⁺, K⁺ & NH₄⁺   salt except Na⁺, K⁺ & NH₄⁺
                            /        |         \
                           /         |          \          mix two soluble salts
                  acid + alkaline  acid + metal
                       acid + metallic oxide   acid + metallic carbonate
```

Flowchart 3.1 - Salt preparation

Preparation of salts

3.15 Explain why, if soluble salts are prepared from an acid and an insoluble reactant:
   a) excess of the reactant is added
   b) the excess reactant is removed
   c) the solution remaining is only salt and water

Key Points: Preparation of soluble salts reacting acid with excess metals, insoluble bases and insoluble carbonates

- **Crystallisation** method is used to prepare soluble salts (except Na^+, K^+ and NH_4^+) from metals, insoluble bases and insoluble carbonates.

- **Procedure:**
  - **Step 1:** Add excess solid, a little at a time into warm acid. **Excess is added** to make sure all the acid has been used up and the reaction is complete.
  - **Step 2:** Excess (unreacted) reactant can be filtered off to leave the salt behind.
  - **Step 3:** Excess (unreacted) reactant can be removed by evaporation to leave the salt behind.

  In example 1 and 3, no more effervescence is observed which confirms that the reaction is completed

- **Some examples:**

  $Fe(s) + 2HCl(aq) \longrightarrow FeCl_2(aq) + H_2(g)$
  $CuO(s) + H_2SO_4(aq) \longrightarrow CuSO_4(aq) + H_2O(l)$
  $CaCO_3(s) + 2HCl(aq) \longrightarrow CaCl_2(aq) + H_2O(l) + CO_2(g)$

  In example 2, the solid reactant no longer dissolves in the acid which confirms that the reaction is completed.

- A summary of this process shown in fig 3.6.

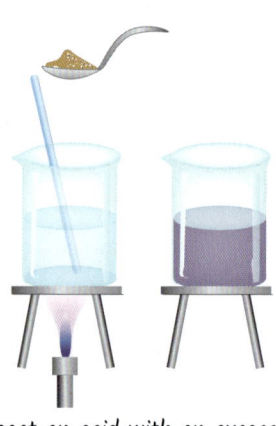

1. React an acid with an excess of metals or insoluble bases or insoluble carbonates until no more reacts.

2. Filter the mixture to get a solution of the salt with the excess solid left behind.

3. Heat the solution to start evaporating the water from the solution.

4. Turn of the heat and leave until all of the water has evaporated, leaving the solid salt behind.

Fig 3.6 - A summary of preparation of soluble salts using metals, insoluble bases and insoluble carbonates

> 3.16 Explain why, if soluble salts are prepared from an acid and a soluble reactant:
> a) titration must be used
> b) the acid and the soluble reactant are then mixed in the correct proportions
> c) the solution remaining, after reaction, is only salt and water
>
> 3.18 Describe how to carry out an acid-alkali titration, using burette, pipette and a suitable indicator, to prepare a pure, dry salt

Key Points: Preparation of soluble salts reacting acid and alkali

- *Titration* is the method used to prepare soluble Na^+, K^+ and NH_4^+ salts.
- Principle behind this method is neutralisation where acid reacts with alkali to form a salt and water.
- Procedure:
  - **Step A:** Pipette a known volume of acid into a conical flask.
  - **Step B:** Add a few drops of indicator into the conical flask.
  - **Step C:** Using a burette, add the alkali, a little at a time, into the conical flask until the indicator changes colour.
  - **Step D:** Stop the addition and note down the volume of alkali used.
  - **Step E:** Repeat the above steps, this time without addition of indicators, using the same volume of alkali into the flask of known volume of acid.
  - **Refer to** fig 3.7 for steps A to D.
  - **The solution** formed is a neutral solution of a salt and water.
  - **Step F:** Heat the solution so that the water will evaporate, and the solution becomes saturated.
  - **Step G:** Crystallise and filter out the pure crystals.
- Refer to step 3 and 4 from fig 2.10 in topic 2.
- Example: $HCl(aq) + NaOH(aq) \longrightarrow NaCl(aq) + H_2O(l)$
  acid   alkali   salt   water

Fig 3.7 - Titration

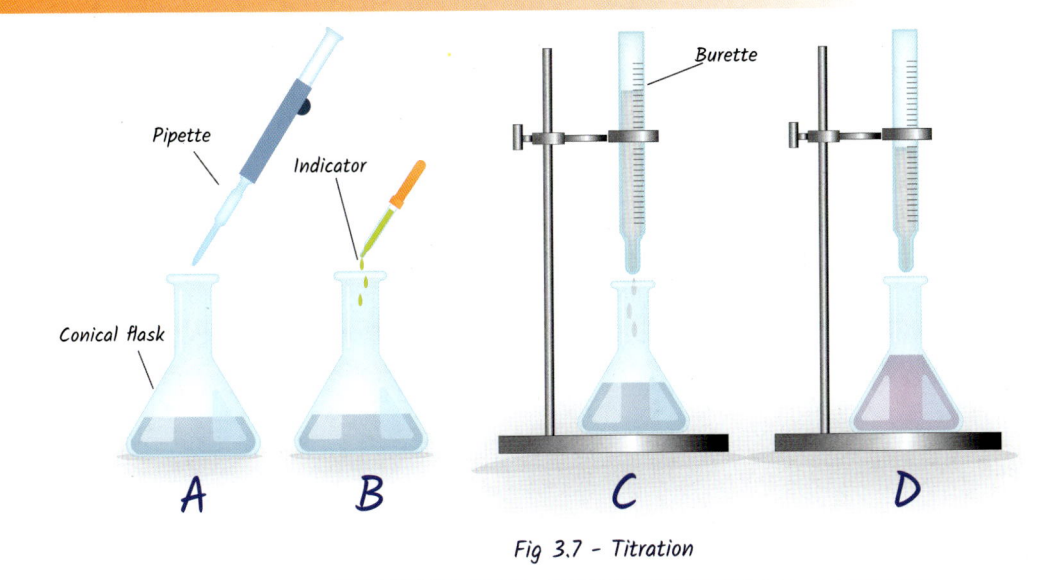

3.21 Describe the method used to prepare a pure, dry sample of an insoluble salt

Key Points: Preparation of insoluble salts using two soluble salts

- **Precipitation** is the method used to prepare insoluble salts using two soluble salts.
- $XY(aq) + AB(aq) \longrightarrow XB(aq) + AY(s)$
- Note Y and B have swapped the places. This is known as displacement.
- Procedure:
    - **Step 1:** Mix two soluble salts and stir until no more precipitate forms.
    - **Step 2:** Filter and collect the precipitate.
    - **Step 3:** The precipitate is washed with distilled water to remove impurities.
    - **Step 4:** Allow the precipitate to dry on (or) between filter papers.
- Refer Fig 3.8.
- Example: $Na_2SO_4(aq) + Pb(NO_3)_2(aq) \longrightarrow 2NaNO_3(aq) + PbSO_4(s)$

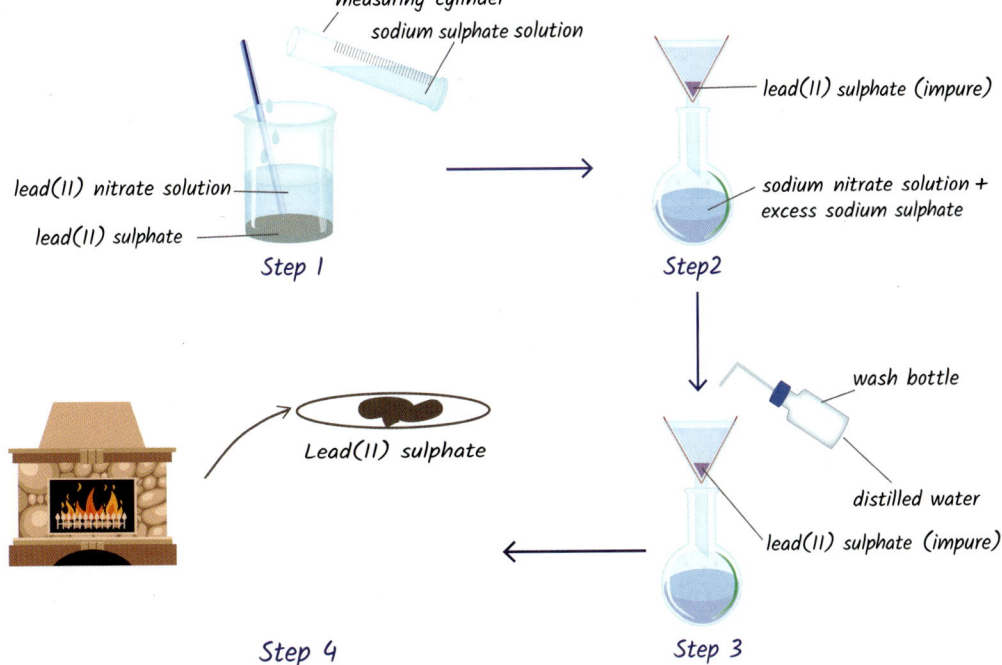

Fig 3.8 Preparation and separation of pure insoluble salt

Electrolytic Processes

Electrolysis

3.22 Recall that electrolytes are ionic compounds in the molten state or dissolved in water
3.23 Describe electrolysis as a process in which electrical energy, from a direct current supply, decomposes electrolytes
3.24 Explain the movement of ions during electrolysis, in which:
  a) positively charged cations migrate to the negatively charged cathode
  b) negatively charged anions migrate to the positively charged anode

Key Points: Electrolytic cell

- An electrolytic cell is used to decompose chemical compounds, in a process called electrolysis.
- An electrolytic cell consists of:
  - Supply of direct current.
  - Electrodes: The substance which passes electric current to the electrolytes.
     Two electrodes, anode (positively charged) and cathode (negatively charged) are attached to a direct current (DC) electricity supply and put into the electrolyte.
  - Electrolytes: The ionic compounds which conducts electricity in molten and aqueous state.
- An electrolytic cell is shown in fig 3.9.

Key definition: Electrolysis is the process of decomposing substance (electrolytes) in molten or aqueous state by passing electrical energy.

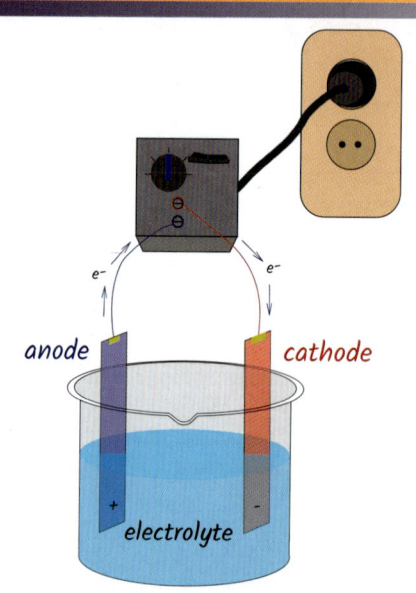

Fig 3.9 - An electrolytic cell

Key Points: Electrolytes

- In electrolysis, electrolytes are usually:
  - Molten or aqueous solutions of ionic compounds
  - Acids or alkalis
- **Strong electrolytes** are strong acids, alkalis and salt solutions
- **Weak electrolytes** are weak acids and alkalis

Key Points: Electrolysis process

- During electrolysis, the cations (+) moves towards the cathode (-) and the anions (-) moves towards anode (+).
- At the anode, anions are discharged through the loss of electrons. Loss of electrons is oxidation.
- At the cathode, the cations are discharged through the gain of electrons. Gain of electrons is reduction.
- Anode (+) ⟶ Oxidation ⟶ loss of electrons [OIL] ⟶ An OX
- Cathode (-) ⟶ Reduction ⟶ gain of electrons [RIG] ⟶ RED Cat

Oil : **O**xidation **i**s **l**oss of electrons.
Rig : **R**eduction **i**s **g**ain of electrons.

Red Cat = **Red**uction at **Cat**hode
An Ox = **Ox**idation at **An**ode

Electrolysis of molten substances

3.26 Predict the products of electrolysis of other binary, ionic compounds in the molten state
3.25 e) molten lead bromide (demonstration)

3.27	Write half equations for reactions occurring at the anode and cathode in electrolysis
3.28	Explain oxidation and reduction in terms of loss or gain of electrons
3.29	Recall that reduction occurs at the cathode and that oxidation occurs at the anode in electrolysis reactions (H)

Key Points: Electrolysis of molten ionic compounds

- A binary ionic compound contains only two elements of a metal and a non-metal.
- **Metallic ions** are **positively charged** cations which **gains electrons** at the **cathode** to form a **metal atom**.
- **Non-metallic ions** are **negatively charged** anions which **loss electrons** at the anode to form its **molecules**.

Worked Example 1: Draw and label the process of electrolysis of molten lead(II) bromide, $PbBr_2$

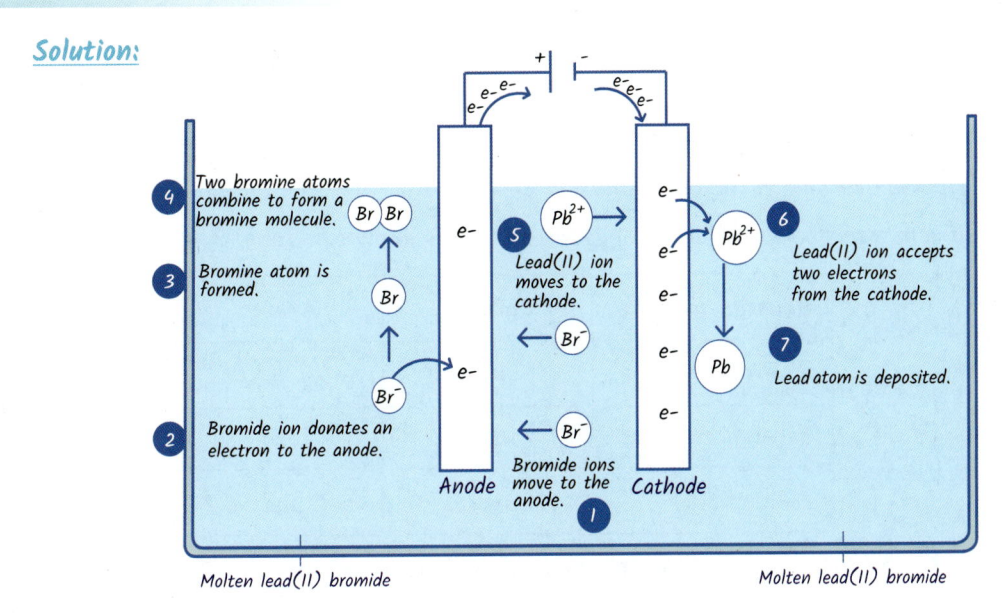

Solution:

```
                              +   -
                        e-e-       e-e-
                      e-              e-

   4  Two bromine atoms
      combine to form a   Br  Br
      bromine molecule.              5   Pb²⁺ →             Pb²⁺   6  Lead(II) ion accepts
                           ↑         e-                e-            two electrons
   3  Bromine atom is                   Lead(II) ion  e-            from the cathode.
      formed.              Br           moves to the  e-
                           ↑            cathode.                ↓
                                                e-
                                      ← Br⁻                Pb    7  Lead atom is
                           Br⁻                    e-              deposited.
                           ↑
                                  e-
   2  Bromide ion donates an      ← Br⁻          e-
      electron to the anode.
                              Anode   Bromide ions  Cathode
                                      move to the
                                      anode.
                                        1

      Molten lead(II) bromide                    Molten lead(II) bromide
```

Worked Example 2: Using half equations, explain the following process of electrolysis.
a) Electrolysis of molten lead(II) bromide, $PbBr_2$
b) Electrolysis of molten magnesium oxide, MgO

Solution:

a) **Reaction at the cathode:** $Pb^{2+}(l) + 2e^- \longrightarrow Pb(l)$
Each lead ion undergoes reduction by gaining 2 electrons at the cathode to form lead atoms.
Reaction at the anode: $2Br^-(l) \longrightarrow 2e^- + Br_2(g)$
Each bromide ion undergoes oxidation by losing 2 electrons at the anode to form bromine atom. 2 bromine atoms will combine to form a Br_2 molecule.

b) **Reaction at the cathode:** $Mg^{2+}(l) + 2e^- \longrightarrow Mg(l)$
Each magnesium ion undergoes reduction by gaining 2 electrons at the cathode to form magnesium atoms.
Reaction at the anode: $2O^{2-}(l) \longrightarrow 4e^- + O_2(g)$
Each oxide ion undergoes oxidation by losing 2 electrons at the anode to form oxygen atom. 2 oxygen atoms will combine to form a O_2 molecule.

Use the trick below to make and balance the half equations
- Loss of electrons, electrons are shown on the right side of the arrow.
Loss – Going away from the arrow.
- Gain of electrons, electrons are shown on the left side of the arrow.
Gain – taking in before the arrow.
- Charges are neutral on both sides of the equation.
- Number of electrons gained at the cathode are the same as the number lost at the anode.

Cathode: Greyish deposit of lead can be found at bottom of electrolytic cell.
Anode: Brown gas of bromine is liberated at anode.

Cathode: shiny, silvery deposit of magnesium can be found at bottom of electrolytic cell.
Anode: Colourless gas of oxygen is liberated at anode.

Electrolysis of aqueous solution

3.25 Explain the formation of the products in the electrolysis, using inert electrodes, of some electrolytes, including:
a) copper chloride solution   b) sodium chloride solution
c) sodium sulphate solution   d) water acidified with sulphuric acid

Key Table: Electrolysis of aqueous solution

- Aqueous solution is a solution in which solute is dissolved in water. The mixture consists of some amount of water irrespective of whether they are diluted or concentrated.
- Water, H_2O ionises to give H^+ & OH^- ions.
- Examples of ions present in different aqueous solutions shown in table 3.4.

Aqueous solution	Cations	Anions
dil. NaCl	H^+ and Na^+	OH^- ad Cl^-
dil. H_2SO_4	H^+	OH^- and SO_4^{2-}
conc. $CuSO_4$	H^+ and Cu^{2+}	OH^- and SO_4^{2-}

Table 3.4 - Examples of aqueous solutions

- As more than one type of anion and cation are present, discharge of ions are based on the following criteria
  - Position of ion in the electrochemical series
  - Concentration of ion
  - Nature of electrode
- Position of ion in the electrochemical series is shown in a table 3.5 in terms of order of difficulty of discharge.
- If solution is concentrated, OH⁻ ion from water gets less preference than the anion from compound.

Key Table: Discharge of cations and anions

Lists of common ions in order of difficulty of discharge	
Cations (aq)	Anions (aq)
K^+	
Na^+	
Ca^{2+}	
Mg^{2+}	
Zn^{2+}	SO_4^{2-}
Fe^{2+}	NO_3^-
Pb^{2+}	Cl^-
H^+	Br^-
Cu^{2+}	I^-
Ag^+	OH^-

Difficulty of discharge decreases down the series

Table 3.5 – Discharge of cations and anions

Worked example 3: Predict the products and deduce the half equations of the following salt solutions.

a) Concentrated copper(II) chloride solution ($CuCl_2$)
b) Copper(II) sulphate solution ($CuSO_4$)
c) Sodium sulphate solution (Na_2SO_4)
d) Brine (concentrated NaCl)

Solution:

a) Concentrated copper chloride solution ($CuCl_2$):

- Copper chloride solution contains 4 aqueous ions.
  Cu^{2+} and Cl^- from the salt
  H^+ and OH^- from the water
- Cu^{2+} ions are **lower** than H^+ in the electrochemical series it gets discharge more easily to gain electrons than H^+ ions at cathode, $Cu^{2+}(aq) + 2e^- \longrightarrow Cu(s)$.
- Cl^- ions lose electrons more readily than OH^- ions at anode, $2Cl^-(aq) \longrightarrow 2e^- + Cl_2(g)$.
- **Copper metal** (from Cu^{2+} ions) is discharged at the cathode and **chlorine gas** (from Cl^- ions) is discharged at the anode.

Concentration of ions At anode it is Cl_2 gas not O_2 gas. This is due to the presence of a high concentration of chloride ions compared to the lower concentration of hydroxide ions from water.

b) Copper(II) sulphate solution (CuSO$_4$):

- Copper(II) sulphate solution contains 4 aqueous ions.
  - Cu^{2+} and SO_4^{2-} from the salt (CuSO$_4$)
  - H^+ and OH^- from the water (H$_2$O)

  Position of ion in the electrochemical series

- Cu^{2+} ions gain electrons more readily than H^+ ions at cathode, $Cu^{2+}(aq) + 2e^- \longrightarrow Cu(s)$.
- OH^- ions lose electrons more readily than SO_4^{2-} ions at anode, $OH^-(aq) \longrightarrow 2H_2O(g) + O_2(g) + 4e^-$.
- **Copper metal** (from Cu^{2+} ions) is discharged at the cathode and **oxygen gas** (from OH^- ions) is discharged at the anode.

c) Sodium sulphate solution (Na$_2$SO$_4$):

- Sodium sulphate solution contains 4 aqueous ions.
  - Na^+ and SO_4^{2-} from the salt (Na$_2$SO$_4$)
  - H^+ and OH^- from the water (H$_2$O)

  Position of ion in the electrochemical series

- H^+ ions gain electrons more readily than Na^+ ions at cathode, $2H^+(aq) + 2e^- \longrightarrow H_2(g)$
- OH^- ions lose electrons more readily than SO_4^{2-} ions at anode, $OH^-(aq) \longrightarrow 2H_2O(g) + O_2(g) + 4e^-$.
- **Hydrogen gas** (from H^+ ions) is discharged at the cathode and **oxygen gas** (from OH^- ions) is discharged at the anode.

d) Brine (Concentrated NaCl):

- Brine is a salt water which contains 4 aqueous ions.
  - Na^+ and Cl^- from the salt
  - H^+ and OH^- from the water

  Concentration of ions

- H^+ ions gain electrons more readily than Na^+ ions at cathode, $2H^+(aq) + 2e^- \longrightarrow H_2(g)$.
- Cl^- ions lose electrons more readily than OH^- ions at anode, as the concentration of chloride ion is higher $2Cl^-(aq) \longrightarrow 2e^- + Cl_2(g)$.
- Hydrogen gas (from H^+ ions) is discharged at the cathode and chlorine gas (from Cl^- ions) is discharged at the anode.
- The ions left out in the solution are Na^+ and OH^-.
- Overall equation for the reaction: $2NaCl(aq) + 2H_2O(l) \longrightarrow 2NaOH(aq) + Cl_2(g) + H_2(g)$.
- The Na^+ and OH^- ions left in solution form a solution of sodium hydroxide (NaOH).
- Electrolysis of brine gives 3 products – hydrogen gas (H$_2$), chlorine gas (Cl$_2$) and sodium hydroxide solution (NaOH).

Worked example 4: Complete the table: Predict the ions and the products in the electrolysis process using inert electrodes.

Question

Solution	Ions present	Ions		Products	
		Cations	Anions	Cathode	Anode
molten NaCl	Na$^+$ & Cl$^-$		Cl$^-$	Na	
water		H$^+$	OH$^-$		
water with few drops of dilute sulphuric acid		H$^+$			
dilute sulphuric acid	H$^+$, OH$^-$ & SO$_4^{2-}$	H$^+$	OH$^-$ & SO$_4^{2-}$	H$_2$	
aqueous sodium chloride					
aqueous copper(II) sulphate					O$_2$
concentrated hydrochloric acid	H$^+$, OH$^-$, Cl$^-$	H$^+$	OH$^-$ & Cl$^-$		

Solution

Solution	Ions present	Ions		Products	
		Cations	Anions	Cathode	Anode
molten NaCl	Na$^+$ & Cl$^-$	Na$^+$	Cl$^-$	Na	Cl$_2$
water	H$^+$ & OH$^-$	H$^+$	OH$^-$	H$_2$	O$_2$
water with few drops of dilute sulphuric acid	H$^+$, OH$^-$ & SO$_4^{2-}$	H$^+$	OH$^-$ & SO$_4^{2-}$	H$_2$	O$_2$
dilute sulphuric acid	H$^+$, OH$^-$ & SO$_4^{2-}$	H$^+$	OH$^-$ & SO$_4^{2-}$	H$_2$	O$_2$
aqueous sodium chloride	H$^+$, Na$^+$, Cl$^-$ & OH$^-$	H$^+$ & Na$^+$	Cl$^-$ & OH$^-$	H$_2$	O$_2$
aqueous copper(II) sulphate	H$^+$, Cu^{2+}, SO$_4^{2-}$ & OH$^-$	H$^+$ & Cu^{2+}	SO$_4^{2-}$ & OH$^-$	Cu	O$_2$
concentrated hydrochloric acid	H$^+$, OH$^-$, Cl$^-$	H$^+$	OH$^-$ & Cl$^-$	H$_2$	Cl$_2$ Since the solution is concentrated, chlorine gets preference over O$_2$

Purification of copper using copper electrodes

3.30 Explain the formation of the products in the electrolysis of copper sulphate solution, using copper electrodes, and how this electrolysis can be used to purify copper

Key Points: Purification of copper using copper electrodes

- Newly extracted copper contains some impurities which can be purified by electrolysis.
- **Impure copper** is used at the **anode** with the thickness of 40-50mm which weigh around 330kg.
- **Pure copper** is taken at the **cathode** with the thickness of 1mm which weigh about 5kg.
- **Electrolyte:** Solution of **copper(II) sulphate** solution acidified with **sulphuric acid**.
- Ions present:
    From the water: **H⁺** and **OH⁻**
    From the copper(II) sulphate: **Cu^{2+}** and **SO_4^{2-}**
- When current flows, copper moves from impure anode to the pure cathode.
- At anode: **OXIDATION**

    - None of OH⁻ and SO_4^{2-} are discharged. The copper electrodes lose electrons more readily than the anions
    - Each copper atoms loses 2 electrons and becomes copper ions, $Cu^{2+}(aq)$.
    - The copper anode dissolves and the mass and the size of the **anode copper** decreases.
    - $Cu(s) \longrightarrow Cu^{2+}(aq) + 2e^-$

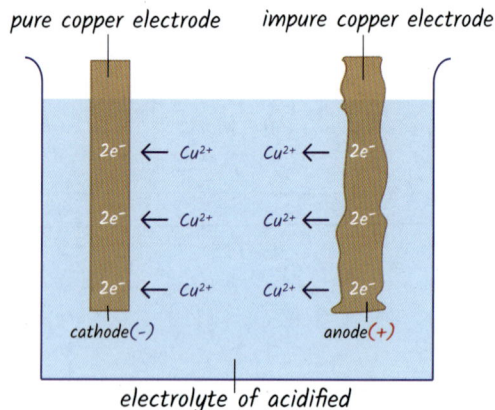

Nature of electrodes

Fig 3.10 Purification of copper (movement of ions)

- At cathode: **REDUCTION**
    - Cu^{2+} ions are preferentially discharged as they are lower than H⁺ in the electrochemical series.
    - Each Cu^{2+} ion gains 2 electrons and the pink solid is deposited on the cathode.
    - Eventually, the mass and the size of the **cathode copper** increases.
    - $Cu^{2+}(aq) + 2e^- \longrightarrow Cu(s)$

- As the exchange of copper ions takes place between electrolyte and electrodes the colour of copper(II) sulphate stays blue.
- During the process, the impurities fall to the bottom of anode in the form of a slime.

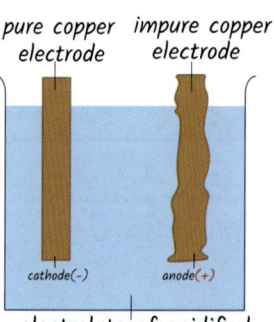

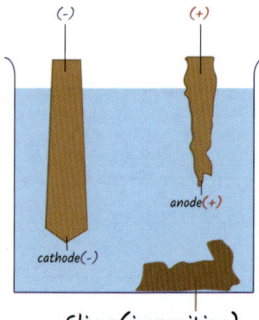

Fig 3.11 - Purification of copper
- a) Before experiment b) After experiment

Slime contains precious metals like silver, gold and platinum metals. Recovery of these metals is economically good for this process.

Extraction of Metals

Reactivity Series of Metals

> 4.3 Explain the reactivity series of metals (potassium, sodium, calcium, magnesium, aluminium, (carbon), zinc, iron, (hydrogen), copper, silver, gold) in terms of the reactivity of the metals with water and dilute acids and that these reactions show the relative tendency of metal atoms to form cations
>
> 4.9 Explain how a metal's relative resistance to oxidation is related to its position in the reactivity series

Key Points: Reactivity series of metals

- Metals can be arranged according to their reactivities and their positions are shown in a series which is known as the reactivity series of metals (Fig 4.1).
- In the series, reactivity of metal **increases from bottom to top**.
- **Most reactive metals** can easily lose electrons and forms stable compounds compared with least reactive metals.
- A metal that is higher up in the reactivity series has a higher tendency to form its positive ions by oxidation.
- A metal that is lower down in the series shows greater resistance to oxidation.
- Tendency to form cations and resistance to oxidation completely depends upon the metal's position in the reactivity series.

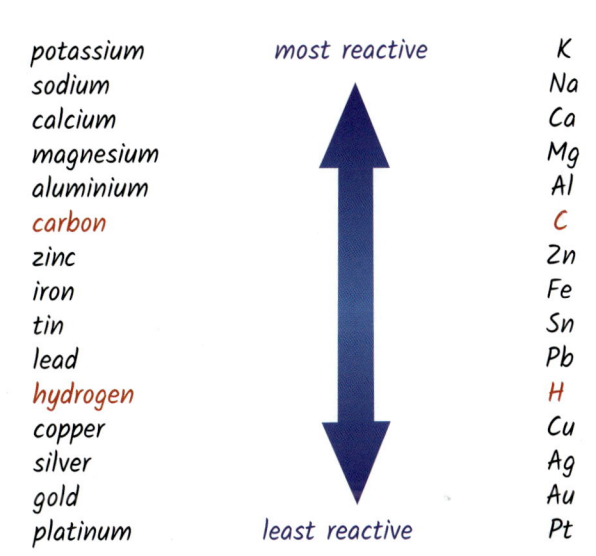

potassium (most reactive)	K
sodium	Na
calcium	Ca
magnesium	Mg
aluminium	Al
carbon	C
zinc	Zn
iron	Fe
tin	Sn
lead	Pb
hydrogen	H
copper	Cu
silver	Ag
gold	Au
platinum (least reactive)	Pt

Fig 4.1 - Reactivity series of metals

- **Least reactive metals** exist in their pure form in uncombined form in nature, such as silver, gold and platinum.
- In general, a more reactive metal will **displace** a less reactive metal from a compound.
- Hydrogen and carbon are two non-metals placed as a reference point to show the most reactive and least reactive metals.
- Metals below hydrogen in the reactivity series do not have the ability to displace hydrogen.
- Using the position of metals in the reactivity series, it is easy to determine the type of chemical reaction that it may undergo. Also, it is very useful to find how these metals can be extracted.

Metals	With Cold Water	With Steam	With Air (oxygen)	With Dilute Acids
	Produces metal hydroxide and hydrogen gas.	Produces metal oxide and hydrogen gas.	Produces metal oxide	Produces metal salt and hydrogen gas
	A more reactive metal will displace a less reactive metal from a compound.			
Potassium (K)	Violently	Violently	Readily	Violently
Sodium (Na)	Vigorously			
Calcium (Ca)	Moderately			
Magnesium (Mg)	Slowly	Vigorously	Slowly	Vigorously
Aluminium (Al)	No	Moderately (Fe - reversible)	In the presence of HEAT	Moderately
Zinc (Zn)				
Iron (Fe)				
Tin (Sn)		No		Slowly
Lead (Pb)				
Copper (Cu)				
Silver (Ag)			No	No
Gold (Au)				
Platinum (Pt)				

Table 4.1 - Reactions of metals in the reactivity series

4.1 Deduce the relative reactivity of some metals, by their reactions with water, acids and salt solutions

Key reactions: With cold water

- **General chemical reaction:** **metal** + water ⟶ **metal hydroxide** + hydrogen gas
- Refer Table 4.1 for nature of reactions.
- $2K(s) + 2H_2O(l) \longrightarrow 2KOH(aq) + H_2(g)$
  – Reaction is very violent and produces hydrogen gas which **catches fire**.
- $Ca(s) + 2H_2O(l) \longrightarrow Ca(OH)_2(aq) + H_2(g)$
  – Reaction is moderately slow and gives off hydrogen gas in the form of **bubbles**.

> Metal hydroxide is formed when metals reacts with cold water.

> Elements below hydrogen are unable to react.

Key reactions: With steam

- **General chemical reaction:** **metal** + steam ⟶ **metal oxide** + hydrogen gas
- Refer table 4.1 for nature of reactions.
- $Mg(s) + H_2O(l) \longrightarrow MgO(s) + H_2(g)$
  – Vigorous reaction and produces hydrogen gas which burns with squeaky pop sound.
- $3Fe(s) + 4H_2O(l) \rightleftharpoons Fe_3O_4(s) + 4H_2(g)$
  – Reaction takes place moderately slow and it is a reversible reaction.

> **Metal oxide** is formed when metals reacts with **steam**.

Key reactions: With acids

- **General chemical reaction:** **metal** + acid ⟶ salt + **hydrogen gas**
- Refer Table 4.1 for nature of reactions.
- Reactions are slower down the reactivity series.
- $2Na(s) + 2HCl(aq) \longrightarrow 2NaCl(s) + H_2(g)$
  – Vigorous reaction and produces hydrogen gas which burns with squeaky **pop sound**.
- $Ca(s) + 2HCl(aq) \longrightarrow 2CaCl_2(aq) + H_2(g)$
  – Vigorous reaction with hydrogen gas.
- $2Al(s) + 6HCl(aq) \longrightarrow 2AlCl_3(aq) + H_2(g)$
  – Slow reaction; warming needed.

> In general, aluminium is protected by an oxide layer which prevents from immediate reaction.

> Metals below hydrogen in the reactivity series do not have the ability to displace hydrogen.

Topic 4 – Extracting metals and Equilibria

Reactivity Series of Metals

4.2 Explain displacement reactions as redox reactions, in terms of gain or loss of electrons (H)

4.5 Explain oxidation as the gain of oxygen and reduction as the loss of oxygen

Key reactions: Displacement reactions

- A more reactive metal displaces a less reactive metal from its compound.
- Displacement reactions are redox reactions where both oxidation and reduction reactions take place by transferring electrons between two species.
- Two types of displacement reaction
  - **Single displacement**: An element reacts with a compound to form a new element and a different compound.
  - **Double displacement**: Two compounds react to form two new compounds.
  - In both cases, the most reactive metal displaces the least reactive metal.
- Oxidation and reduction in terms of electrons.

Fig. 4.2 - Types of displacement reactions

Double displacement: not part of syllabus

Keynote: Redox in terms of electrons
Oil : **O**xidation **i**s **l**oss of electrons.
Rig : **R**eduction **i**s **g**ain of electrons.

- **Displacement in terms of ELECTRONS:**

$$Zn(s) + CuSO_4(aq) \longrightarrow ZnSO_4(aq) + Cu(s)$$
$$Zn(s) + Cu^{2+}(aq) \longrightarrow Zn^{2+}(aq) + Cu(s)$$

Oxidation: Zn atom is oxidized to a zinc ion by losing 2 electrons. Zn is a reducing agent.

$$Zn(s) \longrightarrow Zn^{2+}(aq) + 2e^-$$

Reduction: The copper ion is reduced to copper atom by gaining two electrons. Cu^{2+} is an oxidising agent.

$$Cu^{2+}(aq) + 2e^- \longrightarrow Cu(s)$$

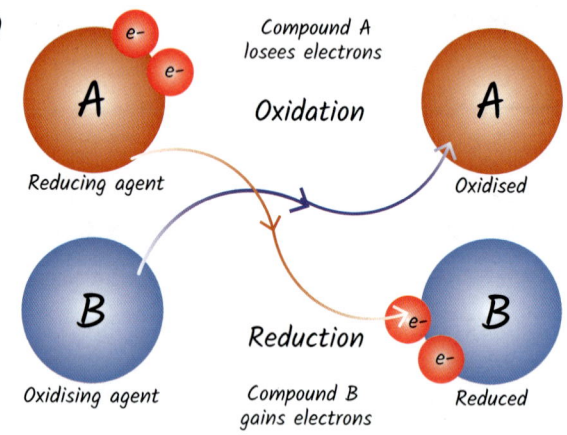

Fig. 4.3 - Oxidation and reduction

Zinc displaces copper from the salt solution, this proves zinc is more reactive than copper. During the reaction, blue solution of copper(II) sulphate changes to colourless zinc sulphate leaving pink/red copper deposit on zinc granules.

- **Single displacement reaction** in terms of OXYGEN.

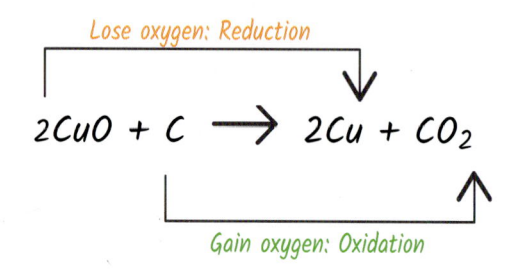

Lose oxygen: Reduction

$$2CuO + C \longrightarrow 2Cu + CO_2$$

Gain oxygen: Oxidation

Oxidising agent: The substance responsible for oxidation (or the substance which has been **reduced**.
Reducing agent: The substance responsible for reduction (or the substance which has been **oxidised**.

Redox in terms of oxygen
Oxidation is **gain** of oxygen.
Reduction is **loss** of oxygen.

4.4 Recall that: a) most metals are extracted from ores found in the Earth's crust
b) unreactive metals are found in the Earth's crust as the uncombined elements
4.6 Recall that the extraction of metals involves reduction of ores

Key Points: Extraction of metals

- Metals are extracted according to their nature of reactivity.
- **Reactive** metals do not exist as an element, but they do combine with other elements to form metal ore.

> Ore is a type of rock that contains minerals with important elements including metals.

- **Unreactive** metals exist in their pure form in uncombined form in nature. Such metals include silver, gold and platinum.
- Metal ores are generally combinations of oxides, sulphides, silcates or carbonates.
- **BAUXITE** is the ore of aluminium which mainly contains **aluminium oxide**.
- **HAEMATITE** is the ore of iron which mainly contains **iron(III) oxide**.
- Methods of extraction is shown in Fig 4.2.

Reactivity of metal increases ↑

potassium
sodium
calcium
magnesium
aluminium
} Most reactive metals extracted by ELECTROLYSIS

zinc
iron
tin
lead
copper
} Less reactive metals extracted by REDUCTION (heating using REDUCING AGENT such as CARBON or HYDROGEN)

silver
gold
} Least reactive metals occurs NATIVE in the ground

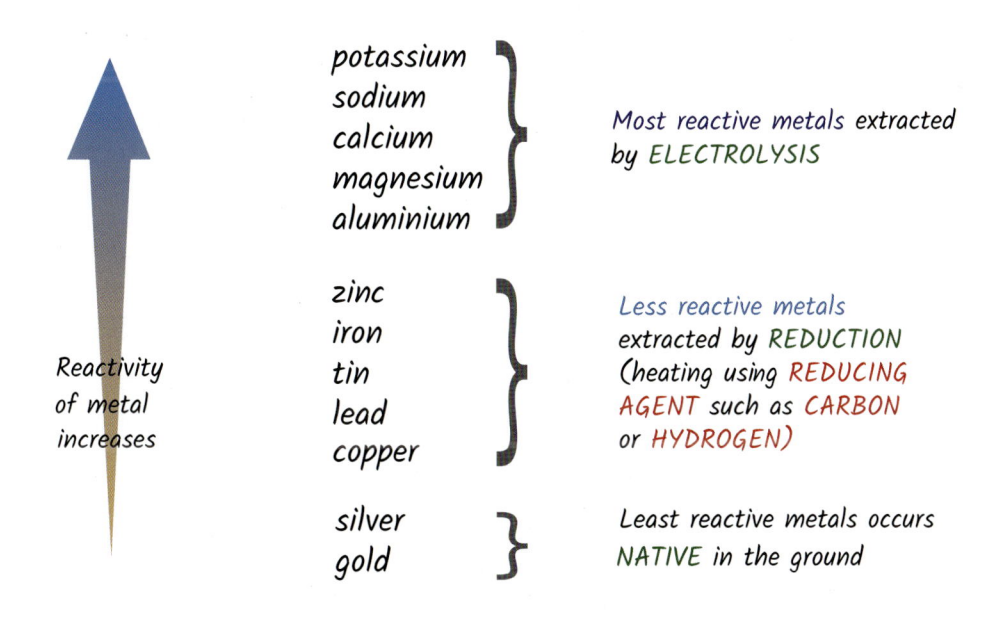

Fig 4.2 - Extraction of metals

Topic 4 – Extracting metals and Equilibria

4.7 Explain why the method used to extract a metal from its ore is related to its position in the reactivity series and the cost of the extraction process, illustrated by
a) electrolysis (including aluminium)
b) heating with carbon (including iron) - knowledge of the blast furnace is not required

Key Points: Extraction of aluminium

- Aluminium is extracted using ELECTROLYSIS from its ore BAUXITE.
- Bauxite consists of aluminium oxide (Al_2O_3 – Al^{3+} & O^{2-}) with the melting point of more than 2000°C
- Bauxite is dissolved in CRYOLITE to lower the melting point of the ore and to act as a solvent.
- Electrolyte of this process is a mixture of molten aluminium oxide and molten cryolite at a temperature of around 950°C.
- The electrodes are made of carbon (graphite) – Refer to Fig 4.3.
- When the current is passed:
  - Aluminium ion moves towards cathode and sinks as aluminium by gaining 3 electrons to the bottom of the tank.
  - Reduction: $Al^{3+}(l) + 3e^- \rightarrow Al(l)$
  - Oxide ion moves towards anode by losing 4 electrons to form oxygen gas
  - Oxidation: $2O^{2-}(l) \rightarrow O_2(g) + 4e^-$
- As the working temperature of the cell is very high, the oxygen burns away the carbon anodes which must be replaced at regular intervals.

> Aluminium is placed above carbon in the reactivity series. Hence it is extracted using electrolysis.

> Cryolite - Sodium aluminium fluoride (Na_3AlF_6).

> The process of aluminium extraction is not required for the syllabus. However, knowledge about the cost of the process is required for this specification.

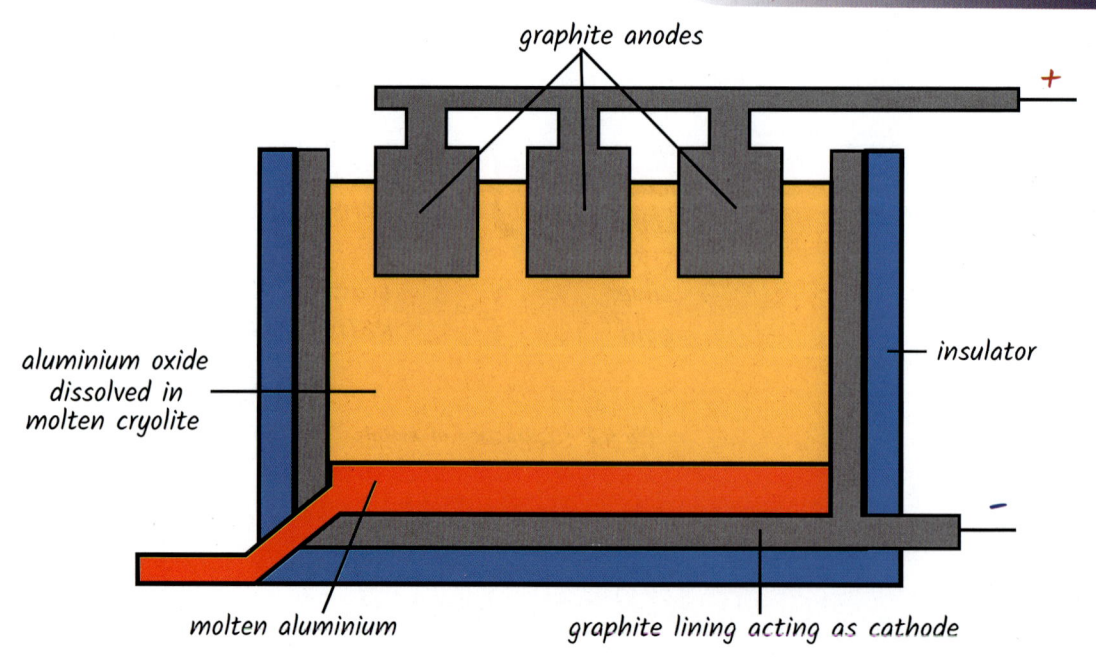

Fig 4.3 - Extraction of aluminium

Worked Example 1: Aluminium is extracted using electrolysis. To reduce the cost of the process cryolite is mixed with bauxite. Explain how the addition of cryolite reduces the cost of this process.

Solution:
Cryolite is added to reduce the melting point of the ore which saves energy and becomes cost effective.

Worked Example 2: Extraction of aluminium is a very expensive process. Suggest any two reasons which makes this process expensive.

Solution:
Large amount of electricity is needed to carry out the process. Anode must be replaced regularly.

Extraction of iron

Key Points: Extraction of iron

- Iron is extracted from the ore, haematite (Fe_2O_3).
- Since haematite is nothing but iron oxide, and the oxygen must be removed to leave the iron behind using reduction reactions.
- As the carbon is more reactive than iron, it can displace the iron from its oxide. Hence the method for extraction of iron is called 'reduction by carbon' and it takes place in the blast furnace (Fig 4.4).

Oxidation – Removal of oxygen.

Knowledge of blast furnace is not required for this specification.

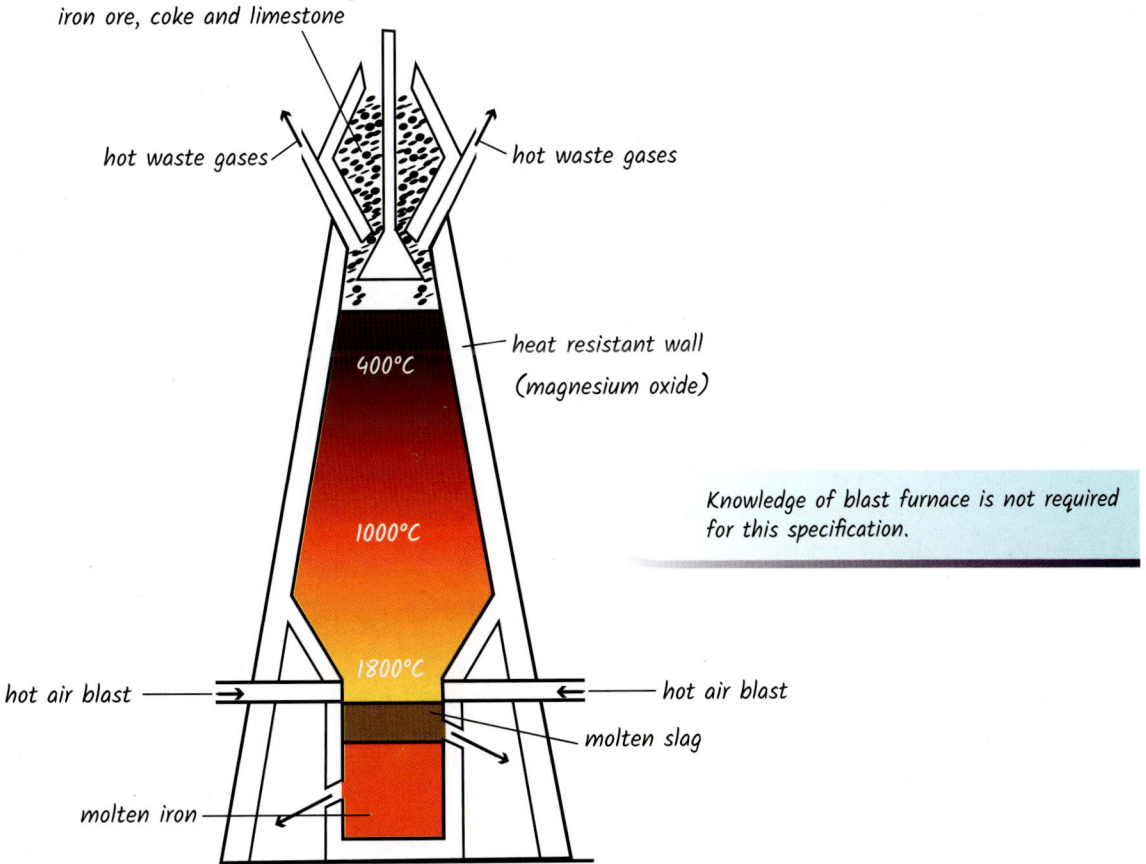

Fig 4.4 - Extraction of iron in a blast furnace

Topic 4 – Extracting metals and Equilibria

Biological extraction of metal

4.8 Evaluate alternative biological methods of metal extraction (bacterial and phytoextraction) (H)

Key Points: Alternative method of extraction - Phytomining and bioleaching

- Ores like copper ore is running out and it needs to be extracted from low grade ore.
    - Since it is harder to extract metal from lower grade ore, alternative methods like phytomining and bioleaching allows us to economically extract metals from lower-grade ores.

    Low grade ore contains very limited amount of metal.

- Phytomining:
    - Plants are grown on land containing the metal compound required.
    - High concentration of metal compound is absorbed in their tissue.
    - Later, higher concentration of the metal compound is extracted from the ashes of plants by burning the plants after harvesting.

    Copper is widely extracted using phytomining and bioleaching method

- Bioleaching:
    - Bioleaching uses bacteria which are mixed with the lower grade ore.
    - Chemical reactions of bacteria produce a solution called a leachate.
    - The leachate contains the metal compound required.

- Once the metal compound is obtained, metal can be extracted using displacement or electrolysis method.
- Biological extraction does not involve digging, transporting and clearing large amounts of waste unlike in traditional mining.

Recycling Metals

4.10 Evaluate the advantages of recycling metals, including economic implications and how recycling can preserve both the environment and the supply of valuable raw materials

Key Points: Recycling metals

- Metal ores are limited in the earth's crust. Therefore, it is essential to recycle the metals.
- The main metals which are recycled include aluminium and iron.
- Recycling has more advantages than disadvantages (Table 4.4).

Advantages	Disadvantages
Reduces environmental air pollution.	More man power is required.
Reduces the space required for the disposal of metals (landfill).	Time consuming process.
Cheaper to recycle than to extract.	Transportation.
Saves energy and reduces the greenhouse gas (CO_2).	

Table 4.4 - Advantages and disadvantages of recycling metals

4.11 - 4.12 Describe & evaluate that a life-cycle assessment for a product involves consideration of the effect on the environment of obtaining the raw materials, manufacturing the product, using the product and disposing of the product when it is no longer useful

Key Points: Key Points: Life-cycle assessments (LCA)

- Impact of manufactured products are analysed by LCA.
- The key stages of LCA are:
    - **Making raw materials for the product** - Removing raw materials from the earth's crust has a lot of impact on nature, like damaging the habitats, which may become unavailable in the future.
    - **Production of the products (manufacture)** - Releasing pollution into the environment and using up the land to build factories and industries which led to destroy nature.
    - **Transportation of both raw materials and the end products** - Transporting raw materials and end products uses lots of energy and pollutants released by the vehicles affects the environment.
    - **Utilising and implementing products** - Handling the product as per the label which needs education and follow up and impact of usage entirely depends upon the type of product (bio-degradable and non-biodegradable).
    - **Disposing at the end of life time** - Non-biodegradable products ends up in landfill sites and burning these products produces lots of air pollution. However, energy released during this process can be used to generate electricity. Recycling products can be further broken down into more useful products. On the other hand, reusable product does not need to be disposed, which can be helpful to the environment.

Reversible reactions and Equilibria

Reversible reactions

4.13 Recall that chemical reactions are reversible, the use of the symbol in equations and that the direction of some reversible reactions can be altered by changing the reaction conditions

Key Points: Reversible reactions

- A **reversible reaction** is a chemical reaction in which reactants react together to produce the products AND the products reacts together to form reactants **simultaneously**.
- Reversible reactions are shown with a symbol $\rightleftharpoons$.
- Reversible reaction can be represented as P + Q $\rightleftharpoons$ R + S.
- Two half headed arrows in the symbol represents the reaction goes forward ($\longrightarrow$), right hand side and backward ($\longleftarrow$), left hand side.
- Magnitude of reactants and products can be changed by altering the conditions of the system.

Key definition: A reversible reaction is a chemical reaction in which reactants react together to produce the products AND products react together to form reactants.

Key Examples: Reversible reactions

- Example 1: Test for water using hydrated copper(II) sulphate is an example of a reversible reaction.
- Blue colour hydrated copper(II) sulphate is heated to remove water molecules to form white colour anhydrous copper(II) sulphate. This reaction is reversible when water is added (Fig 4.6).

Test for water can be carried out by adding water to blue anhydrous cobalt(II) chloride to produce pink hydrated cobalt(II) chloride. This gets reversed on heating.

blue crystals

heat $\rightleftharpoons$ add water

white powder

hydrated copper sulphate
$CuSO_4 \cdot 5H_2O$

endothermic $\rightleftharpoons$ exothermic

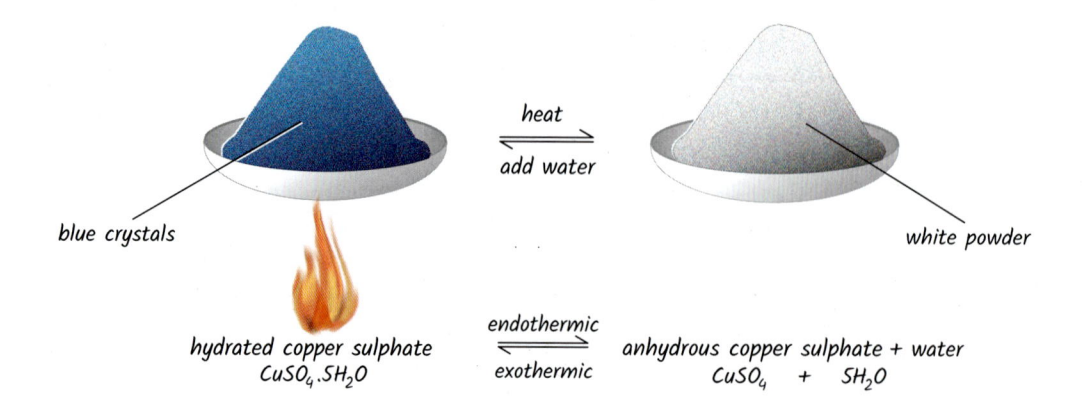

anhydrous copper sulphate + water
$CuSO_4$ + $5H_2O$

Fig 4.6 - Reversible reaction - Test for water

- **Example 2:** Thermal decomposition of ammonium chloride is another example of a reversible reaction.
- Heating white solid ammonium chloride decomposes to form colourless ammonia and hydrogen chloride gas. When these two gases reach the cool part of the test tube, they react together to form a white solid, ammonium chloride again (Fig 4.7).

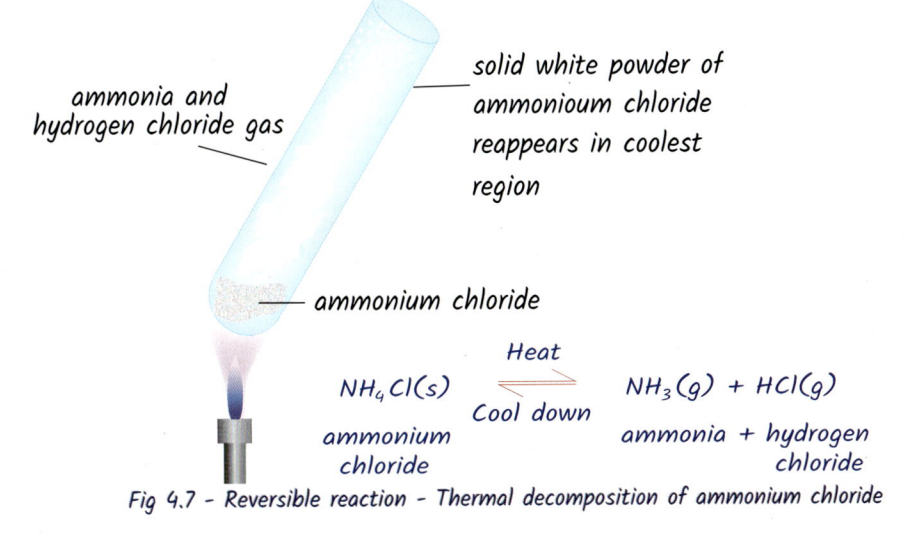

ammonia and hydrogen chloride gas

solid white powder of ammonioum chloride reappears in coolest region

ammonium chloride

$$NH_4Cl(s) \underset{\text{Cool down}}{\overset{\text{Heat}}{\rightleftharpoons}} NH_3(g) + HCl(g)$$

ammonium chloride   ammonia + hydrogen chloride

Fig 4.7 - Reversible reaction - Thermal decomposition of ammonium chloride

Equilibria

4.14 Explain what is meant by dynamic equilibrium

Key Points: Dynamic equilibrium

- Dynamic equilibrium is a reversible reaction.
- **Dynamic equilibrium** is a position in which the forward and the backward reactions are still progressing, but macroscopic properties are **constant**.
    - Examples of macroscopic properties are **colour, pressure, concentration, pH**.
    - Dynamic equilibrium can **only** be reached in a **closed system**.
    - Rate of forward reaction **is equal** to backward reaction.
    - At equilibrium, the concentrations of all reactants and products will remain constant but **NOT** necessarily same.

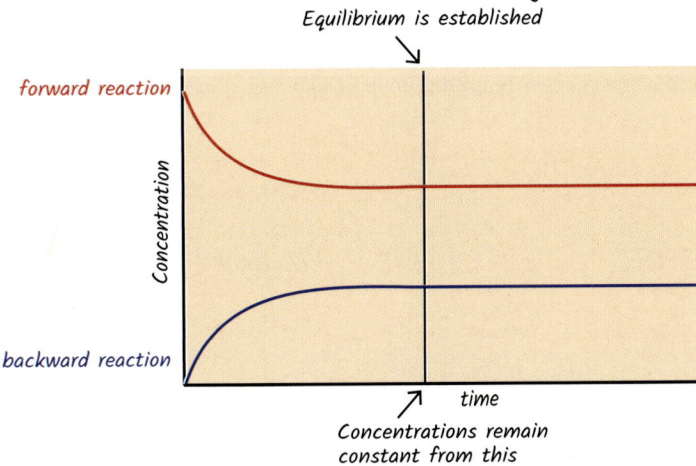

Equilibrium is established

forward reaction

backward reaction

time

Concentrations remain constant from this time on

Fig 4.8 - Dynamic equilibrium

When macroscopic properties are constant the system appears as though nothing is changing.

Key definition: Dynamic equilibrium is a position in which the forward and the backward reactions are still progressing, but macroscopic properties are constant.

4.17 Predict how the position of a dynamic equilibrium is affected by changes in:
a) temperature b) pressure c) concentration (H)

Key Table: Altering the conditions of dynamic equilibrium

Condition	Change	Towards	Position of equilibrium
Concentration	Increase	Reactants	Shift to the right
		Products	Shift to the left
	Decrease	Reactants	Shift to the left (same side - reactant)
		Products	Shift to the right (same side - products)

Forward reactions
ΔH = negative = Exothermic reaction
ΔH = positive = Endothermic reaction

Table 4.6 - The effect of change in concentration on equilibrium position

Condition	Change	Overall reaction	Position of equilibrium
Temperature	Increase	Exothermic	Shift to the left
		Endothermic	Shift to the right
	Decrease	Exothermic	Shift to the right
		Endothermic	Shift to the left

Table 4.7 - The effect of change in temperature on equilibrium position

Condition	Change	Total number of particles	Position of equilibrium
Pressure	Increase	$\Sigma n(R) > \Sigma n(P)$	Shift to the right
		$\Sigma n(R) < \Sigma n(P)$	Shift to the left
	Decrease	$\Sigma n(R) > \Sigma n(P)$	Shift to the left
		$\Sigma n(R) < \Sigma n(P)$	Shift to the right

Table 4.8 - The effect of pressure in temperature on equilibrium position

Worked example 4: Determine the direction in which the equilibrium reaction below will proceed, following a decrease in the external temperature.

$$2SO_2(g) + O_2(g) \rightleftharpoons 2SO_3(g) \qquad \Delta H = -197 kJmol^{-1}$$

Solution

This is an exothermic reaction in the forward direction, so a decrease in temperature will cause the reaction to proceed forward by shifting the equilibrium to the right.
As a result, more sulphur trioxide gas will be produced.

Forward reactions
$\Sigma n(R)$ = Sum of total number of reactants particles.
$\Sigma n(P)$ = Sum of total number of products particles.

The Haber Process

4.15 Describe the formation of ammonia as a reversible reaction between nitrogen (extracted from the air) and hydrogen (obtained from natural gas) and that it can reach a dynamic equilibrium

4.16 Recall the conditions for the Haber process as:
a) temperature 450°C b) pressure 200 atmospheres c) iron catalyst

Key Points: Manufacture of ammonia – The Haber Process

- The Haber Process is used in the manufacture of ammonia.
- Nitrogen from the liquid air and hydrogen from natural gas (methane) are the raw materials in the process.
- The reaction is **reversible**.
- Forward reaction is **exothermic** of $\Delta H = -93 \text{ kJmol}^{-1}$.
- Process is shown in flowchart 4.1.
- **Conditions** to obtain maximum yield of ammonia (NH_3):
  - Finely divided **iron** catalyst
  - **450°C** – Optimum temperature
  - **200** atmospheric pressure
- Iron catalyst does NOT affect the amount of products made. The yield of ammonia stays the same, but ammonia can be obtained faster.
- At each cycle, only about 15% of the nitrogen and hydrogen converts to ammonia. By repeated recycling of the unreacted nitrogen and hydrogen, the overall conversion can be raised to 98%.

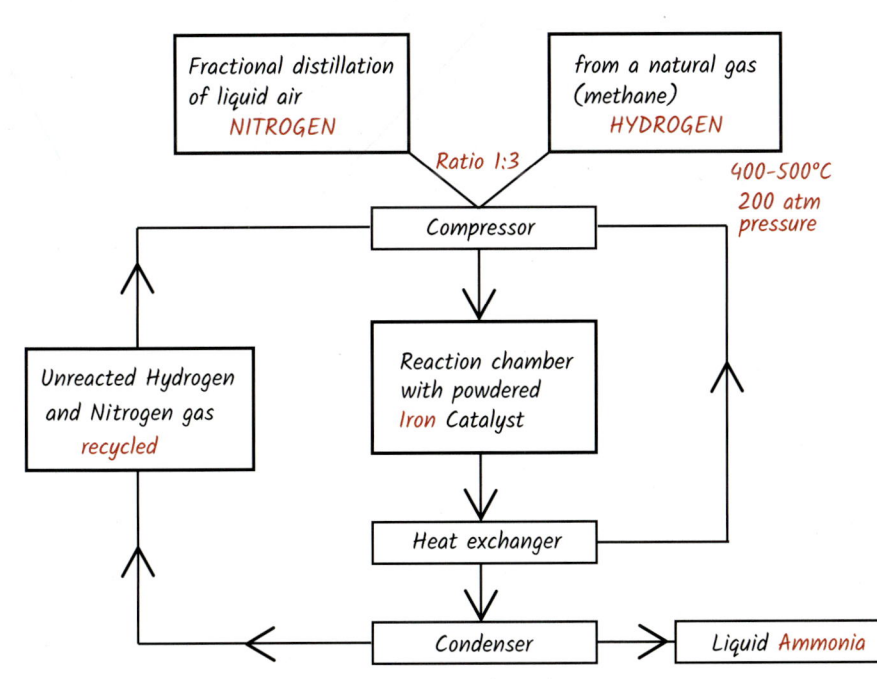

$$N_2 + 3H_2 \rightleftharpoons 2NH_3$$

Flowchart 4.1 – The Haber Process

Transition metals, alloys and corrosion

Transition metals

> **5.1C** Recall that most metals are transition metals and that their typical properties include:
> a) high melting point b) high density
> c) the formation of coloured compounds
> d) catalytic activity of the metals and their compounds as exemplified by iron

Key Points: Transition metals

- The transition metals are found in the middle of the periodic table.
- They are not as reactive as Group I and II metals.
- Some of their physical properties includes:
    - They have high density.
    - They have high melting and boiling point.
    - They are strong and hard metals.
    - They form coloured ions and compounds.
    - They have variable oxidation states.
  For example:
    - Copper forms Cu^+ and Cu^{2+}
    - Iron form Fe^{2+} and Fe^{3+}
- They show catalytic activity in many industrial productions.
  For example:
    - **iron** is used in the industrial production of ammonia
    - **vanadium**(V) oxide is used in the manufacture of sulphuric acid
    - **nickel** is used in the manufacture of margarine from vegetable oil.

Tungsten, with highest melting point is used to make filament for light bulbs.

Rusting of Iron

> **5.2C** Recall that the oxidation of metals results in corrosion
> **5.3C** Explain how rusting of iron can be prevented by:
> a) exclusion of oxygen
> b) exclusion of water
> c) sacrificial protection
> **5.4C** Explain how electroplating can be used to improve the appearance and/or the resistance to corrosion of metal objects

Key Points: Rusting of iron

- Rust is an orange-red powder which consists of mainly hydrated iron(III) oxide ($Fe_2O_3.xH_2O$).
- Water AND oxygen are essential components of rusting.
- Absence of one of these substances prevent rusting.
- The rusting of iron is encouraged by the presence of salt.
- The oxidation of metals result in corrosion.

Oxidation of metal in presence of air (or) some chemicals result in corrosion.

Key Points: Prevention of iron from rusting

- To prevent iron from rusting, iron must be stopped from coming in contact with oxygen AND water.
- This can be achieved in several ways:
- **Barrier methods:**
    - **Painting**: Rusting of ships, lorries, cars, and many other iron products can be protected by making a layer of paint on the surface of iron.
    - **Oiling/greasing**: Machinery parts are coated with oil to prevent them from coming into contact with air or moisture by making a protective film of oil or grease.
- **Galvanising**: Dipping the object into molten zinc. The thin layer of the more reactive zinc metal coating the steel object slowly corrodes and loses electrons to the iron, thereby protecting it.
- **Sacrificial protection**: Attaching the zinc bars on the surface or iron structures. Zinc is above iron in the reactivity series and will react in preference to it (undergoes corrosion).
- **Electroplating**: Coating one metal on top of another metal improves the appearance and/or the resistance of metal corrosion. Car bumpers and bicycle handlebars are electroplated with chromium to prevent rusting.

> Prevention methods are temporary solution. Regular maintenance is required to protect iron from rusting.

> Sacrificial protection - Blocks of magnesium can be used in the place of zinc.

Worked Example 1: In the laboratory, four test tubes were set up with iron nail for rusting. Identify and explain which nail in the test tube gets rusted.

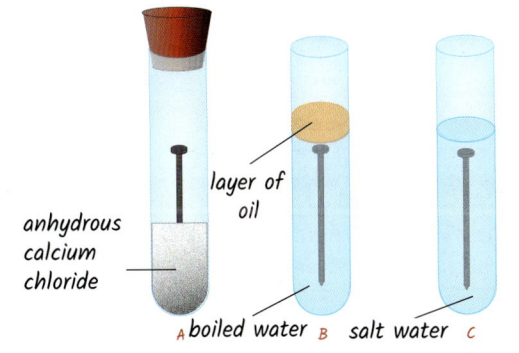

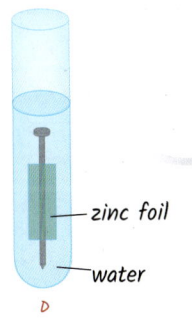

> Drying agents absorbs water from the air and keeps the object dry.

A: anhydrous calcium chloride
B: layer of oil, boiled water
C: salt water
D: zinc foil, water

Rusting experiment with nails.

Solution:
- Test tube C. Nail in test tube C is in direct contact with water and air. Also, salt water increases the pace of rusting.
- Test tube A: Air is present but anhydrous calcium chloride (drying agent) protects the nail from water.
- Test tube B: Water is present, but the layer of oil prevents the air from coming in contact with the nail.
- Test tube D: Water and air is present. However, the more reactive metal zinc gets rusted and protects the iron nail from rusting.

Alloys

> **5.5C** Explain, using models, why converting pure metals into alloys often increases the strength of the product
> **5.6C** Explain why iron is alloyed with other metals to produce alloy steels
> **5.7C** Explain how the uses of metals are related to their properties (and vice versa), including aluminium, copper and gold and their alloys including magnalium and brass

Key Points: Alloys

- Pure metals are too soft to use. To make it useful, it needs to be mixed with another element to make it hard.
- **An alloy** is a mixture of a metal with another element.
- In some cases, alloys itself, like steel is mixed with carbon to make it hard.
- Alloys are often harder than the metal they contain.
- A comparison of pure metals and alloys are shown in Fig 5.1

Pure metals are made up of only one type of atoms
Soft and malleable
Atoms ordered arranged - same size of atoms.
Atoms can slide over each other easily as atoms are of same size

Alloys are made up of more types of atoms.
Strong and hard.
Atoms disorderly arranged - different size of atoms.
Atoms cannot slide over each other easily as foreign atoms are in different size.

Fig 5.1 - Structure of a) pure metals b) alloys

Key Table: Uses of common alloys

Steel	Composition	Uses
Brass	65% copper, 35% zinc	Machine bearing, jewellery
Bronze	90% copper, 10% tin	Casting, parts of machine
Magnalium	70% aluminium, 30% magnesium	Manufacturing aircraft bodies

Table 5.1 - Uses of common alloys

Key Table: Uses of common steel

Steel	Composition	Uses	Properties
Mild steel (low carbon steel)	99.5% iron, 0.5% carbon	Car bodies, building equipment (girders)	Malleable and lost most of brittleness
Hard steel (High carbon steel)	99% iron 1% carbon	Razor blades, cutting tools	Tough and brittle
Stainless steel	74% iron, 18% chromium, 8% nickel	Cutlery, surgical instrumentals	Tough, resistant to corrosion

Table 5.2 - Uses of common steel

Quantitative analysis

Moles calculations

Key Points: Moles calculations

- Moles can be calculated in terms of different **states of matter**.
- Moles: The **mole (mol)** is an SI unit which measures the number of particles in a specific substance.
- Use the hints below to apply different formulas in terms of states of matter.
- **Hints:**
  - **Solid:** g (OR) kg
  - **Solution:** $moldm^{-3}$ AND $molcm^{-3}$
  - **Gas:** cm^3 (OR) dm^3
- One mole of any gas occupies $24dm^3$

Key Formulas: States of matter

- **Solid** – Mass is usually given in g or kg.

  $$Moles = \frac{Mass}{Relative\ formula\ mass/atomic\ mass/molecular\ mass}$$ (further derived to)

  Mass = Moles x Relative formula mass/atomic mass/molecular mass

- **Liquid** – volume is usually given in cm^3 so it must be converted to dm^3 by dividing the volume by 1000 as shown below in the formula. If volume is given in dm^3 do not divide by 1000

  $$Moles = \frac{Concentration\ X\ Volume}{1000}$$ (further derived to) $$Concentration = \frac{Moles}{Volume}$$

- **Gas** – if volume is given in dm^3, 1 mole of any gas occupies $24dm^3$

  $$Moles = \frac{Volume}{24}$$ (further derived to) Volume = Moles x 24

- **Gas** – if volume is given in cm^3, 1 mole of any gas occupies $24000cm^3$

  $$Moles = \frac{Volume}{24000}$$ (further derived to) Volume = Moles x 24000

Calculating number of moles

Worked example 1: a) Calculate the number of moles in 1.25g of sodium chloride, NaCl.

Solution:

$$Moles = \frac{Mass}{Relative\ formula\ mass}$$

Unit grams (g) helps us to use mole formula in terms of solid.

Relative formula mass of NaCl = (1 x 23) + (1 x 35.5) = 58.5

$$= \frac{1.25}{58.5} = \mathbf{0.02\ moles}$$

b) Calculate the mass of 0.5 moles of magnesium hydroxide, $Mg(OH)_2$.

Solution:

Mass = Moles x Relative formula mass

Relative formula mass of $Mg(OH)_2$ = (1 x 24) + [(2 x 16) + (2 x 1)] = 57

= 0.5 x 57 = **28.5g**

c) Calculate the number moles of sulphuric acid, H_2SO_4 in $25cm^3$ of $0.10 mol/dm^3$ solution.

Solution:

$$Moles = \frac{Concentration \times Volume}{1000}$$

$$Moles = \frac{0.10 \times 25}{1000} = \mathbf{2.5 \times 10^{-3} moles}$$

Units cm^3 AND mol/dm^3 helps us to use mole formula in terms of liquid.

To convert gdm^{-3} to $moldm^{-3}$. Use Moles = Mass/Mr and divide by volume in dm^3
Also, if you have gdm^{-3} and you divide by the molar mass ($molg^{-1}$), the grams will cancel out and you will be left with $moldm^{-3}$.

5.16C Describe the molar volume, of any gas at room temperature and pressure, as the volume occupied by one mole of molecules of any gas at room temperature and pressure (The molar volume will be provided as $24dm^3$ or $24000cm^3$ in calculations where it is required) (HC)

d) Calculate the volume of carbon monoxide, CO gas produced when 0.4 moles of carbon is burnt in limited amount of oxygen.

Solution:

$$Volume = Moles \times 24$$

$$= 0.4 \times 24 = \mathbf{9.6 dm^3}$$

This is a straightforward question. As volume is asked for CO gas rearrange the formula of mole formula in terms of gas into volume.

Calculating concentration in terms of g/dm^3

5.8C Calculate the concentration of solutions in $moldm^{-3}$ and convert concentration in gdm^{-3} into $moldm^{-3}$ and vice versa. (HC)

Key Idea: Concentration can be further calculated in terms of g/dm^3

$$Concentration\ of\ solution = \frac{Mass\ of\ solute\ in\ grams}{Volume\ of\ solution\ in\ dm^3}$$

Worked example 2: Calculate the concentration of aqueous magnesium sulphate, $MgSO_4$ solution initially 12.5g of magnesium sulphate dissolved in $50cm^3$ of water.

Solution:

Note: $1dm^3 = 1000cm^3$, so $50cm^3 = 50/1000 = 0.05dm^3$

$$Concentration\ of\ solution = \frac{Mass\ of\ solute\ in\ grams}{Volume\ of\ solution\ in\ dm^3} = \frac{12.5}{0.05} = \mathbf{250 g/dm^3}$$

g/dm^3 is mass (g) over volume (dm^3).

The Percentage Yield

5.11C Calculate the percentage yield of a reaction from the actual yield and the theoretical yield

Key Points: The Percentage Yield

- The percentage yield is the ratio of the actual yield to the theoretical yield, expressed in percentage.
- The percentage yield can be calculated using the formula below:

$$\text{Percentage yield} = \frac{\text{actual yield}}{\text{theoretical yield}} \times 100$$

- **Actual yield** is amount of product obtained through an experiment.
- **Theoretical yield** is the quantity of product formed, expected from a chemical reaction.
- An actual yield is usually less than the theoretical yield due to the following reasons:
    - **Incomplete reactions** – Not always all reactants react to form the product.
    - **Practical losses during the experiment** – Human error while conducting experiment such as considering the filter paper is dry but not dried enough (or) spillage while conducting the experiment.
    - **Undesirable side reactions** – side reactions which compete with the actual reaction.

Worked example 3: At the end of salt preparation, Keti produced 25.5 grams of magnesium oxide, MgO. While performing the calculations, her lab partner Keyana determined that the theoretical yield is 28.5 grams of magnesium oxide. What is Keti's percentage yield?

Solution:

$$\text{Percentage yield} = \frac{\text{Actual yield}}{\text{Theoretical yield}} \times 100$$

Actual yield during the experiment: **25.5** grams

Theoretical data value: **28.5** grams

$$\text{Percentage yield} = \frac{25.5}{28.5} \times 100 = \mathbf{89.5\%}$$

Atom Economy

S.13C Recall the atom economy of a reaction forming a desired product
S.14C Calculate the atom economy of a reaction forming a desired product

Key Points: Atom economy

- **Atom Economy** is used to measure the percentage of atoms wasted in the chemical process.
- The higher the atom economy, the **'greener'** the process.
- 100 percent atom economy means that all the atoms in the reactants have been converted to the desired product.

The higher the atom economy, the greener the process. By having higher atom economy, the maximum amount of all the raw materials gets converted into the product and a minimum amount of waste is produced, which makes the process greener.

$$\text{Atom economy} = \frac{\text{Molecular mass of desired products}}{\text{Sum of molecular mass of all products}} \times 100$$

Example 4: Calculate the atom economy for making hydrogen by reacting magnesium with hydrochloric acid:

$$Mg + 2HCl \longrightarrow MgCl_2 + H_2$$

Solution:

Mr of H_2 = 1 + 1 = **2**
Mr of $MgCl_2$ = 24 + (2 × 35.5) = **95**

Mr = Relative formula mass/ molecular mass/atomic mass

$$\text{Atom economy} = \frac{2 \times 1}{95 + (2 \times 1)} \times 100 = 2.06\%$$

Reaction pathways

S.15C Explain why a particular reaction pathway is chosen to produce a specified product, given appropriate data such as atom economy, yield, rate, equilibrium position and usefulness of by-products (HC)

Key Points: Effective reaction pathways

- Every chemical reaction is expected to produce a desired product.
- Products are obtained in more than one route. However, a route is picked by effective pathways.
- Effective pathway produces a desired product with reasonable amount of yield.
- The pathway chosen depends on factors such as:
    - percentage yield
    - atom economy
    - rate of reaction
    - equilibrium position
    - usefulness of by-products

- Artificial fertiliser ammonium sulphate can be obtained by two different ways:
    a) Batch process   Atom economy: 60 - 65 %
                            By-products: excess ammonia cannot be recycled

    b) Continuous process   Atom economy: 90 - 95 %
                            By-products: excess ammonia can be recycled which can be used to make ammonium nitrate by reacting with nitric acid.

- Considering the above data, the desired product of ammonium sulphate can be obtained effectively through continuous process with highest atom economy and excess ammonia gas can be recycled to make different fertilisers.

Calculating volume and mass involving chemical equations

5.17C Use the molar volume and balanced equations in calculations involving the masses of solids and volumes of gases (HC)

Key Steps: Calculating volume and mass using chemical equations

Step 1: Construct the balanced chemical equation.
Step 2: Find out the number of moles of the known substance.
Step 3: Figure out the molar ratio of the substance involved in the question.
Step 4: Calculate the number of moles of the substance to be found.
Step 5: Using the above step workout the mass (or) concentration (or) volume of the substance need to be found.

Worked example 5: Calculate the volume of carbon dioxide, CO_2 gas produced from the complete combustion of 0.5 moles of butane, C_4H_{10}.

Solution: To find volume first we need to find moles.

Balanced chemical equation.	$C_4H_{10} + 6\frac{1}{2}O_2 \longrightarrow 4CO_2 + 5H_2O$
Number of moles of the known substance	0.5 moles
Mole ratio of the substance involved in the question from equation.	1 mole C_4H_{10} : 4 moles CO_2
Calculate the number of moles of the substance to be found	1 mole of C_4H_{10} gives 4 moles of CO_2 Therefore, 0.5 moles must give 1 = 4 0.5 = x $x = \dfrac{4 \times 0.5}{1} = 2$ moles
Volume of CO_2 produced	Volume = Moles × 24 = 2 × 24 = **48dm³**

Worked example 6: Calculate the mass of sodium chloride, NaCl produced when sodium reacts with 17.5g of hydrochloric acid, HCl.

Solution:

Balanced chemical equation.	$2Na + 2HCl \longrightarrow 2NaCl + H_2$
Number of moles of the known substance	value of HCl is given in grams, use the moles formula related to solid: $= \dfrac{Mass}{Relative\ formula\ mass} = \dfrac{17.5}{36.5} = 0.47$ moles
Mole ratio of the substance involve in the question from equation.	2 moles HCl : 2 moles NaCl
Calculate the number of moles of the substance to be found	2 moles of HCl gives 2 moles of NaCl Therefore, 2 moles must give 2 = 2 0.47 = x $x = \dfrac{2 \times 0.48}{2} = 0.48$ moles
Volume of NaCl produced	Mass = Moles x Relative formula mass Relative formula mass of NaCl = 58.5 = 0.47 x 58.5 = **27.5g**

Titration Calculations

5.10C Carry out simple calculations using the results of titrations to calculate an unknown concentration of a solution or an unknown volume of solution required (HC)

Key Steps: Titration Calculations

- Titration is used to find an unknown concentration of a solution or an unknown volume of solution required.
- Following steps are used to find the unknown value.

    Step 1: Construct the balanced chemical equation.

    Step 2: Figure out the value of concentration - C (or) volume - V (or) both from the question for both reactants (reactant 1 and reactant 2). Refer Table 5.3.

    Step 3: Figure out the number of moles (n) - (coefficient) from the balanced equation.

    Step 4: Substitute the value in the below formula:

$$\frac{C_1 V_1}{n_1} \text{ reactant 1} = \frac{C_2 V_2}{n_2} \text{ reactant 2}$$

C_1 = Concentration of reactant 1	C_2 = Concentration of reactant 2
V_1 = Volume of reactant 1	V_2 = Volume of reactant 2
n_1 = Number of moles of reactant 1 (coefficient from balanced equation)	n_2 = Number of moles of reactant 2 (coefficient from balanced equation)

Table 5.3 - Titration calculation

    Step 5: Using the above formula find the unknown concentration - C (or) volume - V of the reactant need to be found

Worked example 7: 25.0cm³ of a 0.10moldm⁻³ solution of sodium hydroxide, NaOH was titrated against a solution of sulphuric acid, H_2SO_4 of unknown concentration. 27.5cm³ of the acid was required. What was the concentration of the acid?

Step 1: Construct the balanced chemical equation	$2NaOH + 1H_2SO_4 \longrightarrow 1Na_2SO_4 + 2H_2O$
Step 2: Figure out the value of concentration - C AND volume - V from the question for both reactants (reactant 1 and reactant 2). Table 5.1 is used.	NaOH = Reactant 1 $\quad$ H_2SO_4 = Reactant 2 $C_1 = 0.10$ $\quad\quad\quad\quad$ $C_2 = x$ $V_1 = 25.0$ $\quad\quad\quad\quad$ $V_2 = 27.5$
Step 3: Figure out the number of moles (n) - (coefficient) from the balanced equation.	The number of moles (n) - (coefficient) from the balance equation. NaOH $\quad\quad\quad\quad\quad$ H_2SO_4 $n_1 = 2$ $\quad\quad\quad\quad\quad$ $n_2 = 1$
Step 4: Substitute the value in the below formula: $$\frac{C_1V_1}{n_1} = \frac{C_2V_2}{n_2}$$	$$\frac{0.10 \times 25}{2} = \frac{x \times 27.5}{1}$$
Step 5: Using the above formula find the unknown concentration of H_2SO_4 (C)	$$x = \frac{0.10 \times 25 \times 1}{2 \times 27.5} = 0.045$$ Concentration of H_2SO_4 = **0.045moldm⁻³**

Since both volumes are given in cm³, it is not necessary to convert volume from cm³ to dm³ as 1000 will be cancelled out automatically.

Avogadro Law

5.18C Use Avogadro law to calculate volumes of gases involved in a gaseous reaction, given the relevant equation (HC)

Key Points: Avogadro law and volume of gas

- Avogadro law states that equal volumes of gases at the same temperature and pressure contains the same number of particles.
- In a balanced equation, the molar ratio of the reactants and products directly gives the gas volume ratio of reactants and products provided all the gases volumes are measured at the same temperature and pressure.
- This is applicable only to gaseous reactants or products at the same temperature and pressure.

Worked example 8: Calculate the volume of carbon dioxide (CO_2) produced, when $50dm^3$ of carbon monoxide (CO) reacts with $50dm^3$ of oxygen (O_2).

$$2CO(g) + O_2(g) \longrightarrow 2CO_2(g)$$

Solution:

According to the equation, 2 moles of CO reacts with 1 mole of O_2 to give 2 moles of CO_2 which is equal to 2 volumes of CO reacts with 1 volume of O_2 to produce 2 volumes of CO_2

The volume of carbon dioxide, CO_2 produced is **50cm³**

	C	O_2	CO_2
Ratio	2	1	2
Volume	50	$\frac{50 \times 1}{2} = 25$	= 2:2 = 50:50

Worked example 9: Calculate the volume of ammonia (NH_3) produced when $50cm^3$ of nitrogen (N_2) is reacted with $200cm^3$ of hydrogen (H_2). What volume of hydrogen remains?

$$N_2(g) + 3H_2(g) \longrightarrow 2NH_3(g)$$

Solution:

	N_2	H_2	NH_3
Ratio	1	3	2
Volume	50	200	= (2 × 50) = 100
Total	50	50 × 3 = 150	100

The volume of ammonia, NH_3 produced is **100cm³**
The volume of hydrogen, H_2 remain = (initially taken − finally produced)
= 200 − 150 = **50cm³**

Dynamic equilibria

The Haber Process

> **5.19C** Describe the Haber process as a reversible reaction between nitrogen and hydrogen to form ammonia

Key Points: Manufacture of ammonia – The Haber Process

- The Haber Process is used in the manufacture of ammonia.
- Nitrogen from the liquid air and hydrogen from natural gas (methane) are the raw materials in the process.
- The reaction is reversible.
- Forward reaction is exothermic of $\Delta H = -93 kJmol^{-1}$.
- Process is shown in flowchart 5.1.
- Conditions to obtain maximum yield of ammonia (NH_3):
  - Finely divided iron catalyst
  - 450°C – Optimum temperature
  - 200 atmospheric pressure
- Iron catalyst does NOT affect the amount of products made. The yield of ammonia stays the same, but ammonia can be obtained faster.
- At each cycle, only about 15% of the nitrogen and hydrogen converts to ammonia. By repeated recycling of the unreacted nitrogen and hydrogen, the overall conversion can be raised to 98%.

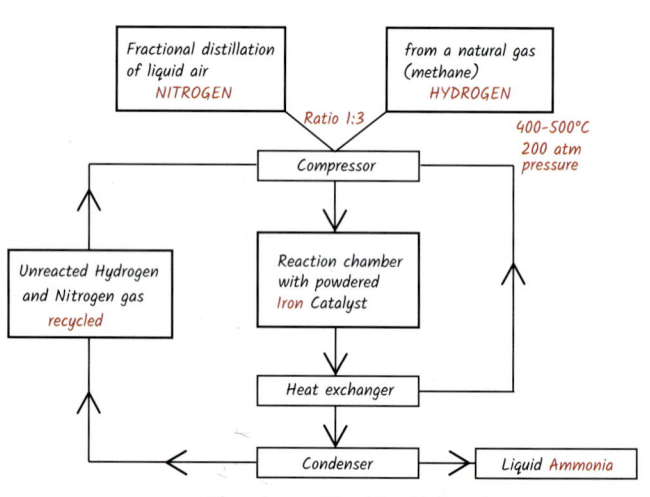

$N_2 + 3H_2 \rightleftharpoons 2NH_3$

Flowchart 5.1 – The Haber Process

> **5.20C** Predict how the rate of attainment of equilibrium is affected by:
> a) changes in temperature
> b) changes in pressure
> c) changes in concentration
> d) use of a catalyst

Key Points: The Haber process – In terms of Le Chatelier's principle:

- **decreasing the temperature**, yields more amount of ammonia, as the forward reaction is exothermic. A lower temperature will favour a high yield of ammonia, but it takes a long time as the rate is slow. Therefore, 450°C (optimum) is a compromise, and still produces a reasonably high proportion of ammonia.
- **increasing the concentration of nitrogen or hydrogen**, increasing concentration on one side shifts the equilibrium to the opposite side, which gives higher yield of ammonia.
- **increasing the pressure**, in the given balanced equation there are 4 moles of gas on the reactants side (left) but 2 moles of gas (ammonia) on the right hand side (products). Therefore, if pressure is increased, the equilibrium shifts to the right with less number of molecules (4:2) to decrease the pressure.

> **5.21C** Explain how, in industrial reactions, including the Haber process, conditions used are related to:
> a) the availability and cost of raw materials and energy supplies
> b) the control of temperature, pressure and catalyst used produce an acceptable yield in an acceptable time
> (HC)

Key Points: The Haber process – raw materials and energy:

- In the manufacture of ammonia, conditions are carefully chosen by considering the availability and cost of raw **materials** and **energy provisions.**
- Hydrocarbons are generally used as the source of hydrogen like natural gas, naphtha, heavy oil. Few more methods are considered like hydrogen produced by electrolysis of water or obtained as a byproduct from chlorine production.
- Considering the method of production in terms of raw materials:
  - Natural gas is a non-renewable resource, whereas water from rivers and oceans are readily available.
- Considering the method of production in terms of energy provisions:
  - For electrolysis, electricity can be generated through natural resources like solar energy (or) water, whereas for natural gas intense heating is needed.

Artificial fertiliser

> **5.22C** Recall that fertilisers may contain nitrogen, phosphorus and potassium compounds to promote plant growth
> **5.23 C** Describe how ammonia reacts with nitric acid to produce a salt that is used as a fertiliser

Key Points: Manufacture of ammonium nitrate, NH_4NO_3

- Ammonia and nitric acid are extremely important in the production of artificial fertilisers.
- The fertilisers which add the three main nutrient nitrogen (**N**), phosphorus (**P**) and potassium (**K**) are called **NPK** fertilisers.
- Ammonium nitrate is the most widely used nitrogenous fertiliser.
- Ammonium nitrate is manufactured by reacting ammonia gas and nitric acid.

$$\text{ammonia} + \text{nitric acid} \longrightarrow \text{ammonium nitrate}$$

$$NH_3(g) + HNO_3(aq) \longrightarrow NH_4NO_3(aq)$$

Ammonium nitrate is otherwise known as NITRAM.

Topic 5 – Separate Chemistry 1

5.24C Describe and compare:
a) the laboratory preparation of ammonium sulphate from ammonia solution and dilute sulphuric acid on a small scale
b) the industrial production of ammonium sulphate, used as a fertiliser, in which several stages are required to produce ammonia and sulphuric acid from their raw materials and the production is carried out on a much larger scale (details of the industrial production of sulphuric acid are not required)

Key Points: Preparation of ammonium sulphate in the lab

- A small amount of ammonium sulphate can be prepared in a lab on a small scale.
- The process of preparing ammonium sulphate in a lab is known as '**batch**' process.
- This can be done by **neutralising** ammonia solution (a base) with dilute sulphuric acid (an acid) using **titration** method followed by **crystallisation** method. Refer to separation technique topic 2.

$$\text{ammonia} + \text{sulphuric acid} \longrightarrow \text{ammonium sulphate}$$

$$2NH_3(aq) + H_2SO_4(aq) \longrightarrow (NH_4)_2SO_4(aq)$$

Key Points: Manufacturing ammonium sulphate - Industrial method

- A large amount of ammonium sulphate can be prepared industrially at a large scale.
- The process of manufacturing ammonium sulphate in a lab is known as '**continuous**' process.
- Raw materials are obtained by the following processes:
  - ammonia – The Haber process
  - sulphuric acid – The contact process

$$\text{ammonia} + \text{sulphuric acid} \longrightarrow \text{ammonium sulphate}$$
$$2NH_3(g) + H_2SO_4(aq) \longrightarrow (NH_4)_2SO_4(aq)$$

- The manufacturing starts with the production of raw materials which is depicted in the flowchart 5.2.

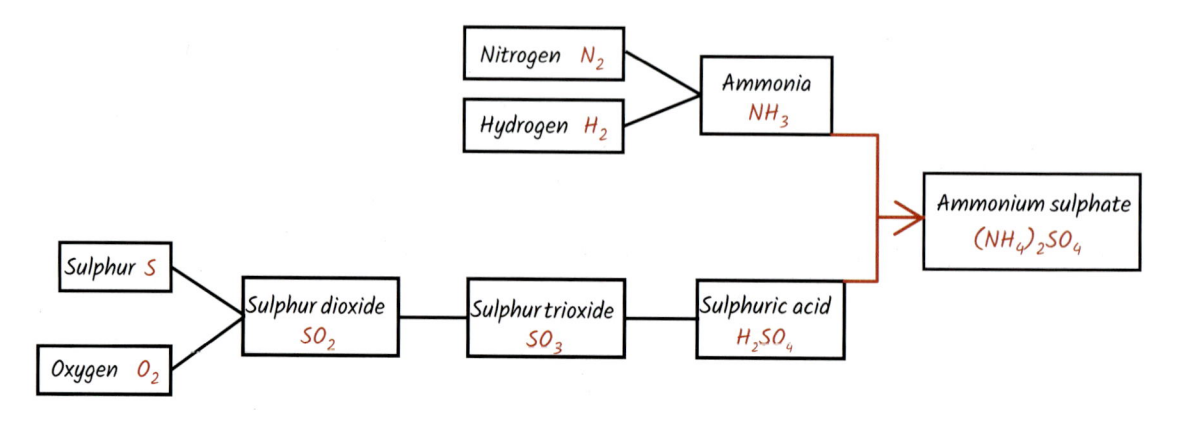

Flowchart 4.2 - Manufacturing of ammonium sulphate - Industrial method

Chemical and Fuel Cell

S.25C	Recall that a chemical cell produces a voltage until one of the reactants is used up
S.26C	Recall that in a hydrogen-oxygen fuel cell hydrogen and oxygen are used to produce a voltage and water is the only product
S.27C	Evaluate the strengths and weaknesses of fuel cells for given uses

Key Points: Chemical cells

- Chemical cell is a stored source of energy.
- Converts chemical energy into electrical energy.
- Two different metals acts as the electrodes.
- The far away in the reactivity series the two metals are, more voltage it can produce.
    - Example:
      Combination of zinc and copper produce more voltage than zinc and iron.
- Each electrode is dipped into a solution of one of their salts (electrolyte).
  Example:
    zinc dipped into zinc sulphate, whereas copper is dipped into copper(II) sulphate solution.
- The circuit is connected by the salt bridge. In most cases filter paper is soaked in a salt solution which act as a salt bridge.
- When one of the reactants is used up, the chemical reaction stops, and no more voltage is produced, and cell goes dead.
- Since electric energy is transferred to the surrounding, it is an **exothermic reaction** (Fig S.2).

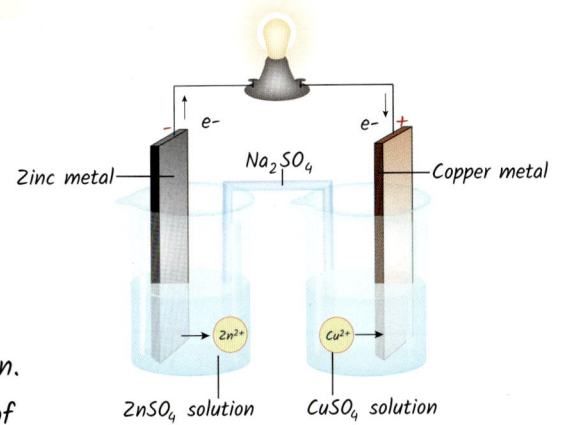

Fig S.2 - The Daniel Cell (A type of electrochemical cell)

Refer to reactivity series of metals.

Knowledge about the experimental setup and salt bridge is not required in this specification.

Key Points: Fuel cells

- A fuel cell is a device that uses hydrogen and oxygen to create electricity by producing water as the only by product.
- No combustion reaction takes place within the cell.
- A single fuel cell consists of an electrolyte sandwiched between the two thin electrodes
- Hydrogen is passed to the catalysed anode which separates hydrogen ion (H^+) and electrons (e^-).

$$2H_2(g) \longrightarrow 4H^+(aq) + 4e^-$$

- At the cathode, oxygen combines with electrons and hydrogen ions resulting in water or hydroxide ions.

$$4H^+(aq) + O_2(g) + 4e^- \longrightarrow 2H_2O(g)$$

Cancelling out the Hydrogen ions and electrons gives the overall reaction as:
$2H_2(g) + O_2(g) \longrightarrow 2H_2O(g)$

- The electrons from the anode cannot pass through the membrane to the positively charged cathode; they must travel around it via an electrical circuit to reach the other side of the cell. This movement of electrons is an electrical current.
- As long as the fuel is supplied, they produce voltage lifelong.

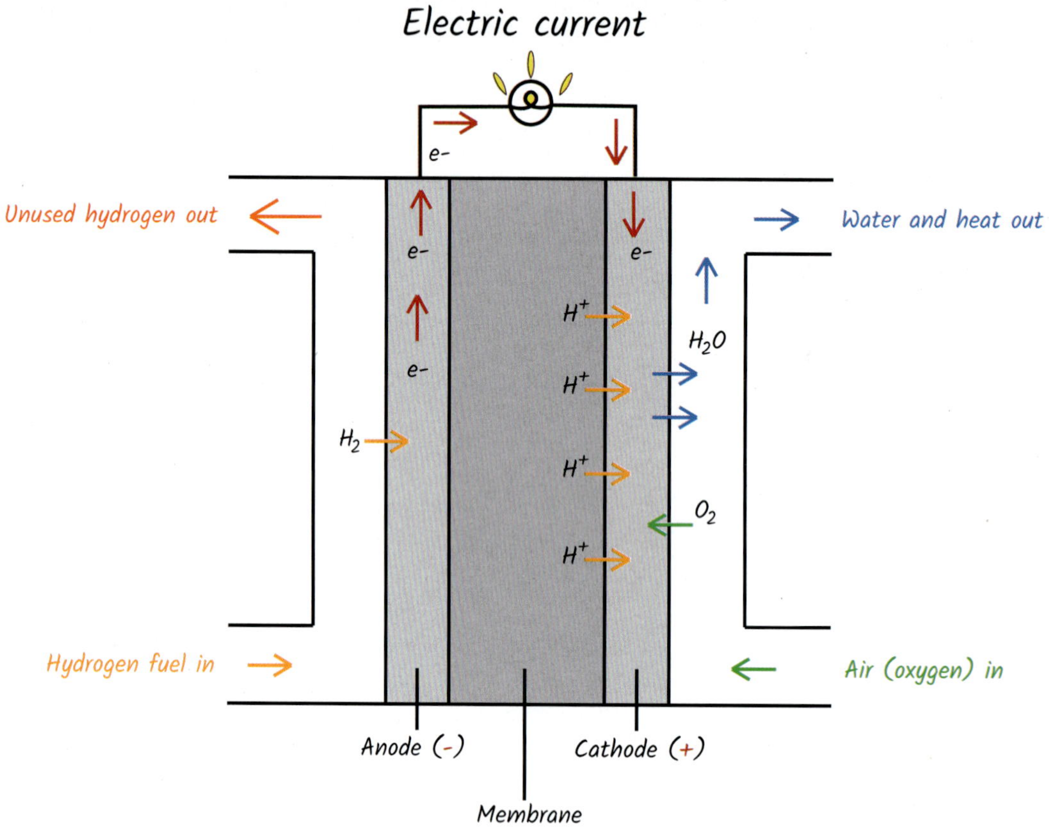

Fig S.3 - A hydrogen-oxygen fuel cell

> Anode is negative, and cathode is positive, just opposite of electrolytic cell.

Key Points: Evaluation of fuel cells

- **Fuel cells in spacecraft:**
    - It produces electricity in the absence of solar energy. However, it needs refilling once initial fuel is over.
    - No need to move around which reduces the maintenance level.
    - By-product (water) can be used as drinking water, so no need to worry about disposal.
    - A quiet environment is created, reducing sound pollution.

- **Fuel cells in vehicle:**
    - It produces no greenhouse gases, however the production of hydrogen using natural gas (or) coal does release carbon dioxide in the environment.
    - Free from sound pollution is good, compared with other vehicles. However, it can cause accidents particularly with pedestrians.
    - It uses renewable energy resources, however storage and distribution are still a problem.
    - Water as a by-product has lots of advantages. However, operating in cold weather is a problem as water is present in and around the cell, while it is in operation.

Group 1

The Periodic Table

> 6.1 Explain why some elements can be classified as alkali metals (group 1), halogens (group 7) or noble gases (group 0), based on their position in the periodic table

Key Points: Elements in the periodic table

- In the periodic table, elements are arranged according to increasing atomic number.
- The periodic table consists of Periods and Groups.
- Vertical column in the periodic table is known as a **Group**. There are eight groups in the periodic table (0 to 7).
- Horizontal row in the periodic table is known as a **Period**. There are seven periods in the periodic table (1 to 7).
- Elements in the **same group have the same number of outermost electrons**. The total number reflects a group number.
   - E.g: Total number of electrons in the outermost shell of magnesium, Mg is 2. Magnesium belongs to group 2 of the periodic table.
- Elements in the same period have same number of shells in their structure.
   - E.g: Total number of shells in sodium, Na is 3. Sodium belongs to period 3 of the periodic table.
- Some elements are classified as:
   - **Alkali metals (Group 1):** The alkali metals, found in Group 1 of the periodic table, have one electron in their outermost shell. Therefore, they can readily lose its outermost electron to form positive ions with +1 charge and become stable.
   - **Halogens (Group 7):** The halogens, found in Group 7 of the periodic table, have 7 electrons in their outermost shell. A halogen gains one electron to form negative ions with -1 charge to become stable.
   - **Noble gases (Group 0 or 8):** The noble gases, found in group 8 of the periodic table, have eight electrons in their outermost shell, making them stable in nature.

> Group 0 elements are also known as group 8 elements.

> Maximum occupancy of electron in a shell is known as stable or complete.

> Key Exception: Helium has only two electrons in its outermost shell.

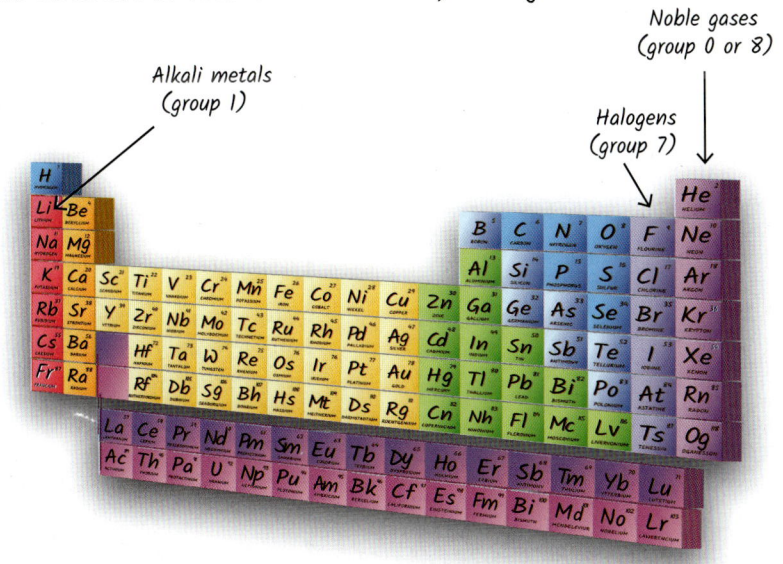

Fig 6.1 - Location of Group 1, 7 and 0 elements in the periodic table

Topic 6 – Groups in the periodic table

Group 1 - Alkali metals

6.2 Recall that alkali metals: a) are soft
b) have relatively low melting points
6.5 Explain this pattern in reactivity in terms of electronic configurations

Key Points: Group 1 elements and its physical properties

- Group 1 elements are called **alkali metals.**
- They are soft metals which can be cut with a knife.
- They are shiny.
- They have low melting and boiling points which decreases down the group.
- They have low densities which increases down the group, as the size of the atom increases.
- They are good conductors of heat and electricity.

As the number of shells in an atom increases the size of the atom also increases.

Key Points: Reactivity of group 1 elements

- Reactivity increases down the group.
- This is due to the ability of the element to **lose** one outer electron increases, as the number of electron shells increases down the group.
- The number of **electron shells increases** which means that the size of the atom increases resulting in **decrease in electrostatic attraction between the outermost shell and nucleus**. Therefore, as the distance from the nucleus and outer shell electron increases it becomes easy to lose electrons from the outermost shell.
- Fig 6.2 shows the relationship between reactivity, electronic configuration and the size of the element.

Group 1 elements are stored in oil as they react easily with oxygen and water vapour in the atmosphere.

lithium: 2,1

sodium: 2,8,1

potassium: 2,8,8,1

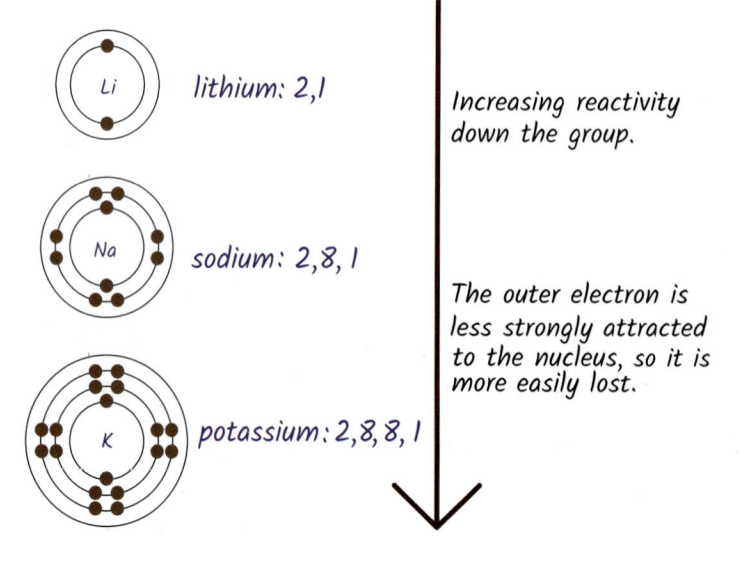

Increasing reactivity down the group.

The outer electron is less strongly attracted to the nucleus, so it is more easily lost.

Fig 6.2 - Reactivity of group 1 elements

6.3 Describe the reactions of lithium, sodium and potassium with water
6.4 Describe the pattern in reactivity of the alkali metals, lithium, sodium and potassium, with water; and use this pattern to predict the reactivity of other alkali metals

Key Points: Reactions with water

- Alkali metals reacts vigorously with water to form an alkaline solution and hydrogen gas.
- Reactions become more vigorous down the group and these reactions are **exothermic** (reactions that give out heat to the surrounding).

Since Group I metals have the same number of outermost shell electron, their chemical reactions are similar.

- **General equation:**
  Metal + water ⟶ metal hydroxide + hydrogen
  $2M(s) + 2H_2O(l) \longrightarrow 2MOH(aq) + H_2(g)$

- **Examples:**
  Lithium + water ⟶ Lithium hydroxide + hydrogen
  $2Li(s) + 2H_2O(l) \longrightarrow 2LiOH(aq) + H_2(g)$

  sodium + water ⟶ sodium hydroxide + hydrogen
  $2Na(s) + 2H_2O(l) \longrightarrow 2NaOH(aq) + H_2(g)$

  potassium + water ⟶ potassium hydroxide + hydrogen
  $2K(s) + 2H_2O(l) \longrightarrow 2KOH(aq) + H_2(g)$

Lithium	Sodium	Potassium
Floats on the surface of water	Floats on the surface of water	Floats on the surface of water
Fizzes	Fizzes, reacts vigorously	Fizzes, reacts vigorously
Melts steadily	Melts quickly and becomes ball shape	Melts rapidly and disappears in quick time

Fig 6.2 - Reactivity of group I elements

Topic 6 – Groups in the periodic table

Group 7 - Halogens

6.6 Recall the colours and physical states of chlorine, bromine and iodine at room temperature

6.7 Describe the pattern in the physical properties of the halogens, chlorine, bromine and iodine, and use this pattern to predict the physical properties of other halogens

Key Points: Group 7 elements and its physical properties

- Group 7 elements are non-metals and they are known as **halogens**.
- They are reactive non-metals which are not found free in nature.
- They have low melting and boiling points.
- They form diatomic molecules (F_2, Cl_2 etc.)
- Pattern **down the group**:
  - Density increases;
  - Colour becomes darker;
  - Melting and boiling points increase due to stronger intermolecular forces of attraction;
  - Reactivity decreases, where the most reactive halogen is fluorine.
- Colour and physical state of halogens shown in Table 6.2.

> For Group 7 elements, the melting and boiling points increases down the group, as the size of the molecule increases. Therefore At_2 will have higher melting and boiling points than the other elements.

Halogens	Colour	Physical state
Fluorine (F_2)	Pale yellow	Gas
Chlorine (Cl_2)	Pale green	Gas
Bromine (Br_2)	Orange - Red	Liquid
Iodine (I_2)	Grey solid (sublimes to purple vapour)	Solid
Astatine (At_2)	Black	Solid

Fig 6.2 - Reactivity of group 1 elements

6.13 Explain the relative reactivity of the halogens in terms of electronic configurations

Key Points: Reactivity of halogens

- Reactivity increases up the group. The most reactive element is fluorine.
- This is due to the ability of the halogen to gain an electron increases, as the number of electron shells decreases from bottom to top of the group.
- The number of electron shells decreases, which means that the size of the atom decreases resulting in stronger attraction between the outermost shell and nucleus. Therefore, it becomes easier to attract the electrons towards the nucleus.

Fluorine 2,7

Chlorine 2,8,7

Bromine 2,8,18,7

↑ More reactive

More easily attracts the electrons towards the nucleus.

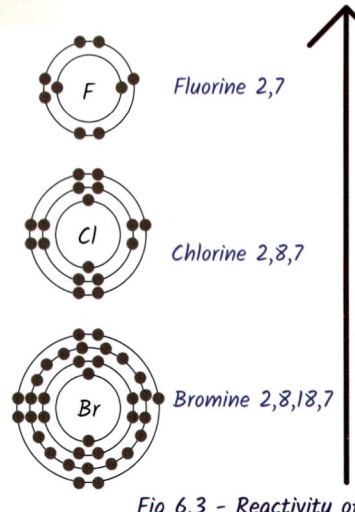

Fig 6.3 - Reactivity of halogens

- Fig 6.3 shows the relationship between reactivity, electronic configuration and the size of the element.

6.8 Describe the chemical test for chlorine

Key Chemical Test I: Chlorine gas, Cl_2

Test: Pass the gas over **damp blue litmus paper**
Result: It turns damp blue litmus paper to **red**, and then **bleaches it white**.

Chlorine has sharp choking smell.

Key Chemical Test II: Chlorine gas, Cl_2

Test: Pass the gas in to **damp starch-iodide paper**
Result: It turns damp starch-iodide paper to **blue-black**.

6.9 Describe the reactions of the halogens, chlorine, bromine and iodine, with metals to form metal halides, and use this pattern to predict the reactions of other halogens.

Key Points: Reactions with metals

- Halogens readily gains 1 outer electron to become stable.
- Reactivity decreases down the group as the size of the atom increases, resulting in decrease in attraction between the nucleus and the electrons in the outermost shell.
- With metals they form **metal halides**.
- **General equation:**
    Metal + halogen ⟶ metal halide
- **Examples:**
    Metals:
    $2Na(s) + Cl_2(g) \longrightarrow 2NaCl(s)$
    $2Li(s) + Br_2(l) \longrightarrow 2LiBr(s)$
    $Mg(s) + Cl_2(g) \longrightarrow MgCl_2(s)$
    $2Al(s) + 3Cl_2(g) \longrightarrow 2AlCl_3(s)$

    Transition metals:
    $2Fe(s) + 3Cl_2(g) \longrightarrow 2FeCl_3(s)$
    $2Fe(s) + 3Br_2(l) \longrightarrow 2FeBr_3(s)$

Transition metals reacts with halogens to form metal halides of higher oxidation states.
Exception: *Iodine forms Iron(II) iodide as it is less reactive, located lower in the group.*

6.10 Recall that the halogens, chlorine, bromine and iodine, form hydrogen halides which dissolve in water to form acidic solutions, and use this pattern to predict the reactions of other halogens

Key Points: Reactions with hydrogen

- Halogens react with hydrogen to produce **hydrogen halides**.
- Hydrogen reacts with fluorine vigorously. The reactivity decreases down the group.
- **General equation:**
$$\text{Hydrogen} + \text{halogen} \longrightarrow \text{hydrogen halide}$$
- **Examples:**
$$\text{Hydrogen} + \text{chlorine} \longrightarrow \text{hydrogen chloride}$$
$$H_2(g) + Cl_2(g) \longrightarrow 2HCl(g)$$
- Hydrogen halides dissolves in water to produce **acidic** solution.

Key Points: Reactions with water

- Halogens react with water to form acidic solutions.
- With fluorine:
$$2F_2(g) + 2H_2O(l) \longrightarrow 4HF(g) + O_2(g)$$
$$3F_2(g) + 3H_2O(l) \longrightarrow 6HF(g) + O_3(g)$$
Fluorine reacts with water vapour to form oxygen and ozone
- With chlorine:
$$Cl_2(g) + 2H_2O(l) \rightleftharpoons HCl(aq) + HOCl(aq)$$

Chlorine reacts with water to give **green solution**. This is a **reversible reaction** to produce mixture of hydrochloric acid and chloric(I) acid (hypochlorous acid)

6.11 Describe the relative reactivity of the halogens chlorine, bromine and iodine, as shown by their displacement reactions with halide ions in aqueous solution, and use this pattern to predict the reactions of astatine

Key Points: Displacement reactions with halide ions in aqueous solutions

- A more reactive halogen displaces a less reactive halogen from its aqueous salt solution.

- **Examples:**
$$F_2(g) + 2KBr(aq) \longrightarrow 2KF(aq) + Br_2(aq)$$
$$Cl_2(g) + 2KI(aq) \longrightarrow 2KCl(aq) + I_2(aq)$$
$$Br_2(g) + 2KI(aq) \longrightarrow 2KBr(aq) + I_2(aq)$$

- Refer Table 6.3.

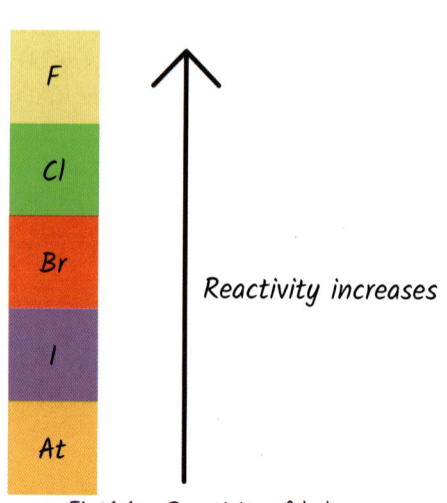

Fig 6.4 - Reactivity of halogens

salt(aq) \ halogen	Potassium chloride	Potassium bromide	Potassium iodide	explanation
chlorine		2KCl + Br₂ orange	2KCl + I₂ red - brown	Chlorine is more reactive than bromine and iodine, so reaction takes place.
bromine	no reaction		2KBr + I₂ red - brown	Bromine is more reactive than iodine, so reaction takes place ONLY with iodine.
iodine	no reaction	no reaction		Iodine is least reactive than other halogens in the table, so no reaction takes place.

Table 6.3 - Displacement reactions with halide ions in aqueous solutions

Iodine may be a grey solid but in solution it forms a red-brown solution.

Worked example 1: Write the chemical reaction between following halogen and metal halides.
a) Chlorine and sodium bromide
b) Iodine and magnesium fluoride

Solution:

a) $Cl_2(g) + 2NaBr(aq) \longrightarrow 2NaCl(aq) + Br_2(aq)$
Chlorine is more reactive than bromine and can displace bromine from sodium bromide to form orange bromine solution.

As iodine is above astatine displacement between iodine and potassium astatide can take place to form black solid of astatine.

b) Iodine is less reactive than fluorine, therefore reaction is not possible.

6.12 Explain why these displacement reactions are redox reactions in terms of gain and loss of electrons, identifying which of the substances are oxidised and which are reduced (H)

Key Points: Displacement reactions as redox reactions

Redox in terms of electrons
Oil : Oxidation is loss of electrons.
Rig : Reduction is gain of electrons.

- Displacement reactions with halogens and metal halides are redox reactions.
- Redox reactions are the reaction in which both reduction and oxidation takes simultaneously.
- **Example:**

  Chlorine + Sodium bromine → Sodium chlorine + Bromine
  $Cl_2(g) + 2NaBr(aq) \longrightarrow 2NaCl(aq) + Br_2(aq)$

- Above reaction can be written as below.

  $Cl_2(g) + 2Br^-(aq) \longrightarrow 2Cl^-(aq) + Br_2(aq)$

- As sodium ions are not taking part in the reaction they are ignored in the above chemical equation. These types of ions are called as **spectator ions.**
- Looking at the transfer of electrons, the above reaction can be split into two half equations.

117

$$Cl_2(g) + 2Br^-(aq) \rightarrow 2Cl^-(aq) + Br_2(l)$$

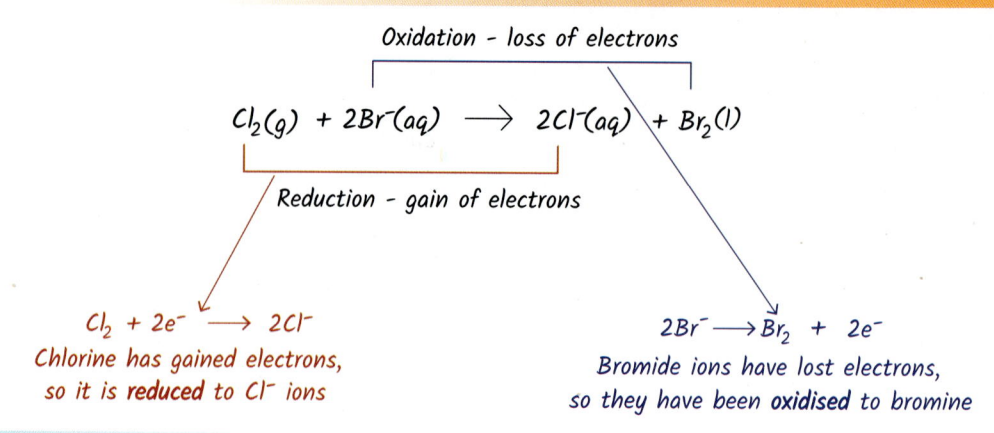

Oxidation - loss of electrons (top bracket over $2Br^-$ to Br_2)
Reduction - gain of electrons (bottom bracket over Cl_2 to $2Cl^-$)

$Cl_2 + 2e^- \rightarrow 2Cl^-$
Chlorine has gained electrons, so it is **reduced** to Cl^- ions

$2Br^- \rightarrow Br_2 + 2e^-$
Bromide ions have lost electrons, so they have been **oxidised** to bromine

Worked example 2 Deduce the half equation and identify which species is oxidised and reduced when fluorine solution is added to potassium chloride solution.

Solution:

$F_2 + 2e^- \rightarrow 2F^-$ fluorine is **reduced** by gaining two electrons.
$2Cl^- \rightarrow Cl_2 + 2e^-$ chloride is **oxidised** by losing two electrons.

Group 0 - Noble gas

6.14 Explain why the noble gases are chemically inert, compared with the other elements, in terms of their electronic configurations
6.15 Explain how the uses of noble gases depend on their inertness, low density and/or non-flammability
6.16 Describe the pattern in the physical properties of some noble gases and use this pattern to predict the physical properties of other noble gases

Key Points: Physical properties of group 0 elements

- Group 0 elements are known as noble gases.
- Noble gases are all monoatomic gas (He, Ne etc.).
- They are inert.
- As they already have full outer shells of electrons, noble gases are unreactive.
- They have very low melting and boiling points.
- Down the group, the size of the atom increases, the number of electrons increases, hence the force of attraction. Due to strong force of attraction, it needs lots of energy to overcome the force, which results in increasing boiling point.
- As the mass of the atom increases, the density increases down the group.

Key Points: Uses of noble gases

- Helium is less dense than air and non-flammable. Therefore, it is used to fill airships and gas balloons.
- Like other noble gases, neon is unreactive. It is used to fill light tubes for neon signs.
- It is also used to fill light bulbs, as it will not react with the hot filament.

Rates of reaction

Collision theory

7.3 Explain how reactions occur when particles collide and that rates of reaction are increased when the frequency and/or energy of collisions is increased

Key Points: Collision theory

- Collision theory states that for reactant particles to react with each other, their particles must collide successfully.
- Particles must not only collide with each other but collide with enough energy AND in correct orientation.
- A successful collision between molecules requires the correct geometry to break bonds and form products.
- The minimum amount of energy required to start a reaction is called the activation energy, Ea.

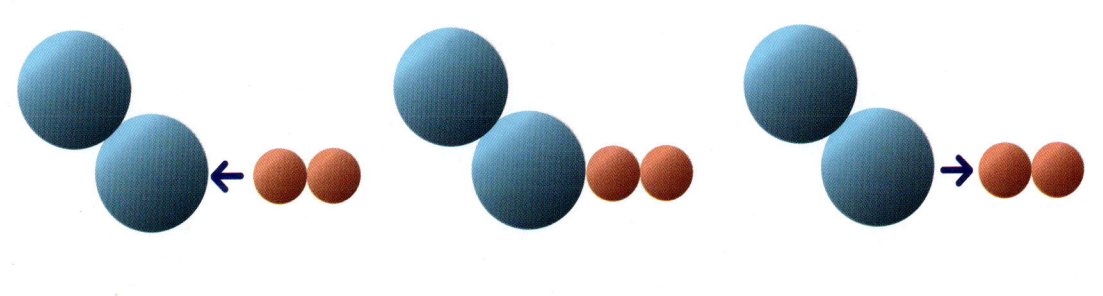

reactants set to collide

reactants collides in side ways (incorrect orientation)

reactants remains SAME

Fig 7.1 (a) - Collision theory (unsuccessful collision)

reactants set to collide

head to head collision between reactants (correct orientation)

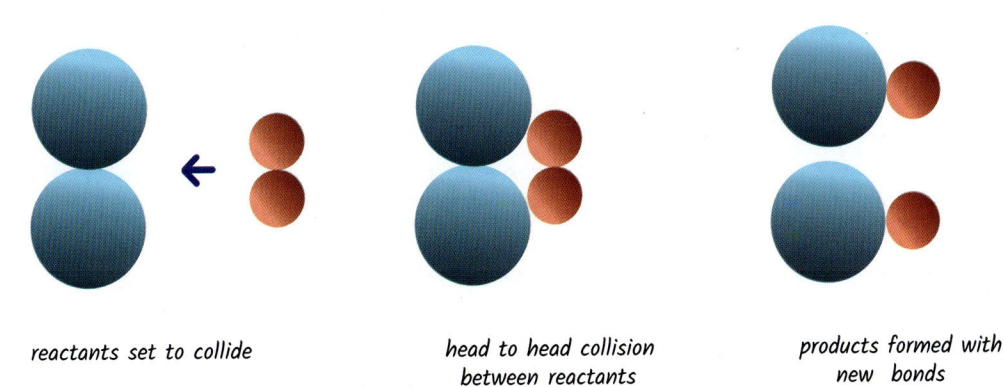

products formed with new bonds

Fig 7.1 (b) - Collision theory (successful collision)

Topic 7 – Rate of reactions and energy changes

119

Factors to increase the rate of reaction

7.4 Explain the effects on rates of reaction of changes in temperature, concentration, surface area to volume ratio of a solid and pressure (on reactions involving gases) in terms of frequency and/or energy of collisions between particles

Key Table: Factors to increase the rate of reaction

> The higher the rate, the shorter the time taken for a reaction to finish.

Factors to INCREASE the rate of reaction	Explanation
An increase in **temperature** of a reaction system	At a higher temperature there will be a **greater number of successful collisions per second** because: • particles gain kinetic energy and moves faster. • more particles will have enough energy to make the collision successful.
An increase in reactant **concentration**	Higher concentration means that there are more reactant particles in the same space or same volume. This results in a **greater number of successful collisions in the same amount of time** making the reaction go faster.
An increase in **surface area** (smaller particle size)	A greater surface area means a larger number of particles exposed each other, so there will be a **greater number of successful collisions per same unit of time.**
An increase in **pressure**	Increased pressure reduces the volume in which the reactants are, and this brings particles closer together resulting in a **greater number of successful collisions per same unit of time.**

Table 7.1 – Factors to increase the rate of reaction

Experimental methods for measuring rate of reaction

> 7.2 Suggest practical methods for determining the rate of a given reaction
> 7.5 Interpret graphs of mass, volume or concentration of reactant or product against time

Rate = Speed

Key Points: Experimental methods for measuring rate of reaction

$$\text{rate of reaction} = \frac{\text{change in amount of a reactant or a product}}{\text{time}}$$

- The rate of a reaction can be calculated using the equation below:
- Some common experimental methods for measuring rate of reaction:
  - **A change in mass:** the reaction vessel (minus the syringe) can be placed on a top-loading balance and the mass of the apparatus and solution is recorded over time, and graphed.
  - **A change in gas volume:** if the reaction produces a gas; this gas will escape as the reaction progresses. The volume of oxygen being produced can be measured by collecting it in a gas syringe, attached to the reaction vessel.
  - **A change in electrical conductivity:** if ions are produced or used up during a reaction, the electrical conductivity will change.
  - **Colorimetry:** the colour of the reaction mixture will change with time and a colorimeter can be used to monitor the strength of colour in the mixture.

Common methods of measuring the rate of reaction

> 7.4 Explain the effects on rates of reaction of changes in temperature, concentration, surface area to volume ratio of a solid and pressure (on reactions involving gases) in terms of frequency and/or energy of collisions between particles

Key Experiment: Calcium carbonate (marble chips) with hydrochloric acid

$$CaCO_3(s) + 2HCl(aq) \longrightarrow CaCl_2(aq) + H_2O(l) + CO_2(g)$$

Method 1: Collection of carbon dioxide gas using syringe:

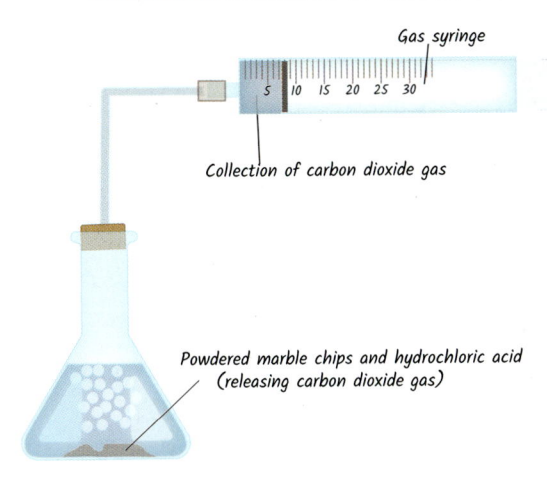

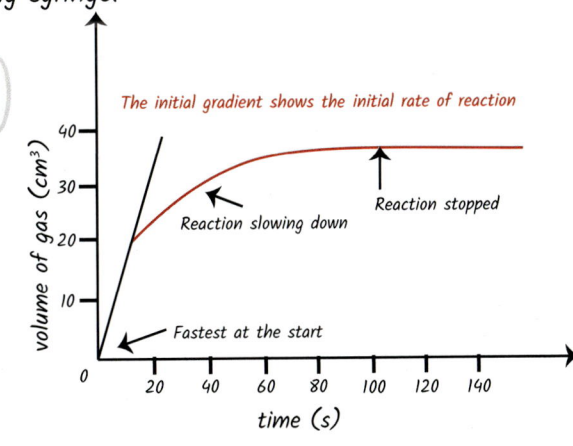

Graph 7.1 - Calcium carbonate (marble chips) with hydrochloric acid

Fig 7.2 (a) - Calcium carbonate (marble chips) with hydrochloric acid

Topic 7 - Rate of reactions and energy changes

121

Key Points: Collection of carbon dioxide gas

- The experimental set up has been shown in Fig 7.2 (a).
- Collect the gas produced in a gas syringe and record the volume every 20 seconds.
- Plot a graph of volume of gas (cm³) against time as shown in graph 7.1.
- The gradient of the graph at any one point relates to the rate of reaction.
- From the graph it is evident that the gradient is the largest at the start of the experiment which shows that the initial rate of reaction is fast.
- **"more number of particles are exposed to each other which takes part in a greater number of successful collisions"**.
- Over time, the gradient decreases as **the particles are used up and the number of successful collisions decreases**, which decreases the rate of reaction.
- The gradient becomes zero at 158s shows **particles are used up so no more successful collision is taking place** meaning that the rate is zero and the reaction is completed.

> Same procedure can be used for: Decomposition of hydrogen peroxide with catalyst manganese(IV) oxide. Metal and acid (different concentrations).

> Reaction stops when one of the reactant is used up.

Method 2: Measuring the mass loss of marble chips

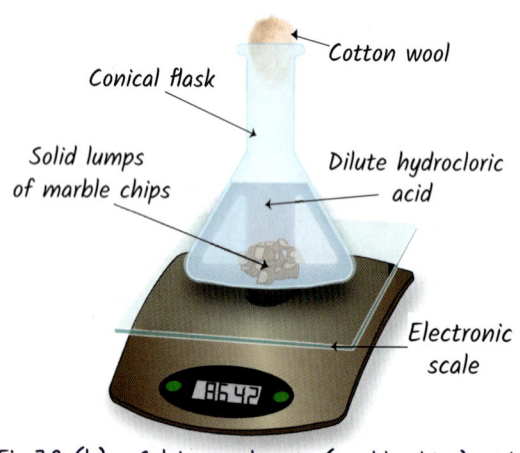

Fig 7.2 (b) - Calcium carbonate (marble chips) with hydrochloric acid

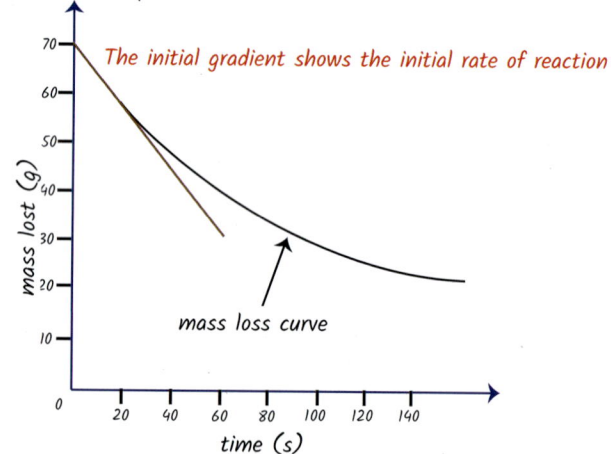

Graph 7.2 - Calcium carbonate (marble chips) with hydrochloric acid

Key Points: Mass loss of marble chips

- The experimental set up has been shown in Fig 7.2 (b).
- Record the initial mass and follow it up for every 20 seconds.
- Plot a graph of mass loss (g) against time as shown in graph 7.2.
- From the graph it is evident that the gradient is the largest at the start of the experiment which shows that the initial rate of reaction is fast.
- Over time, the gradient decreases as **the particles are used up. The number of successful collisions decreases** which makes the rate to decrease.
- The gradient becomes zero at one-point **particles are used up so no more successful collision is taking place** meaning that the rate is zero and the reaction is completed.

Experimental evidence – Factors affecting the rate of reaction

Key Points: Effect of temperature

- **Experiment:** sodium thiosulphate with hydrochloric acid

$$Na_2S_2O_3(aq) + 2HCl(aq) \longrightarrow 2NaCl(aq) + S(s) + H_2O(l) + SO_2(g)$$

- **Condition:** Carry out four similar experiments by keeping all factors the same **EXCEPT** the temperature of reaction mixture.
- Water bath for all four experiments was set at 30°C, 40°C, 50°C and 60°C respectively.
- 25cm³ of sodium thiosulphate was added into a conical flask and placed on a piece of white paper marked with black cross (**X**).
- 5cm³ of hydrochloric acid was added into the flask and allowed to react by shaking the mixture.
- A stop clock was used to measure the time taken for the cross to disappear as the yellow precipitate of sulphur starts to develop. A snapshot of observations at different temperatures are shown in Fig 7.3.

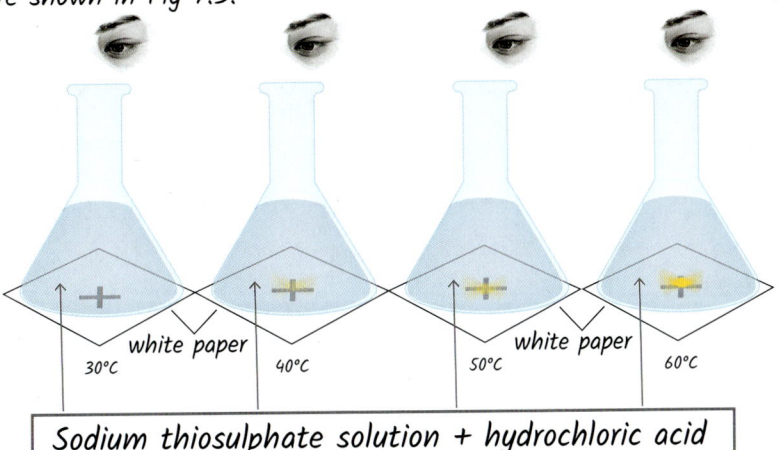

Fig 7.3 - Formation of sulphur (yellow precipitate) at different temperature

- Data were recorded for the different temperatures. See Table 7.2.

Experiment	Temperature of reaction (°C)	Time taken for cross to disappear (s)
1	30	106
2	40	81
3	50	61
4	60	50

Table 7.2 - Reaction of sodium thiosulphate and hydrochloric acid

- **Data analysis:**
  - Time taken for cross to disappear in experiment 4 is less than experiment 1.
  - At 30°C, it took 106 seconds for the cross to disappear, whereas at 60°C it took only 50 seconds.
  - This data proves that experiment 4 with higher temperature is faster than experiment 1 with lower temperature.
- **Theory:**
  - Higher the temperature, the faster (shorter time) the reaction is.
  - At higher temperature, particles gain energy and move faster with greater number of successful collisions, which increases the rate of reaction.

Key Points: Effect of concentration

- **Experiment:** magnesium with hydrochloric acid
$$Mg(s) + 2HCl(aq) \longrightarrow MgCl_2(aq) + H_2(g)$$
- **Condition:** Carry out two similar experiment by keeping all factors the same **EXCEPT** the concentration of acid.

Experiment 1	Experiment 2
0.5 g of magnesium	0.5 g of magnesium
25 cm³ of 1 mol/dm³ HCl solution	25 cm³ of 2 mol/dm³ HCl solution

Table 7.3 - Calcium carbonate (marble chips) with hydrochloric acid

- The volume of hydrogen gas given off was recorded at every 1-minute interval for both experiments.
- A graph has been plotted with the data from both experiments (Graph 7.3).

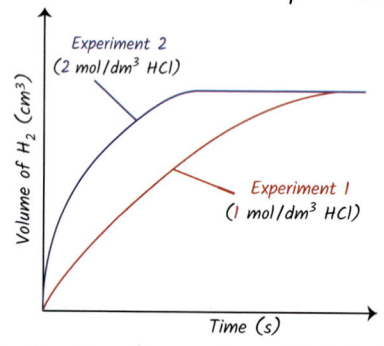

Graph 7.3 - Reaction of magnesium with hydrochloric acid

- **Graphical analysis:**
  - Graph of experiment 2 is steeper than experiment 1.
  - Graph of experiment 2 levels off and becomes straight much earlier than experiment 1.
  - This graphical data proves that experiment 2 with higher concentration is faster than experiment 1 with lower concentration.
- **Theory:**
  - Increase in the concentration of one of the reactants increases the rate of reaction.
  - Increasing the concentration of hydrochloric acid **increases the H⁺ ions** in a given volume. Hence, the number of successful collisions increases, and the rate of reaction increases.

Key Points: Effect of surface area

- **Experiment:** Calcium carbonate (marble chips) with hydrochloric acid
$$CaCO_3(s) + 2HCl(aq) \longrightarrow CaCl_2(aq) + H_2O(l) + CO_2(g)$$
- **Condition:** Carry out two similar experiment by keeping all factors the same **EXCEPT** the surface area of marble chips.

Experiment 1	Experiment 2
0.5g of marble chips (powdered - larger surface area)	0.5g of marble chips (solid lumps - smaller surface area)
25cm³ of 1mol/dm³ HCl solution	25cm³ of 1mol/dm³ HCl solution

Table 7.4 - Reaction of powdered and solid lumps of marble chips with hydrochloric acid

- The volume of carbon dioxide gas given off was recorded at every 1-minute interval for both experiments.
- A graph has been plotted with the data from both experiments (Graph 7.4).

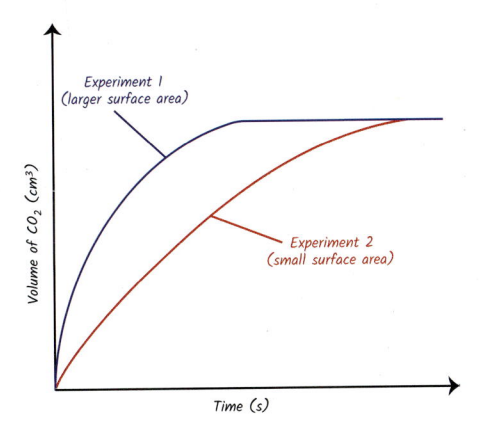

Fig 7.2 (a) - Calcium carbonate (marble chips) with hydrochloric acid

- Graphical analysis:
    - Graph of experiment 1 is steeper than experiment 2.
    - Graph of experiment 1 levels off and becomes straight much earlier than experiment 2.
    - This graphical data proves that experiment 1 with larger surface area is faster than experiment 2 with smaller surface area.

- Theory:
    - Increased surface area of the reactant, increases the rate of reaction.
    - When the surface area increases a greater number of particles of marble chips are exposed to hydrochloric acid, resulting in greater number of successful collisions taking place between the reactants, which increases the rate of reaction.

Key Points: Effect of pressure

- When pressure increases, the rate of reaction also increases.
- As the volume of the system reduces, the pressure increases which allows the reacting particles to get closer, leading to a greater number of successful collisions.

a) Low pressure   b) High pressure

Fig 7.4 - Effect of pressure

Reactions used in rates of reaction experiments

Some common reactions used in rates of reaction experiments (Table 7.5)

pH can be changed when acid is used.

Experiment	Factors	What variables can be measured?
calcium carbonate and acid: $CaCO_3(s) + 2HCl(aq) \rightarrow CO_2(g) + CaCl_2(aq) + H_2O(l)$	· Increase the surface area of calcium carbonate · Increase the concentration of hydrocloric acid	· mass loss · volume of CO_2 produced · decrease in concentration of acid
decomposition of hydrogen peroxide: $2H_2O_2(aq) \rightarrow O_2 + 2H_2O(l)$	· Adding catalyst (manganese(VI) oxide)	· volume of O_2 produced · mass loss of system
metal and acid: $Zn(s) + 2HCl(aq) \rightarrow ZnCl_2(aq) + H_2(g)$	· Increase of surface area of zinc · Increase of concentration of hydrocloric acid · Increase the temperature of reaction	· mass loss · volume of H_2 produced · decrease in concentration of acid
sodium thiosulphate and hydrocloric acid: $Na_2S_2O_3(s) + 2HCl(aq) \rightarrow 2NaCl(aq) + SO_2(g) + S(s) + H_2O(l)$	· Increase of surface area of zinc · Increase of concentration of hydrocloric acid · Increase the temperature of reaction	· Time it takes to block view of a cross by producing enough sulphur

Table 7.5 - Rates of reaction experiments

Catalyst

> 7.6 Describe a catalyst as a substance that speeds up the rate of a reaction without altering the products of the reaction, being itself unchanged chemically and in mass at the end of the reaction
>
> 7.7 Explain how the addition of a catalyst increases the rate of a reaction in terms of activation energy

Key Points: Catalyst

- A catalyst is any substance that speeds up the rate of a reaction without being used up.

  Ea is the symbol of activation energy.

- Catalysts are able to increase the rate of a reaction by providing an alternative pathway that has lower activation energy.
- With lower activation energy at room temperature, most collisions have enough energy for a reaction to occur.
- With higher activation energy at room temperature, fewer collisions have enough energy for a reaction to occur.
- The enthalpy level diagram for a catalysed and uncatalysed reaction is shown in Fig 7.5.
- The lower activation energy pathway provided by the catalyst enables more reactant particles to have sufficient energy to react.

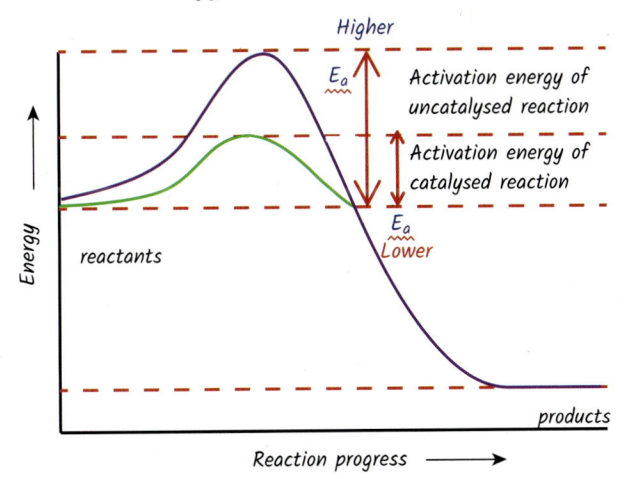

Fig 7.5 - Activation energy with and without catalyst

> 7.8 Recall that enzymes are biological catalysts and that enzymes are used in the production of alcoholic drinks

Key Points: A biological catalyst

- A catalyst which is produced organically is known as a **biological catalyst**.
- Biological catalysts are called enzymes.
- Enzymes are large chains of protein molecules with a specific part and shape, called the active site.
- Reacting molecules and enzymes go together as a lock and key.
- Enzymes in yeast are used in the production of alcoholic drinks such as wine and beer by the process of fermentation, where glucose is converted into ethanol and carbon dioxide in the presence yeast at room temperature.

Worked example 1: This question is about decomposition of hydrogen peroxide to produce oxygen and water using manganese(IV) oxide. Data were recorded at regular intervals and a graph was plotted as shown below:

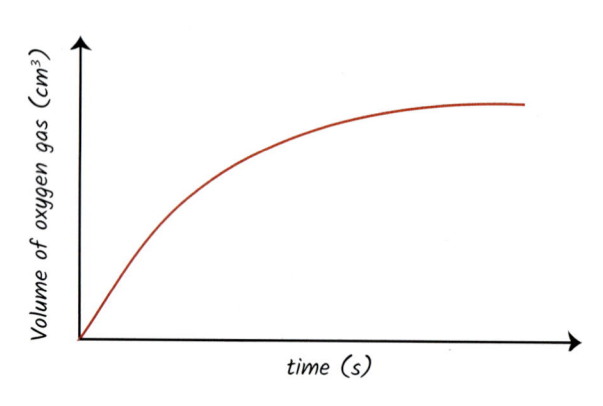

[Graph: Volume of oxygen gas (cm³) vs time (s) — curve rising steeply then levelling off]

a) Using the graph describe how the rate of reaction changes as the reaction progresses.
b) Write the balanced equation for the above reaction with state symbols.
c) State and explain the purpose of manganese(IV) oxide.
d) On the same graph, plot another **dotted curve** you expect to see if manganese(IV) oxide is not used and label it as **M**.

Solution:

a) Initially, the reaction is fast. As the reaction progresses the gradient of the graph decreases. Later, rate of reaction slows down until the point where the graph starts to level off, indicating that the rate of reaction is zero as the volume of oxygen gas produced remains constant.

b) $2H_2O_2(aq) \longrightarrow O_2(g) + 2H_2O(l)$

c) A catalyst. It increases the rate of reaction by providing an alternative pathway that has a lower activation energy to increase the greater number of successful collisions.

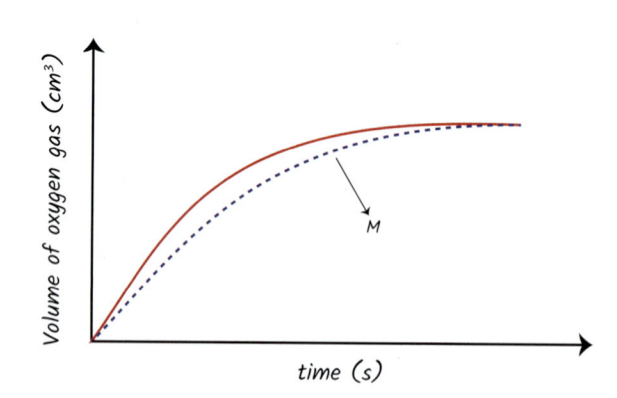

[Graph: Volume of oxygen gas (cm³) vs time (s) — solid curve (original) and dotted curve labelled M below it, both levelling off at the same value]

Heat energy changes in chemical reactions

Heat energy

7.9 Recall that changes in heat energy accompany the following changes:
   a) salts dissolving in water   b) neutralisation reactions
   c) displacement reactions   d) precipitation reactions
   and that, when these reactions take place in solution, temperature changes can be measured to reflect the heat changes

7.10 Describe an exothermic change or reaction as one in which heat energy is given out

7.11 Describe an endothermic change or reaction as one in which heat energy is taken in

Key Points: Heat energy

- Energy cannot be created nor destroyed. However, it can be transferred from one form to another.
- All chemical components store chemical energy.
- This energy can be transferred into heat, light, electrical and in some cases sound energy.
- Energy changes occur in chemical reactions and even in some physical processes, these changes can be observed by measuring initial and final temperature during the reaction.
- Some examples of reactions take place in solution:
  - **salts dissolving in water** – making a salt solution
  - **neutralisation reactions** – acid reacts with base to form a salt and water
  - **displacement reactions** – a higher reactive substance displaces lesser reactive substance
  - **precipitation reactions** – formation of solid in a solution

Thermometer can be used to measure the temperature change.

Key Points: Heat energy (or) thermal energy

- Energy changes in terms of heat is classified into two types:
  - Exothermic
  - Endothermic
- Change in heat energy of the reaction is represented as ΔH
- Exothermic, a reaction in which heat is given out to the surrounding and the surrounding temperature increases.
- ΔH is negative
- Endothermic, a reaction in which heat is taken in from the surrounding and the surrounding temperature decreases.
- ΔH is positive

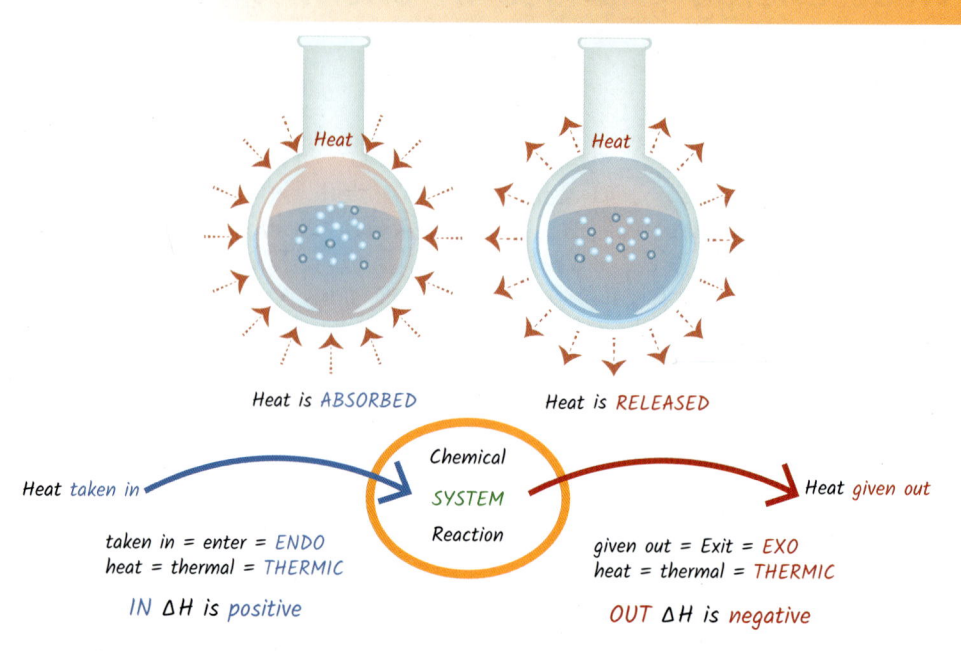

Fig 7.6 – Exothermic and Endothermic reaction

Energy changes in terms of bond breaking and bond making

7.12 Recall that the breaking of bonds is endothermic and the making of bonds is exothermic
7.13 Recall that the overall heat energy change for a reaction is:
   a) exothermic if more heat energy is released in forming bonds in the products than is required in breaking bonds in the reactants
   b) endothermic if less heat energy is released in forming bonds in the products than is required in breaking bonds in the reactants

Key Points: Bond breaking and bond making

- The change from reactants to products is known as a chemical reaction.
- Reactants:
  - It involves bond breaking as old bonds break to release the substance
  - To break, energy is taken in
  - Reactants side is ENDOTHERMIC
- Products:
  - It involves bond making as new bond forms to make new substance
  - To make, energy is given out
  - Products side is EXOTHERMIC
- If total energy absorbed when old bonds are broken is more than the total energy released when new bonds are made, then the overall reaction is ENDOTHERMIC. Overall energy change (ΔH) becomes positive
- If total energy absorbed when old bonds are broken is less than the total energy released when new bonds are made, then the overall reaction is EXOTHERMIC. Overall energy change (ΔH) becomes negative
- Overall energy of the reaction can be calculated with bond energy values using the formula:

$$\Delta H = \Sigma E_r - \Sigma E_p$$

ΣE_r = Sum of energy absorbed (taken in) to **break** the old bond in the reactants (Endothermic reaction)

ΣE_p = Sum of energy released (given out) to make the new bond in the products (Exothermic reaction)

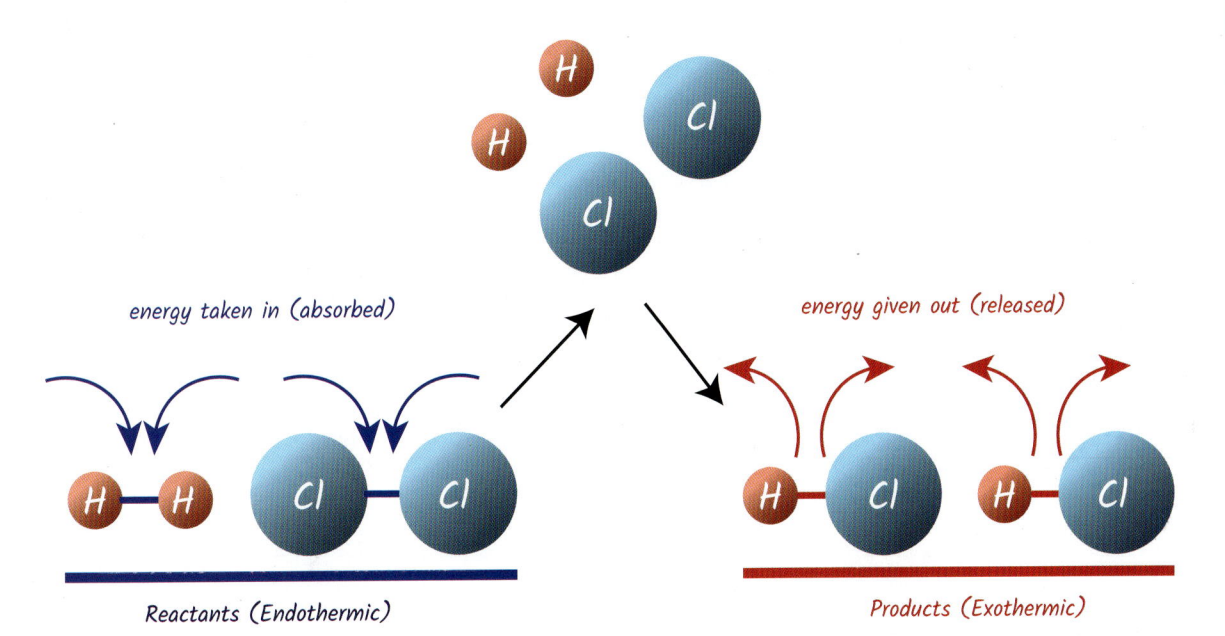

Fig 7.7 - Energy changes in terms of bond breaking and bond making

Key Table: Relationship between bond breaking and bond making in terms of chemical reaction

ENDOTHERMIC				EXOTHERMIC			
Reactants	Energy taken IN	Bond breaks	ΔH is positive	Products	Energy given OUT	Bond forms	ΔH is negative

Table 7.6 - Relationship between bond breaking and bond making in terms of chemical reaction

Topic 7 - Rate of reactions and energy changes

Calculating the energy changes using bond energy values

7.14 Calculate the energy change in a reaction given the energies of bonds (in kJmol⁻¹) (H)

Key Steps: To calculate the energy changes using bond energy values

Step 1: Deduce the chemical equation showing all the bonds between molecules.
Step 2: Count all the similar types of bond on the reactants side.
Step 3: Look up the bond energies of the bonds from data table.
Step 4: Multiply the bond energies by the number of bonds broken.
Step 5: Add up all the bond energies value of the reactants side.
Step 6: Repeat the above steps (2 to 5) with products side.
Step 7: Use the energy change formula below to find out ΔH in kJ/mol.

$$\Delta H = \Sigma E_r - \Sigma E_p$$

> Bond, a linkage between two elements.
> (Single (-), double (=) and triple (≡))

> Bond energy data will be provided in the question.

> Watch out for the following types of bond in a molecule.
> N_2 (N≡N)
> O_2 (O=O)
> CO_2 (O=C=O)
> Alkene (C=C)

Step 8: Determine whether the overall reaction was endothermic or exothermic by using the answer from step 7.
- If ΔH is positive, then the overall reaction is Endothermic.
- If ΔH is negative, then the overall reaction is Exothermic.

Worked example 2: Use the table below to find total energy change of the given reaction (ΔH) and determine whether the overall reaction is endothermic or exothermic. You must show your working.

$$H_2 + O_2 \longrightarrow 2H_2O$$

Bond	Bond energy (kJ/mol)
H-H	436
O=O	464
O-H	498

Solution:

Step 1: Draw the chemical equation showing all the bonds between molecules.

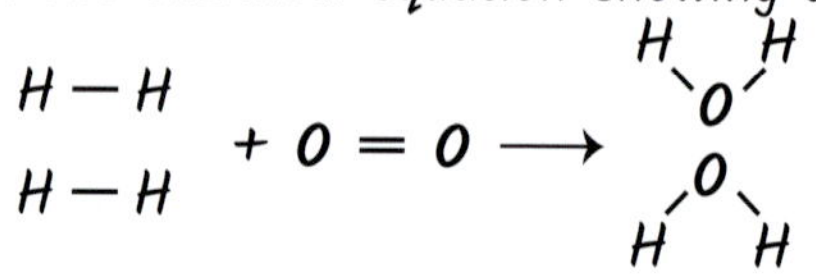

H — H
H — H + O = O ⟶ H-O-H, H-O-H

Step 2: Count all the similar types of bond on the reactants side.

Total no. of H-H bonds = 2
Total no. of O=O bonds = 1

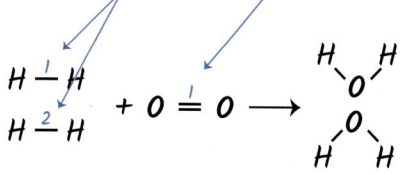

Step 3: Look up the bond energies of the bonds from data table.

Bond energy of H-H is **436**
Bond energy of O=O is **464**

Step 4: Multiply the bond energies by the number of bonds broken

(2 x H-H) = (2 x 436) = **872**
(1 x O=O) = (1 x 464) = **464**

Step 5: Add up all the bond energies value of the reactants side.

(872 + 464) = **1336**
ΣE_r = **1336**

Step 6: Repeat the above steps (2 to 5) with products side

Total no. of O-H bonds = 4

$$H-H$$
$$H-H \quad + \quad O=O \quad \longrightarrow \quad \begin{array}{c} H \quad H \\ {}_1O_2 \\ {}_3O_4 \\ H \quad H \end{array}$$

Bond energy of O-H is **436**
(4 x O-H) = (4 x 436) = **1744**
ΣE_p = **1744**

Step 7: Use the energy change formula below to find out ΔH in kJ/mol

$$\Delta H = \Sigma E_r - \Sigma E_p$$

= 1336 - 1744
= **- 408kJ/mol**

Total energy of the given reaction is **- 408kJ/mol**

Step 8: Determine whether the overall reaction was endothermic or exothermic by using the answer from step 7.

Since, ΔH is *negative,* the overall reaction is *Exothermic.*

Reaction profile

7.15 Explain the term activation energy
7.16 Draw and label reaction profiles for endothermic and exothermic reactions, identifying activation energy

Key Points: Reaction profile diagram

- In the process of converting the reactants to products, the reactant particles must collide with sufficient amount of energy.
- If the particles do not collide with correct orientation along with enough energy, formation of product is not possible.
- This sufficient amount of energy is shown as activation energy in reaction profile diagram.

> **Activation energy (E_a)** is defined as the minimum amount of energy required to start the chemical reaction.

- Reaction profile is drawn between energy (y-axis) and progress of reaction (x-axis).
- **Reactants** starts with a horizontal line.
    - For endothermic, line starts from the lower side of energy (y-axis).
    - For exothermic, line starts from the higher side of energy (y-axis).
- **Activation energy** shown with **E_a**.
    - For endothermic, hump raised from reactant side and drops midway and ends **above** reactants with a horizontal line.
    - For exothermic, hump raised from reactant side and drops midway and ends **below** reactants with a horizontal line.
- Double headed arrow shown between top middle of the hump and the reactant.
- **Overall energy change** is shown with **ΔH** value in kJ/mol.
    - For endothermic, upward arrow from reactants to products with **ΔH** value.
    - For exothermic, downward arrow from reactants to products with **ΔH** value.
- Refer to Fig 7.8.

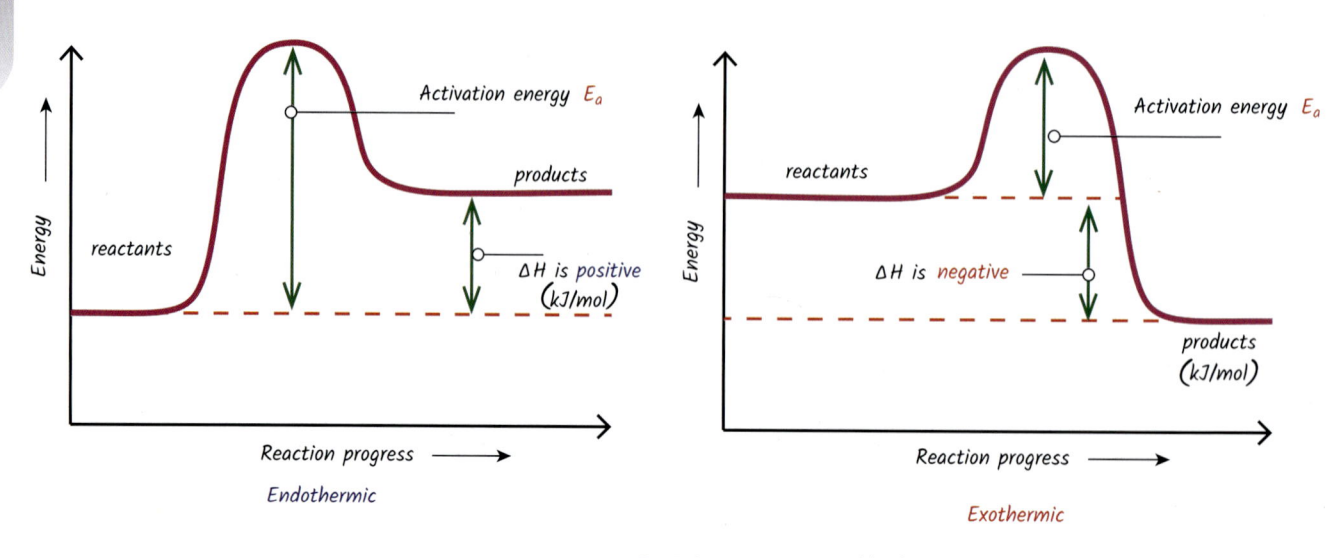

Endothermic

Exothermic

Fig 7.8 - Reaction profile diagram

Fuel

Hydrocarbons and crude oil

8.1 Recall that hydrocarbons are compounds that contacarbon and hydrogen only
8.2 Describe crude oil as:
   a) a complex mixture of hydrocarbons
   b) containing molecules in which carbon atoms are in chains or rings (names, formulae and structures of specific ring molecules not required)
   c) an important source of useful substances (fuels and feedstock for the petrochemical industry)
   d) a finite resource

Key Points: Hydrocarbon and crude oil

- Over many million years of action of high pressure and temperature, fossil remains of plants and marine animals are converted into fossil fuels such as crude oil, coal, natural gas or heavy oils.
- Fossil fuels contains hydrocarbons.

Hydrocarbons are substances which contains hydrogen and carbon only.

- Crude oil is a naturally occurring petroleum product composed of mixture of complex hydrocarbon deposits and other organic materials.
- Crude oil is a **finite resource**; the supply of oil in the Earth's crust will be exhausted, at some point in the long run.
- Crude oil is a **non-renewable resource**.
- Crude oil is a major source of fuels such as petrol, kerosene, diesel, etc.
- On the other hand, methane is a non-renewable fuel, however it is obtained from natural gas.
- Crude oil is also considered as an important source of feedstock for the petrochemical industry.
- For example, naphtha which is obtained from fractional distillation of crude oil is considered as feedstock for petrochemical and fertilizer industries.

> A non-renewable resource (or) finite resource is a resource which will run out over time.

> Non-renewable fuels from crude oil can be remembered as:
> "Poor kitties determine fluffy bubbles"
> Poor - Petrol
> Kitties - Kerosene
> Determine - Diesel
> Fluffy - Fuel oil
> Bubbles – Bitumen

> Feedstock is the raw material which is used for powering up the industrial processes.

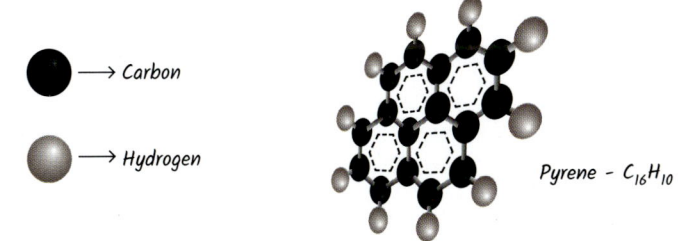

● → Carbon
● → Hydrogen

Pyrene - $C_{16}H_{10}$

> Pyrene is a combination of four benzene rings.

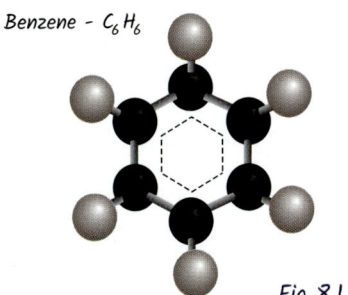

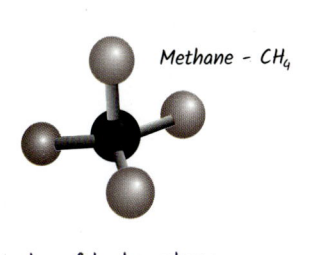

Benzene - C_6H_6

Methane - CH_4

Fig 8.1 - Examples of hydrocarbons

Topic 8 – Fuels & earth science

Topic 8 – Fuels & earth science

8.3 Describe and explain the separation of crude oil into simpler, more useful mixtures by the process of fractional distillation

8.4 Recall the names and uses of the following fractions:
   a) gases, used in domestic heating and cooking
   b) petrol, used as fuel for cars
   c) kerosene, used as fuel for aircraft
   d) diesel oil, used as fuel for some cars and trains
   e) fuel oil, used as fuel for large ships and in some power stations
   f) bitumen, used to surface roads and roofs

8.5 Explain how hydrocarbons in different fractions differ from each other in:
   a) the number of carbon and hydrogen atoms their molecules contain
   b) boiling points
   c) ease of ignition
   d) viscosity and are mostly members of the alkane homologous series

8.15 Recall that petrol, kerosene and diesel oil are non-renewable fossil fuels obtained from crude oil and methane is a non-renewable fossil fuel found in natural gas

Fractional distillation of crude oil

Key Points: Fractional distillation of crude oil

Fractions are different components of hydrocarbons.

- Crude oil is a mixture which contains different types of fractions.
- Fractional distillation is carried out to separate crude oil into its fractions.
- The different fractions separate at different level because they have **different boiling points**.

The separation process is also known as petroleum refining.

- Crude oil is heated, vapourised, and pumped into a fractionating column, which is coolest at the top and hottest at the bottom.

cool (25°C)

refinery gases → bottled gas

gasoline (petrol) → fuel for cars

naphtha → making chemicals

kerosene → aircraft fuel

diesel oil → fuel for cars, lorries, buses

fuel oil → fuel for ships, power stations

heated crude oil

hot (350°C)

residue → bitumen for roads and roofs

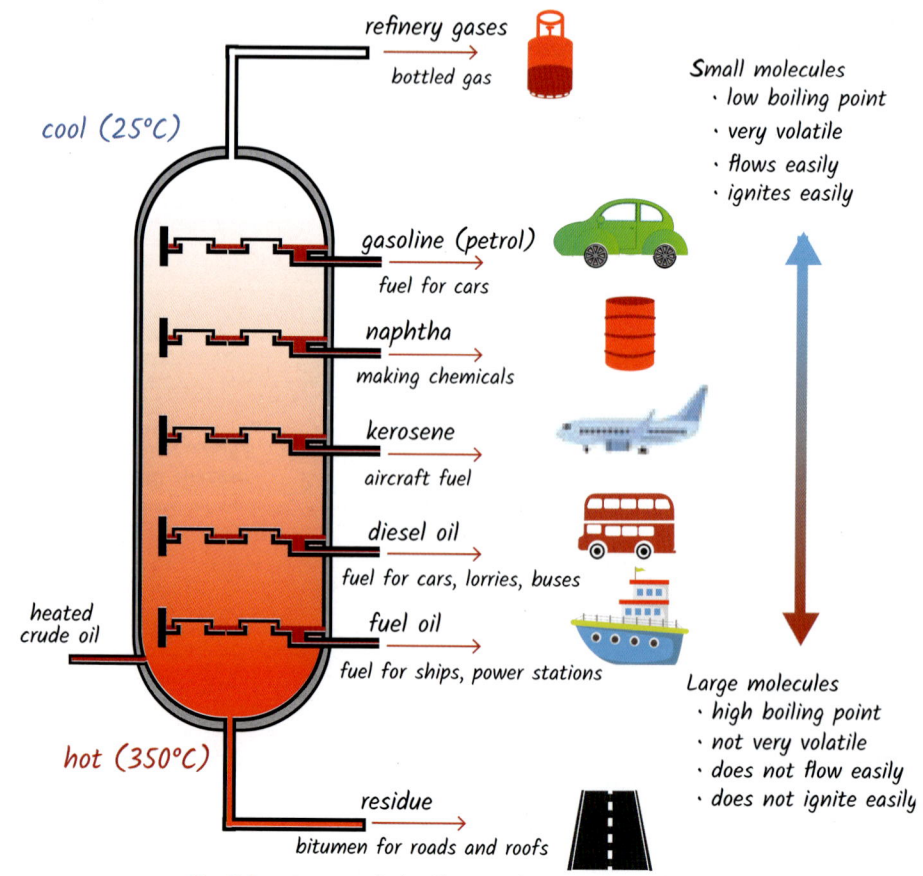

Small molecules
· low boiling point
· very volatile
· flows easily
· ignites easily

Large molecules
· high boiling point
· not very volatile
· does not flow easily
· does not ignite easily

Fig 8.2 - Fractional distillation of crude oil in a refinery

- The principle used: when the number of carbon atom increases the boiling point increases.
- The larger hydrocarbons (longest chain with more carbons) boils at bottom whilst the smaller hydrocarbons (smallest chain with less carbons) rise up and boils at the top.
- The gases are passed through a fractionating column which becomes cooler as the height increases.
- When a compound in the gaseous state cools below its boiling point, it condenses into a liquid.
- The liquids may be drawn off the fractionating column at various heights.

Key Table: Uses of different fractions

Name	No. of Carbon atoms	Boiling point °C	Uses
Refinery gas below	3 or 4	30	Bottled gas for domestic heating and cooking.
Petrol or Gasoline	7 to 9	100 to 150	Fuel for car engines.
Naphtha	6 to 11	70 to 200	Solvents and used in petrol.
Kerosene (paraffin)	11 to 15	200 to 300	Fuel for aircraft and stoves
Diesel Oil	16 to 18	250 to 300	Fuel for some road vehicles (cars, trucks and lorries) and trains.
Fuel Oil	20 to 27	350 to 450	Fuel for ships and heating in power stations.

Table 8.1 - Uses of different fractions

Homologous series

8.6 Explain an homologous series as a series of compounds which:
   a) have the same general formula
   b) differ by CH_2 in molecular formulae from neighbouring compounds
   c) show a gradual variation in physical properties, as exemplified by their boiling points
   d) have similar chemical properties

8.7 Describe the complete combustion of hydrocarbon fuels as a reaction in which:
   a) carbon dioxide and water are produced
   b) energy is given out.

Key Points: Homologous series

- A homologous series is a family of compounds with increasing carbon numbers where 1 member differs from the other by a $-CH_2$ unit.
- Features of members of a homologous series:
  - The same general formula.
  - Similar chemical properties.
  - Physical properties change gradually. For example, the melting and boiling point increases gradually when the number of carbon atom increases.

Gradual increase is due to an increase in the intermolecular forces as the size and mass of the molecules increases.

Try this out to remember the first four names of alkanes.
Monkey – Meth – 1 carbon
Eat – Eth – 2 carbons
Peeled – Prop – 3 carbons
Banana – But – 4 carbons

Key Points: Combustion Reactions

- The reaction in which hydrocarbons burn in the presence of oxygen to produce heat and other gaseous products.
- Since heat is produced, it is an exothermic process.
- Combustion reaction is an example of an **oxidation** reaction.
- Types of combustion:

Complete Combustion
- When there is an excess amount of oxygen, complete combustion occurs.
- In a complete combustion reaction, the main products are carbon dioxide and water.

$$CH_4(g) + 2O_2(g) \longrightarrow CO_2(g) + 2H_2O(g)$$

Incomplete combustion
- When there is a limited supply of oxygen, incomplete combustion occurs.
- In an incomplete combustion reaction, the main products are water and carbon monoxide or elemental carbon.

$$2C_8H_{18}(l) + 17O_2(g) \longrightarrow 16CO(g) + 18H_2O(g)$$

Products of combustion reactions include pollutants such as carbon (smoky flame) – SOOT, sulphur dioxide and oxides of nitrogen.

Same concept applies for alkene and alcohol (keep an eye on balancing oxygen as alcohol itself has an oxygen).

Key Steps: Balancing combustion equations

Step 1: Balance 'C' & 'H' from **left** to *right*
Step 2: Balance 'O' from *right* to **left**
Step 3: If you get fraction numbers, multiply the whole equation by 2.

Pollutants

8.8 Explain why the incomplete combustion of hydrocarbons can produce carbon and carbon monoxide
8.9 Explain how carbon monoxide behaves as a toxic gas
8.10 Describe the problems caused by incomplete combustion producing carbon monoxide and soot in appliances that use carbon compounds as fuels
8.11 Explain how impurities in some hydrocarbon fuels result in the production of sulphur dioxide
8.12 Explain some problems associated with acid rain caused when sulphur dioxide dissolves in rain water
8.13 Explain why, when fuels are burned in engines, oxygen and nitrogen can react together at high temperatures to produce oxides of nitrogen, which are pollutants

Key Points: Soot (C)

- Soot is a deposit of tiny black carbon particles which is released during combustion reactions.
- Deposit of soot blackens the materials and buildings and also blocks the chimneys and boilers.
- It causes health issues such as skin irritation, breathing difficulties and asthma.

Key Points: Carbon monoxide (CO)

- Carbon monoxide is formed during the incomplete combustion of hydrocarbons.
- It is a toxic gas.
- It causes health issues such as drowsiness and unconsciousness. It may cause death if the concentration of carbon monoxide is high.
    - *Carbon monoxide is a toxic gas which combines with haemoglobin preventing the absorption of oxygen by red blood cells. Due to its interference with oxygen transport in the human body, it is considered as a poisonous gas, which even causes death when the concentration of carbon monoxide is sufficiently high.*

Key Points: Sulphur dioxide (SO_2)

- Main component of coal is sulphur.
- Burning coals in factories and industries oxidise sulphur to form sulphur dioxide.
$$S(s) + O_2(g) \longrightarrow SO_2(g)$$
- Sulphur dioxide further dissolves in droplets of rainwater to form acid rain.
- Acid rain contains weak acid of sulphurous acid.
$$SO_2(g) + H_2O(l) \rightleftharpoons H_2SO_3(aq)$$
- Effects of acid rain:
    - Kills aquatic life in rivers and lakes by making water too acidic.
    - Increases the acidity of soil which destroys the vegetation.
    - Dissolves buildings made up of limestone and produces carbon dioxide.
    - Corrodes the metal buildings.

Key Points: Oxides of nitrogen (NO_x)

- Internal combustion of fuel in vehicle engine at high temperature produces nitrogen monoxide.
$$N_2(g) + O_2(g) \longrightarrow 2NO(g)$$
- Nitrogen monoxide which is released from vehicles combine with oxygen in the air to form nitrogen dioxide.
$$2NO(g) + O_2(g) \longrightarrow 2NO_2(g)$$
- Nitrogen dioxide further dissolves in droplets of rainwater to form acid rain.
$$2NO_2(g) + H_2O(l) \longrightarrow HNO_2(aq) + HNO_3(aq)$$
- Nitrogen dioxide is a toxic gas which causes lung diseases.

Oxides of nitrogen are nitrogen monoxide and nitrogen dioxide.

HNO_2 – Nitrous acid

HNO_3 – Nitric acid

Evaluating the use of hydrogen fuel over petrol

8.14 Evaluate the advantages and disadvantages of using hydrogen, rather than petrol, as a fuel in cars

Key Points: Advantages of using hydrogen instead of petrol

- Crude oil is very limited which is the source of petrol. Whereas, hydrogen is readily available to use.
- Hydrogen as a fuel does not produce harmful emissions. Hydrogen reacts with oxygen to form water only, whereas burning petrol produces:
  - **carbon monoxide** which is a toxic gas.
  - **carbon dioxide** which causes global warming.
  - **soot** which makes materials dirty and harmful to health.
  Furthermore, water which is obtained as a product can be recycled to make more hydrogen.
- It is **renewable** compared to petrol which is non-renewable from crude oil.
- It is **fuel efficient** compared to petrol or any other products of crude oil as it can produce more energy per pound of fuel.

Key Points: Disadvantages of using hydrogen instead of petrol

- Manufacturing hydrogen is **expensive and produces harmful gas** during the production compared to petroleum refining.
- It is **difficult to store**. Transporting and storing hydrogen is considered as impractical, whereas petrol can be transferred through pipelines and trucks.
- Replacing storage fuel tank in vehicles makes it expensive, as most of the vehicle uses gasoline, so it is **not easy to replace existing infrastructure**.

Cracking

> 8.16 Explain how cracking involves the breaking down of larger, saturated hydrocarbon molecules (alkanes) into smaller, more useful ones, some of which are unsaturated (alkenes)
> 8.17 Explain why cracking is necessary

Cracking = Splitting

Key Points: Cracking hydrocarbons

- Most of the hydrocarbons obtained from crude oil are larger hydrocarbons. Larger hydrocarbons are not useful until it is broken down into smaller hydrocarbons.
- Breaking up of larger molecules of hydrocarbon can be done by the process called cracking. Since catalyst is used in this process it is also known as catalytic cracking.

> **Cracking:** Breaking up of larger alkane in to smaller alkane AND alkene in the presence of catalyst at high temperature.

- Cracking is done by passing the vapourised paraffin oil over a solid catalyst, where the larger molecules break up on the surface of catalyst (Fig 8.3).

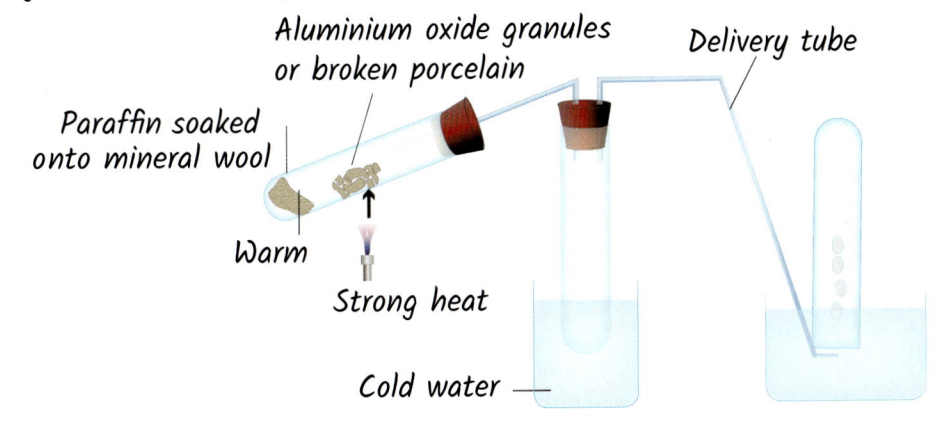

Fig 8.3 - The cracking process in the laboratory

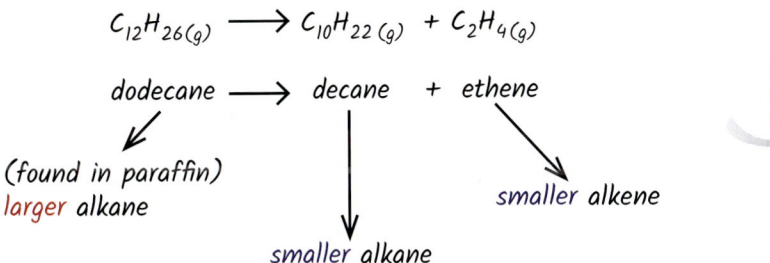

$$C_{12}H_{26(g)} \longrightarrow C_{10}H_{22(g)} + C_2H_{4(g)}$$

dodecane ⟶ decane + ethene

(found in paraffin)
larger alkane ⟶ smaller alkane + smaller alkene

Conditions of cracking:
Catalyst: Aluminium oxide
Temperature: About 650°C

- Some examples of cracking:

$$C_2H_6 \longrightarrow C_2H_4 + H_2$$
ethane ⟶ ethene + hydrogen

$$C_8H_{18} \longrightarrow C_2H_4 + C_6H_{14}$$
octane ⟶ ethene + hexane

Key Points: Uses of cracking

- Cracking larger hydrocarbons into smaller one is the most important process for the commercial production of gasoline and diesel fuel.
- It can also produce alkenes, such as ethene which can be useful in the manufacture of ethanol and polythene (plastics).
- Hydrogen can be obtained by cracking, which has plenty of uses.

Earth and atmospheric science

> 8.18 Recall that the gases produced by volcanic activity formed the Earth's early atmosphere
> 8.19 Describe that the Earth's early atmosphere was thought to contain:
>   a) little or no oxygen   b) a large amount of carbon dioxide
>   c) water vapour   d) small amounts of other gases and interpret evidence relating to this
> 8.20 Explain how condensation of water vapour formed oceans
> 8.21 Explain how the amount of carbon dioxide in the atmosphere was decreased when carbon dioxide dissolved as the oceans formed
> 8.22 Explain how the growth of primitive plants used carbon dioxide and released oxygen by photosynthesis and consequently the amount of oxygen in the atmosphere gradually increased

The Earth's early atmosphere and its changes

Key Points: The Earth's early atmosphere and its evidence

- The Earth formed about 4.6 billion years ago.
- It was not clear enough for scientists to be certain about the gases present in the Earth's early atmosphere.
- Lots of evidence have been developed since the early days but nothing was concrete to be certain about the formation of atmosphere.
- Theory about early atmosphere:
    - At one stage, the Earth began to solidify, volcanic eruptions released gases in a process called **outgassing**.
    - The Earth's early atmosphere was mainly composed of carbon dioxide (CO_2), nitrogen (N_2), ammonia (NH_3), methane (CH_4), water vapour (H_2O) and other gases but with little or no oxygen.
- As the Earth cooled down, water vapour condensed to form the oceans.

Key Points: Evidence of high quantities of carbon dioxide with no (or) little oxygen

- Carbon dioxide is the main component of Mars and Venus today, which is similar to the early atmosphere of Earth.
- Evidence from ancient rocks which contains iron pyrite (Iron(II) disulphide, FeS_2) which can be easily broken by oxygen and water could have only formed with no oxygen or little oxygen.

Key Points: Changes to the Earth's atmosphere

- As the Earth underwent condensation process, changes to the Earth's atmosphere happened in the form of **decrease in carbon dioxide, CO_2** and **increase in oxygen, O_2**.

- **Decrease in carbon dioxide:**
  - Carbon dioxide dissolved in the oceans to form coral reefs and shells made of calcium carbonate, $CaCO_3$.
  - Formation of shells and coral reefs decreases the amount of carbon dioxide in the atmosphere.
- **Increase in oxygen:**
  - Sun breaks up water with UV rays to form 2% of OXYGEN along with ozone (O_3) in the process known as **Photochemical dissociation**
  - Photosynthesis: carbon dioxide and water in the presence of sunlight produce OXYGEN with some organic compounds by cyanobacteria and higher plants.

Cyanobacteria are aquatic and photosynthetic microorganism which lives in shallow water and makes its own food.

Photochemical dissociation not a part of this specification

8.23 Describe the chemical test for oxygen

Key Points: Test of oxygen, O_2 gas

- **Test:** Insert the glowing splint
- **Result:** Relights the glowing splint

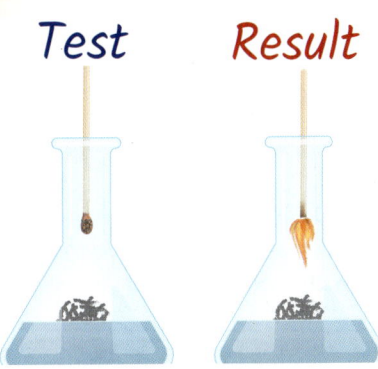

Fig 8.4 - Test of oxygen gas

The Earth's atmosphere today

8.26 Describe: a) the composition of today's atmosphere
b) the potential effects on the climate of increased levels of carbon dioxide and methane generated by human activity, including burning fossil fuels and livestock farming
c) that these effects may be mitigated: consider scale, risk and environmental implications

8.24 Describe how various gases in the atmosphere, including carbon dioxide, methane and water vapour, absorb heat radiated from the Earth, subsequently releasing energy which keeps the Earth warm: this is known as the greenhouse effect.

Key Points: The modern Earth's atmosphere

- The modern Earth's atmosphere has several gases mixed together known as air.
- The air contains carbon dioxide needed for photosynthesis and oxygen needed for respiration.
- Ozone present in the air protects us from ultraviolet radiation from the sun.

- Composition of air:

Composition of air

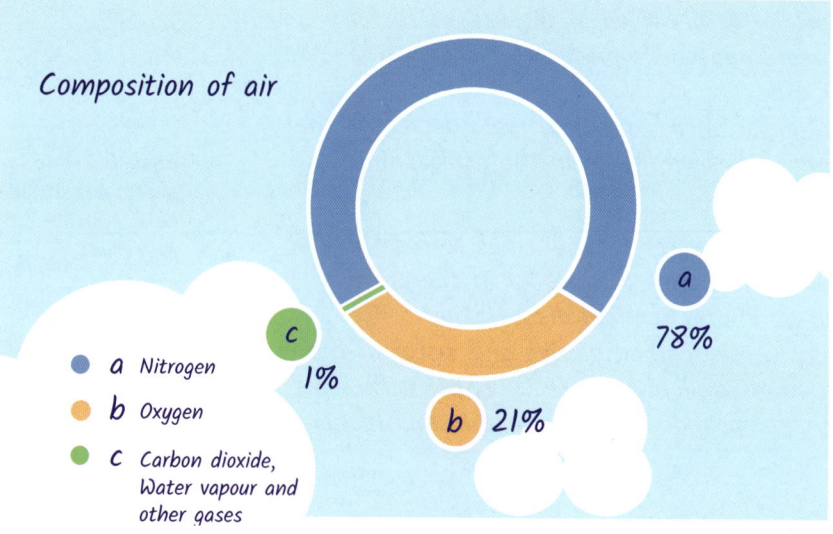

- a Nitrogen
- b Oxygen
- c Carbon dioxide, Water vapour and other gases

a 78%
b 21%
c 1%

Fig 8.5 - Composition of air

Key Points: Current climatic conditions

The five major greenhouse gases are carbon dioxide, methane, water vapour, ozone and nitrous oxide.

- Increase in human activities increases the amount of greenhouse gases in the atmosphere.
- The major greenhouse gases are methane and carbon dioxide.
    - **Methane:** Increase in methane is due to the increased decay of vegetation which is due to deforestation and increase in farming.
    - **Carbon dioxide:** Increase in carbon dioxide is due to burning of fossil fuels.

Key Points: Mitigating climate changes

- Mitigating climate change is all about reducing the release of greenhouse gases into the atmosphere.
- Limiting the release of greenhouse gases includes:
    - Retrofitting buildings makes it more energy efficient.
    - Building flood defenses to prevent the flood into the land.
    - Installing renewable energy sources like solar panels, wind mills and small hydro panels.
    - Increasing sustainable transportation such as electric vehicles and biofuel vehicles.
    - Promoting more sustainable uses of land and forests.
- These developments also have some risks:
    - Some countries are behind in technologies to move forward.
    - Lack of money to invest in innovative projects.
    - Installing panels and building dams destroy the habitats.

Key Points: Greenhouse effect

- The process that warms the Earth's surface naturally is known as Greenhouse effect.
- It has various steps which leads to global warming:
    Step 1: Heat from the sun in the form of infrared radiation reaches the Earth's atmosphere and some of the radiation escapes by reflecting into space.
    Step 2: The rest of the heat is absorbed by the land and the oceans, heating up the Earth's atmosphere.

Step 3: During the process, heat radiates from Earth towards space.
Step 4: Greenhouse gases traps the heat in the atmosphere and keeps the Earth warm.
Step 5: Human activities increase the amount of greenhouse gases released into the atmosphere.
Step 6: Greenhouse gases traps the extra heat and causes the Earth's temperature to rise.

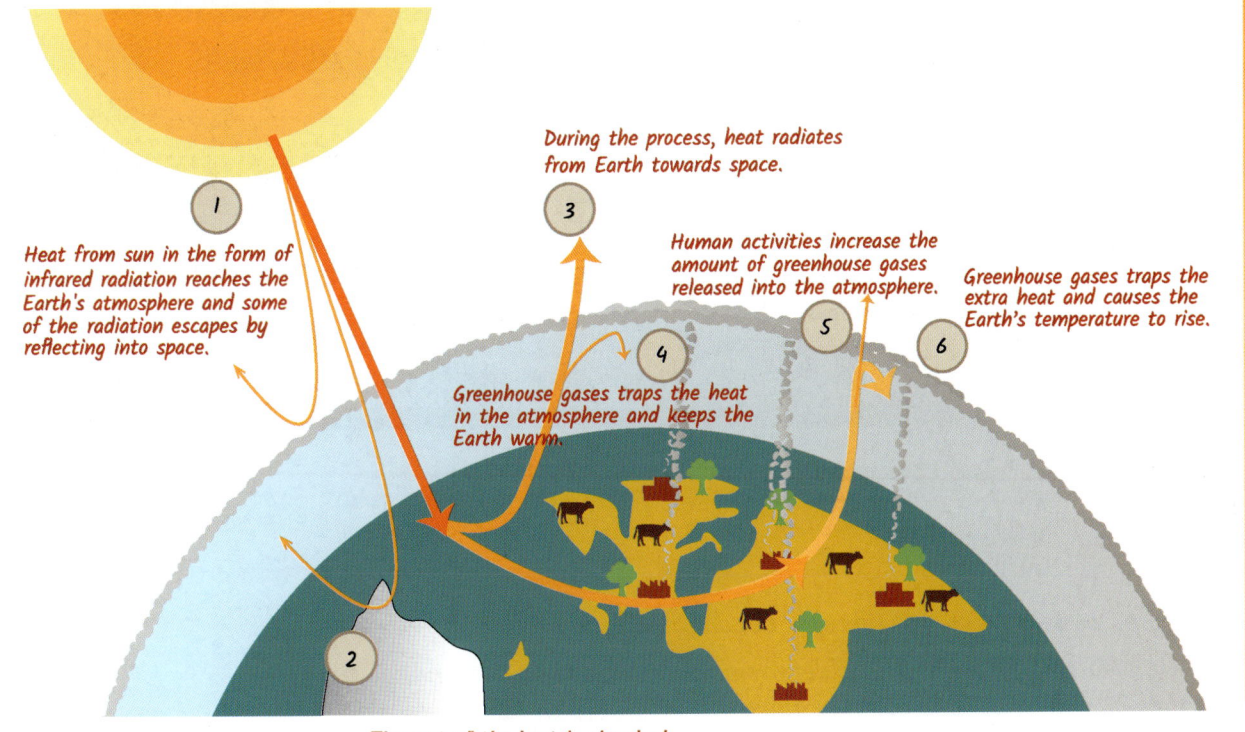

Fig 8.6 - The Greenhouse effect

Key Point: Effects of global warming

- Leads to polar ice caps melting, resulting in world wide floods.
- As sea water expands, the rising sea levels cause floods in low lying land.
- Changing weather patterns, such as increased rainfall in some areas and also the increase in number of deserts in other areas, possibly results in famine due to crop disruptions.

8.25 Evaluate the evidence for human activity causing climate change, considering:
   a) the correlation between the change in atmospheric carbon dioxide concentration, the consumption of fossil fuels and temperature change
   b) the uncertainties caused by the location where these measurements are taken and historical accuracy

Key Point: Correlation between carbon dioxide concentration and temperature change

- Magnitude of carbon dioxide increasing day by day, month by month and year by year.
- As the concentration of carbon dioxide increases, the global average temperature also increases.
- This proves that increase in carbon dioxide affects the Earth's atmosphere in the form of global warming.

Qualitative analysis – Test of ions

Tests for ions – Flame Test

> 9.1C Explain why the test for any ion must be unique
> 9.2C Describe flame tests to identify the following ions in solids:
>   a) lithium ion, Li^+ (red)
>   b) sodium ion, Na^+ (yellow)
>   c) potassium ion, K^+ (lilac)
>   d) calcium ion, Ca^{2+} (orange-red)
>   e) copper ion, Cu^{2+} (blue-green)
> 9.8C Describe that instrumental methods of analysis are available and that these may improve sensitivity, accuracy and speed of tests
> 9.9C Evaluate data from a flame photometer:
>   a) to determine the concentration of ions in dilute solution using a calibration curve
>   b) to identify metal ions by comparing the data with reference data (no knowledge of the instrument or how it works is required)

Key Points: Test of ions

- Ions present in compounds can be identified using different ion test.
- Conducting ion test should determine the presence of ions rather than predicting what ions could be present.
- Therefore, it is vital to test an ion to distinguish it from other ions.

Key Points: Test of solid ions using flame test

Platinum wire can be used instead of nichrome wire.

- Flame test is used to identify metal ions.
- It can be carried out by the following steps:
  - Dip the wire loop (nichrome wire) in hydrochloric acid to ensure the wire is clean.
  - Pick a small amount of sample using the wire.
  - Hold the sample in the blue part of the flame in the Bunsen burner.
- Certain metal ions may be detected in their compounds by observing their characteristic flame colours (Table 9.1).

Metal ion	Flame colour
Lithium, Li^+	Red
Sodium, Na^+	Yellow
Potassium, K^+	Lilac
Calcium, Ca^{2+}	Orange - red
Copper, Cu^{2+}	Blue - green

Table 9.1 - Characteristic flame colours of some metal ions

Key Points: Flame photometer

- Quality of flame test using flame photometer can be more accurate than using wire loop flame test.
- The flame photometer is used to measure light intensity of the flame colour.
- The data obtained from the experiment is used to find the concentration of metal ions in a given diluted solution using calibration curve.

- Colour observed in flame test using wire loop is usually mixture of different colours. However, spectrum of light can be seen for each metal ion while using flame photometer.
- An unknown metal ion can be identified by comparing with spectrum reference data table of known metal ions.
- Using instrumental method of analysis may improve:
  - Sensitivity (detect with small sample).
  - Accuracy (more precise).
  - Speed (in quick time).

Tests for cations in solution

9.3C Describe tests to identify the following ions in solids or solutions as appropriate:
a) aluminium ion, Al^{3+} b) calcium ion, Ca^{2+} c) copper ion, Cu^{2+}
d) iron(II) ion, Fe^{2+} e) iron(III) ion, Fe^{3+}
f) ammonium ion, NH_4^+, using sodium hydroxide solution

9.4C Describe the chemical test for ammonia

Key Table: Test of cations in solution

Cation	Test	Result
Aluminium, Al^{3+}	Add aqueous sodium hydroxide	White precipitate formed. Soluble in excess of sodium hydroxide solution to form colourless solution. $3Al^{3+}(aq) + 3OH^-(aq) \longrightarrow Al(OH)_3(s)$ white precipitate
Calcium, Ca^{2+}	Add aqueous sodium hydroxide	White precipitate formed. Insoluble in excess of sodium hydroxide solution. $Ca^{2+}(aq) + 2OH^-(aq) \longrightarrow Ca(OH)_2(s)$ white precipitate
Ammonium, NH_4^+	Add aqueous sodium hydroxide	No precipitate formed. Warm the solution produces ammonia gas which changes red litmus to blue.
Copper, Cu^{2+}	Add aqueous sodium hydroxide	Light blue precipitate formed. Insoluble in excess of sodium hydroxide solution. $Cu^{2+}(aq) + 2OH^-(aq) \longrightarrow Cu(OH)_2(s)$
Iron(II), Fe^{2+}	Add aqueous sodium hydroxide	Green precipitate formed. Insoluble in excess of sodium hydroxide solution. $Fe^{2+}(aq) + 2OH^-(aq) \longrightarrow Fe(OH)_2(s)$ Green precipitate
Iron(III), Fe^{3+}	Add aqueous sodium hydroxide	Red - brown precipitate formed. Insoluble in excess of sodium hydroxide solution. $Fe^{3+}(aq) + 3OH^-(aq) \longrightarrow Fe(OH)_3(s)$ Red - brown precipitate

Table 9.2 - Test of cations in solution

Ammonia gas has a distinct pungent smell.

Tests for anions in solution

> **9.5C** Describe tests to identify the following ions in solids or solutions as appropriate:
> a) carbonate ion, CO_3^{2-}, using dilute acid and identifying the carbon dioxide evolved
> b) sulfate ion, SO_4^{2-}, using dilute hydrochloric acid and barium chloride solution
> c) chloride ion, Cl^-, bromide ion, Br^-, iodide ion, I^-, using dilute nitric acid and silver nitrate solution
>
> **9.7C** Identify the ions in unknown salts, using results of the tests above

Key Table: Test of anions in solution

Anions	Test	Result
Carbonate, CO_3^{2-}	Add dilute hydrochloric acid	Effervescence (bubbles) seen. Bubble the gas into limewater turns into milky white precipitate. The gas is carbon dioxide. $CO_3^{2-}(aq) + 2H^+(aq) \longrightarrow CO_2(g)\text{ (bubbles)} + H_2O(l)$ $Ca(OH)_2(aq) + CO_2(g) \longrightarrow CaCO_3(s)\text{ (white precipitate)} + H_2O(l)$
Sulphate, SO_4^{2-}	Acidify with dilute hydrochloric acid, then add aqueous barium chloride or barium nitrate solution.	A white precipitate is formed. $Ba^{2+}(aq) + SO_4^{2-}(aq) \longrightarrow BaSO_4(s)$ white precipitate
Chloride, Cl^-	Acidify with dilute nitric acid, then add aqueous silver nitrate solution.	A white precipitate is formed. $Ag^+(aq) + Cl^-(aq) \longrightarrow AgCl(s)$ white precipitate
Bromide, Br^-	Acidify with dilute nitric acid, then add aqueous silver nitrate solution.	A cream precipitate is formed. $Ag^+(aq) + Br^-(aq) \longrightarrow AgBr(s)$ cream precipitate
Iodide, I^-	Acidify with dilute nitric acid, then add aqueous silver nitrate (or) lead(II) nitrate solution.	A yellow precipitate is formed. $Ag^+(aq) + I^-(aq) \longrightarrow AgI(s)$ yellow precipitate $Pb^{2+}(aq) + 2I^-(aq) \longrightarrow PbI_2(s)$ yellow precipitate

Table 9.3 - Test of anions in solution

Test and results of anions can be remembered as below:
Chemistry **S**tudent **W**anted
Chloride **S**ilver nitrate **W**hite precipitate
Bring **S**ome **C**ake
Bromide **S**ilver nitrate **C**ream precipitate
I **L**ike **Y**ou
Iodide **L**ead(II) nitrate **Y**ellow precipitate
I **S**ee **Y**ou
Iodide **S**ilver nitrate **Y**ellow precipitate

Worked example 1: A sample X dissolves in dilute acid, giving off effervescence which turns limewater milky. When aqueous sodium hydroxide is added to coloured solution, a light blue precipitate is formed. What is X?

Solution:
- X gives off effervescence which shows that gas is given off, as its turns
- limewater milky, presence of CO_3^{2-} anion is confirmed.
- Since X forms a light blue precipitate, the cation present is Cu^{2+} is confirmed.

Therefore, considering the combination of cation and anion, X is **Copper(II) carbonate, $CuCO_3$**

Hydrocarbon

Alkanes

> 9.10C Recall the formulae of molecules of the alkanes, methane, ethane, propane and butane, and draw the structures of these molecules, showing all covalent bonds
> 9.11C Explain why the alkanes are saturated hydrocarbons

Key Points: Family of alkane compounds

- The alkane family of molecules contain carbon atoms covalently bonded to four other atoms by **single** bonds.
- As these possess only single bond between carbon – carbon atoms they are referred as **saturated**.
- No further atoms can be added. However, atoms can be substituted.
- The general formula of alkane is C_nH_{2n+2}.
- Names end with suffix **'ane'**.

In general, molecules of carbons up to 4C are gases, those with 5C to 16C are liquids and greater than 16C are solids.

Key Table: Physical properties of alkanes

Carbon atoms	Molecular name	Molecular formula	Relative molecular mass	Boiling point(°C)	Physical state	Structural formula
1	Methane	CH_4	16	-164	gas	H–C(H)(H)–H
2	Ethane	C_2H_6	30	-89	gas	H–C(H)(H)–C(H)(H)–H
3	Propane	C_3H_8	44	-42	gas	H–C(H)(H)–C(H)(H)–C(H)(H)–H
4	Butane	C_4H_{10}	58	-1	gas	H–C(H)(H)–C(H)(H)–C(H)(H)–C(H)(H)–H
5	Pentane	C_5H_{12}	72	36	liquid	H–C(H)(H)–C(H)(H)–C(H)(H)–C(H)(H)–C(H)(H)–H

Table 9.4 - Physical properties of alkanes

Try this out to remember the first four names of alkanes.
Monkey – Meth – 1 carbon
Eat   – Eth – 2 carbons
Peeled – Prop – 3 carbons
Banana – But – 4 carbons

Tips to draw the structure of alkane.
Carbon – Surrounded by total of 4 **single** bonds
Hydrogen – 1 **single** bond

Topic 9 – Separate chemistry 2

Worked example 1: This question is about empirical formula and structural formula of alkane.

a) Draw the structural formula of hexane, C_6H_{14}

<u>Solution:</u>

Hexane, C_6H_{14}

$$H-\underset{\underset{H}{|}}{\overset{\overset{H}{|}}{C}}-\underset{\underset{H}{|}}{\overset{\overset{H}{|}}{C}}-\underset{\underset{H}{|}}{\overset{\overset{H}{|}}{C}}-\underset{\underset{H}{|}}{\overset{\overset{H}{|}}{C}}-\underset{\underset{H}{|}}{\overset{\overset{H}{|}}{C}}-\underset{\underset{H}{|}}{\overset{\overset{H}{|}}{C}}-H$$

b) Derive the empirical formula of the above pentane and hexane.

<u>Solution:</u>

Pentane, C_5H_{12}
Pentane cannot be further simplified so the empirical formula of pentane, C_5H_{12} is C_5H_{12}

Hexane, C_6H_{14}
Hexane can be further simplified from C_6H_{14} to C_3H_7 so the empirical formula of hexane, is C_3H_7

Key Points: Isomerism of Alkanes

- Isomerism is the phenomenon in which more than one compound have the same molecular formula but different structural arrangement of the atoms.
- Isomers are substances which have the same molecular formula but different structural formulae.
- As isomers have different structures, their physical properties vary, such as melting points and boiling points.
- **Isomers of butane (C_4H_{10}) properties:**

C_4H_{10} C_4H_{10}

Butane   2-methylpropane

Isomerism not a part of this specification.

Alkenes

9.12C Recall the formulae of molecules of the alkenes, ethene, propene, butene, and draw the structures of these molecules, showing all covalent bonds (but-1-ene and but-2-ene only)

9.13C Explain why the alkenes are unsaturated hydrocarbons, describing that their molecules contain the functional group C=C

Key Points: Family of alkene compounds

- Alkene form another homologous series of hydrocarbons.
- The general formula of alkene is C_nH_{2n}.
- They possess one **double** bond between carbon – carbon atoms and are referred as **unsaturated**.
- They are reactive compared with alkanes as they can break the double bond and add extra atoms to the molecule.
- Names ends with suffix **'ene'**.

Tips to draw the structure of alkene.
Carbon – Surrounded by total of 4 bonds which includes one double bond between carbon atoms.
Hydrogen – 1 single bond

Key Table: Physical properties of alkenes

Carbon atoms	Molecular name	Molecular formula	Relative molecular mass	Boiling point (°C)	Physical state	Structural formula
2	Ethene	C_2H_4	28	-104	gas	
3	Propene	C_3H_6	42	-47	gas	
4	Butene	C_4H_8	56	-6	gas	

Table 9.5 - Physical properties of alkenes

Key Points: Isomers of Alkenes

- Isomer of butene is shown below.
- Butene (C_4H_8)

Isomerism not a part of this specification.

but-1-ene   but-2-ene   2-methylprop-1-ene (not required for exam)

Topic 9 – Separate chemistry 2

> **9.14C** Recall the addition reaction of ethene with bromine, showing the structures of reactants and products, and extend this to other alkenes
> **9.15C** Explain how bromine water is used to distinguish between alkanes and alkenes
> **9.16C** Describe how the complete combustion of alkanes and alkenes involves the oxidation of the hydrocarbons to produce carbon dioxide and water
> *(refer topic 8)*

Key Points: Addition reaction of alkenes with bromine

- Alkenes contain double bond between carbon atoms. Due to its double bond they undergo **addition reactions**.
- In an addition reaction, two reactants react together to form a **single product**.
- Ethene and bromine

$$C_2H_4(g) + Br_2(aq) \longrightarrow C_2H_4Br_2(aq)$$

ethene + bromine ⟶ 1,2-dibromoethane

- Propene and bromine

$$C_3H_6(g) + Br_2(aq) \longrightarrow C_3H_6Br_2(aq)$$

Propene + Bromine ⟶ 1,2-dibromopropane

Key Points: Distinguish between Alkane and Alkene

- The reaction between alkenes and bromine water **(Yellow Orange in solution)** is used to distinguish between an alkene (unsaturated hydrocarbons) and an alkane (saturated hydrocarbons).
- Test of saturated and unsaturated hydrocarbons:
    - **Reagent**: Add bromine water solution
    - **Result with Alkene**: The colour of the bromine disappears immediately – decolourisation takes place.
        - **Reason**: Addition reaction occurs.
    - **Result with Alkane**: the colour of the bromine does not disappear immediately – no decolourisation takes place.
        - **Reason**: Substitution reaction occurs, it takes a while to disappear completely.

Polymers

Types of polymerisation

> 9.17C   Recall that a polymer is a substance of high average relative molecular mass made up of small repeating units
>
> 9.25C   Recall that:
> a) DNA is a polymer made from four different monomers called nucleotides (names of nucleotides not required)
> b) starch is a polymer based on sugars
> c) proteins are polymers based on amino acids

Key Points: Polymerisation

- The process of joining smaller identical units chemically together into a large chain molecule is known as polymerisation.
- The large chain molecule is known as a polymer and its identical single unit is known as monomer. Therefore, polymers have a very large relative molecular mass.
- Some examples of polymers are:
    - Plastics
    - PVC
    - Protein
    - DNA

polymer (poly = many; mer = unit)
polymerise = to join together

- Some examples of monomers ar
    - ethene molecule is the monomers for making polythene (plastic)
    - sugar is the monomer for making make starch
    - amino acid is the monomer for making protein
    - four different types of nucleotide monomers make up DNA
- There are two types of polymers:
    - Synthetic polymers
    - Natural polymers

Key Points: Synthetic Polymers

- Synthetic polymers are man-made polymers.
- Synthetic polymers are formed by:
    - **Addition polymerisation:** A reaction in which one type of many monomers with a carbon-carbon double bond react together in addition reactions to form an addition polymer without any by-product.
    - **Condensation polymerisation:** A reaction in which more than one type of many monomers join together by losing water molecule in a condensation reaction to form a condensation polymer.

Addition polymerisation

> **9.18C** Describe: a how ethene molecules can combine together in a polymerisation reaction b that the addition polymer formed is called poly(ethene) (conditions and mechanisms not required)
> **9.19C** Describe how other addition polymers can be made by combining together other monomer molecules containing C=C, to include poly(propene), poly(chloroethene) (PVC) and poly(tetrafluoroethene) (PTFE) (conditions and mechanisms not required)
> **9.20C** Deduce the structure of a monomer from the structure of an addition polymer and vice versa

Key Points: Addition Polymers

- Addition polymers are made from unsaturated monomer (alkene) through an addition reaction.
- During the reaction the double bond breaks up to share the electrons to make new covalent bonds between the monomers to make a large molecule of a polymer.
- Conditions: high pressure, high temperature and a catalyst.
- As one type of reactant is used, the name of the product is always the same as that of the reactant with '**poly**' added as a prefix.
- Polymerisation equation can be written as follows, where '*n*' represents the number of repeating units in the polymer chain.

$$n\,CH_2CH_2 \rightarrow (CH_2CH_2)_n$$
$$\text{ethene} \qquad \text{poly(ethene)}$$

$$E + E + E + \ldots \longrightarrow -E-E-E-$$
$$\text{ethene monomers} \qquad \text{poly(ethene)}$$

ethene monomers → poly(ethene) segment → usually represented like this

Poly(ethene) or Polythene

propene → Poly(propene) → poly(propene)

vinyl chloride → polyvinyl chloride

PVC (polyvinyl chloride (or) polychloroethene)

tetrafluoroethene → polytetrafluoroethene

PTFE (polytetrafluoroethene (or) Teflon)

> Keep ethene as a base monomer and replace the hydrogen with different substituent as below:
> **Propene** – replace one 'H' with one 'CH$_3$'
> **PVC** – replace one 'H' with one 'Cl'
> **PTFE** – replace four 'H' with four 'F'

9.21C Explain how the uses of polymers are related to their properties and vice versa: including poly(ethene), poly(propene), poly(chloroethene) (PVC) and poly(tetrafluoroethene) (PTFE)

Key Table: Uses and properties of addition polymer

Polymer	Properties	Uses
Polythene	Low density	Plastic bags
	High density	Plastic bottles
Polypropene	Tough, durable	Ropes, crates
Polyvinylchloride	Strong, hard	Pipes, electric insulator, guttering
Polytetrafluoroethene	Non-stick surface, withstands high temperature	Soles of iron, non-stick pans

Table 9.6 – Uses and properties of some addition polymers

Topic 9 – Separate chemistry 2

Condensation polymerisation

9.22C Explain:
a) why polyesters are condensation polymers
b) how a polyester is formed when a monomer molecule containing two carboxylic acid groups is reacted with a monomer molecule containing two alcohol groups
c) how a molecule of water is formed each time an ester link is formed (HC)

Key Points: Condensation Polymers

- Condensation polymer is made from the two different starting monomer molecules arranged alternatively, as these molecules react and link up by losing water molecule.
- To make a new covalent bond to connect large number of monomers, atoms or groups of atoms need to be removed first at either end of the monomers, so that there are spare electrons to make the connections to other monomers.
- Polyester (e.g. Terylene), polyamide (e.g. nylon) are common examples of condensation polymers.

Key Points: Polyester

- Polyester can be obtained by reacting dicarboxylic acid and diol groups.
- During the reaction, water molecule is lost in every link they make. Since water is lost with two different types of monomers it is known as condensation polymer.
- The linkage which forms between the monomer is known as ester linkage.

In condensation polymerisation, sometimes instead of water molecule hydrogen chloride is lost.

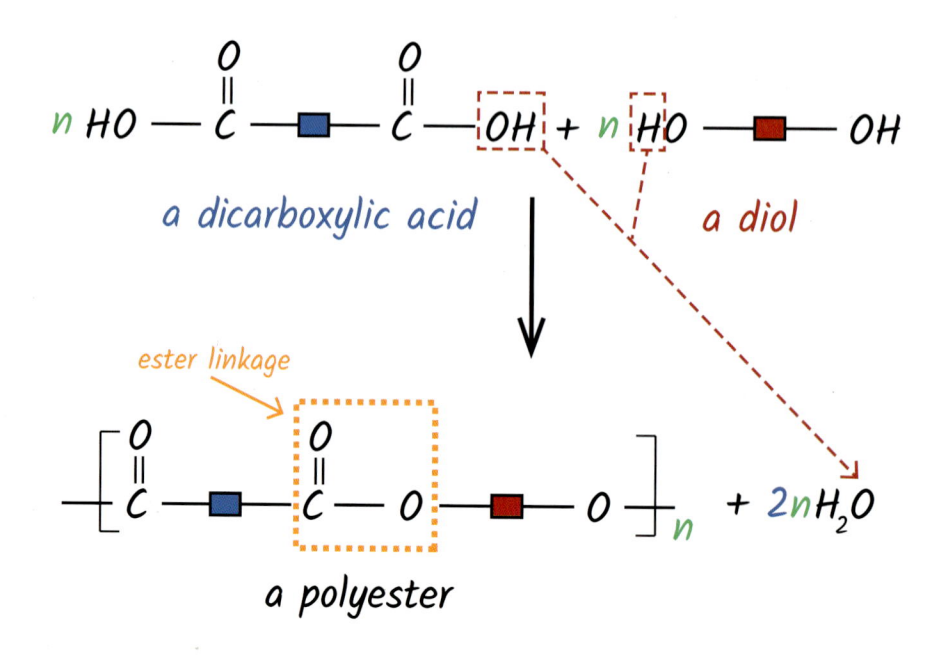

$$n\ HO-\underset{\substack{\| \\ O}}{C}-\blacksquare-\underset{\substack{\| \\ O}}{C}-OH + n\ HO-\blacksquare-OH$$

a dicarboxylic acid   a diol

$$\left[\underset{\substack{\| \\ O}}{C}-\blacksquare-\underset{\substack{\| \\ O}}{C}-O-\blacksquare-O \right]_n + 2nH_2O$$

ester linkage

a polyester

Problems with polymers

9.23C Describe some problems associated with polymers including the:
  a) availability of starting materials
  b) persistence in landfill sites, due to non-biodegradability
  c) gases produced during disposal by combustion
  d) requirement to sort polymers so that they can be melted and reformed into a new product

9.24C Evaluate the advantages and disadvantages of recycling polymers, including economic implications, availability of starting materials and environmental impact

Key Points: Problems with polymers

- Fractions from crude oil are the key raw materials of making polymer.
- Crude oil is a finite and non-renewable resource, so alternative raw materials are required for future.
- Unfortunately, polymers have advantages and disadvantages.
- Advantages:
  - Polymers are unreactive.
  - Cheap to manufacture.
  - Last long as they are non-biodegradable.
- Disadvantages:
  - Polymers are non-biodegradable and cannot be decomposed by bacteria.
  - Increases the litter day by day and last for years in landfill sites.
  - Plastics are carbon-based polymers which burn easily to release toxic fumes.

Key Points: Biodegradable biopolyesters

- The biopolyesters are biodegradable, made from biological monomers which can break down more quickly than other polymers.
- Biological monomers like lactic acid can be used to make biodegradable polymers such as biodegradable plastic bags.
- These biodegradable biopolyesters can be used as food for several microorganisms.

Key Points: Incineration of polymers

- Unused and waste polymers can be incinerated.
- Energy released during incineration can be used to generate electricity. However, it releases greenhouses gases and toxic fumes. Therefore, precautionary measures need to be taken before burning the plastic materials.
- Products of incineration can be reduced by reusing and recycling the polymer products. In this way finite resources can be used for longer.

Key Points: Reuse and recycle polymers

- Recycling can eliminate many issues of landfill. However, recycling is an expensive process where it needs to be collected, sorted, purified and melted before making a new product.
- A clear symbol of reuse on the product can help customer to avoid throwing away after a single use.

Alcohols

Homologous series of alcohols

> **9.26C** Recall the formulae of molecules of the alcohols, methanol, ethanol, propanol (propan-1-ol only) and butanol (butan-1-ol only), and draw the structures of these molecules, showing all covalent bonds
>
> **9.27C** Recall that the functional group in alcohols is –OH and that alcohols can be dehydrated to form alkenes

Key Points: Homologous series of alcohols:

- Alcohols are a series of compounds with a hydroxyl group (-OH) attached to a carbon atom in a hydrocarbon chain.
- The have similar general formula as the homologous series of alkane, where -OH is the functional group which replaces a hydrogen in an alkane to form alcohol family: $C_nH_{2n+1}OH$.
- Differ by CH_2 in molecular formulae from neighbouring compounds.
- Name ends with suffix 'ol'.
- Show a gradual change in physical properties.
- Have similar chemical properties.
- First four members of alcohols are shown in Table 9.7.

"n" value $C_nH_{2n+1}OH$	Formulae	Name	Structure
n=1 $C_{(1)}H_{2(1)+1}OH$	CH_3OH	Methanol	H-C(H)(H)-O-H
n=2 $C_{(2)}H_{2(2)+1}OH$	C_2H_5OH	Ethanol	H-C(H)(H)-C(H)(H)-O-H
n=3 $C_{(3)}H_{2(3)+1}OH$	C_3H_7OH	Propan-1-ol	H-C(H)(H)-C(H)(H)-C(H)(H)-O-H
n=4 $C_{(4)}H_{2(4)+1}OH$	C_4H_9OH	Butan-1-ol	H-C(H)(H)-C(H)(H)-C(H)(H)-C(H)(H)-O-H

Table 9.7 - First four members of alcohols

Dehydration of alcohols

Key Points: Dehydration of alcohol

- Alcohol can be dehydrated to form its parent alkene.
- For example: ethanol can be dehydrated to form ethene. Similarly, propan-1-ol can be used to make propene.
- Conditions: At 180°C with concentrated sulphuric acid as a catalyst.

$$CH_3-CH_2-OH \xrightarrow{\text{Conc. } H_2SO_4, \text{ Heat}} CH_2=CH_2 + H_2O$$

ethanol → ethene

- Dehydration can be also carried out at a small-scale, where ethanol vapour is passed over heated aluminium oxide powder to give ethene and water vapour.

$$CH_3-CH_2-OH \xrightarrow{Al_2O_3} CH_2=CH_2 + H_2O$$

ethanol → ethene

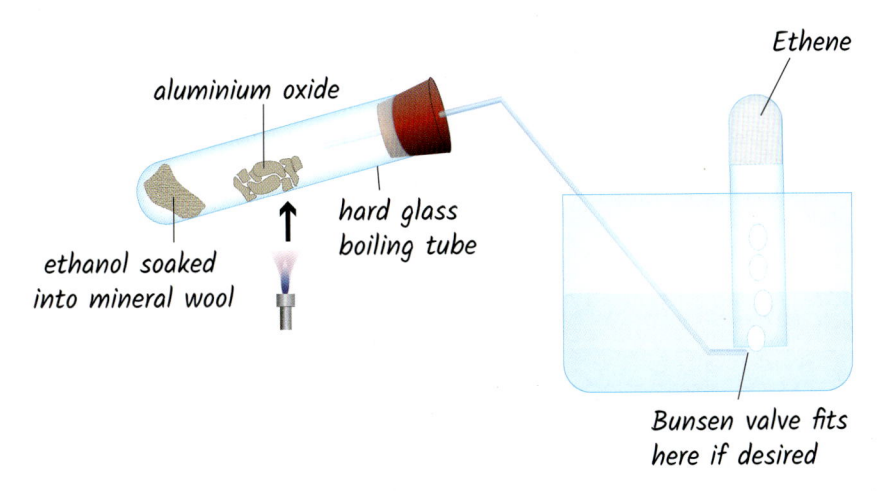

Fig 9.1 - Dehydration of ethanol

Carboxylic acids

Homologous series of carboxylic acids

9.29C Recall the formulae of molecules of the carboxylic acids, methanoic, ethanoic, propanoic and butanoic acids, and draw the structures of these molecules, showing all covalent bonds

9.30C Recall that the functional group in carboxylic acids is –COOH and that solutions of carboxylic acids have typical acidic properties

Key Points: Homologous series of carboxylic acid

- Carboxylic acids are a series of compounds with a carboxyl group (-COOH) attached to a carbon atom in a hydrocarbon chain.
- A carboxyl group is composed of a carbon atom double bonded to an oxygen atom and bonded to a hydroxyl group.
- They have similar general formula as the homologous series of alkane, where -COOH is the functional group which replaces a hydrogen in an alkane to form carboxylic acid family: $C_nH_{2n+1}COOH$.
- Differ by CH_2 in molecular formulae from neighbouring compounds.
- Show a gradual change in physical properties.
- Have similar chemical properties.
- Name ends with suffix 'oic' acid.
- First four members of carboxylic acids are shown in Table 9.8.

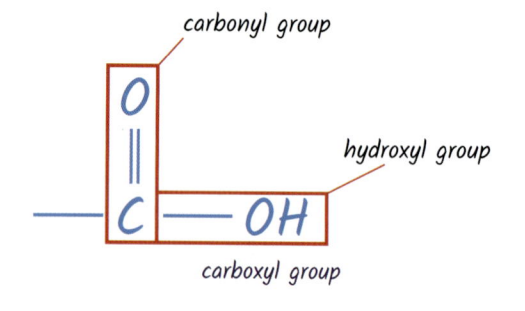

Naming the carboxylic acid goes wrong if you ignore the carbon in carboxyl group.
Example: Propanoic acid starts with C_2H_5 however, there is one more carbon in -COOH which gives a total of 3 carbons, so name starts with prop.

"n" value $C_nH_{2n+1}COOH$	Formulae	Name	Structure
n=0 $C_{(0)}H_{2(0)+1}COOH$	HCOOH	Methanoic acid	H—C(=O)—OH
n=1 $C_{(1)}H_{2(1)+1}COOH$	CH_3COOH	Ethanoic acid	H—CH₂—C(=O)—OH
n=2 $C_{(2)}H_{2(2)+1}COOH$	C_2H_5COOH	Propanoic acid	H—CH₂—CH₂—C(=O)—OH
n=3 $C_{(3)}H_{2(3)+1}COOH$	C_3H_7COOH	Butanoic acid	H—CH₂—CH₂—CH₂—C(=O)—OH

Table 9.8 - First four members of carboxylic acids

Properties of carboxylic acids

Key Points: Carboxylic acid and its chemical properties

- It is a **weak acid** which dissolves in water to form acidic solutions.
- Dilute solution of ethanoic acid is known as **vinegar**.
- Some chemical properties:
  - react with metals to form salt and hydrogen
  - react with carbonates to form salt, water and carbon dioxide
  - react with base to form salt and water
- Functional group, -COOH is responsible for similar types of reactions which helps to predict the product of other member of carboxylic acid family.

Key Points: Chemical properties of carboxylic acid

- With metal:

$$\text{Acid + Metal} \longrightarrow \text{Salt + Hydrogen}$$

$$2CH_3COOH + Mg \longrightarrow (CH_3COO)_2Mg + H_2$$

ethanoic acid   magnesium ethanoate

- With metal carbonates:

$$\text{Acid + carbonate} \longrightarrow \text{Salt + Water + Carbon dioxide}$$

$$2CH_3COOH + Na_2CO_3 \longrightarrow 2CH_3COONa + H_2O + CO_2$$

ethanoic acid   sodium ethanoate

- With base:

$$\text{Acid + Base} \longrightarrow \text{Salt + Water}$$

$$CH_3COOH + NaOH \longrightarrow CH_3COONa + H_2O$$

ethanoic acid   sodium ethanoate

Preparation of carboxylic acids using oxidation

> **9.31C** Recall that ethanol can be oxidised to produce ethanoic acid and extend this to other alcohols (reagents not required)
>
> **9.32C** Recall members of a given homologous series have similar reactions because their molecules contain the same functional group and use this to predict the products of other members of these series

Key Points: Oxidation of alcohols

- Alcohols can be oxidised into carboxylic acids.
- Oxidation can be done by heating in the presence of oxidising agents such as acidified potassium dichromate(VI) (or) acidified potassium manganate(VII). Dilute sulphuric acid is used to acidify the oxidising agent.
- Example: oxidation of ethanol
  - Ethanol can be converted into ethanoic acid.
  - Propanol can be converted into propanoic acid.

$CH_3CH_2OH + 2[O] \longrightarrow CH_3COOH + H_2O$

> [O] = oxidation.
> It is a two steps process.
> **Step 1** alcohol converts into aldehyde.
> **Step 2** aldehyde converts into alcohol.
> (This is not required for exam purpose)

Propan-1-ol + 2[O] → (oxidising agent, -H₂O) → Propanoic acid

Fermentation of ethanol

> **9.33C** Describe the production of ethanol by fermentation of carbohydrates in aqueous solution, using yeast to provide enzymes
> **9.34C** Explain how to obtain a concentrated solution of ethanol by fractional distillation of the fermentation mixture

Key Points: Manufacture of ethanol using fermentation

- **Fermentation process** is a laboratory process of preparing ethanol.
- In this process, sugar is converted into ethanol and carbon dioxide in the presence of yeast.
- Yeast is a single-celled organism which acts as a biological catalyst.
- This reaction is also known as anaerobic respiration as no oxygen is involved in the reaction.
- Yeast is added to sugar at room temperature around 30°C for several days in the absence of air.
- Enzymes in the yeast lower the activation energy, increasing the rate of conversion of sugar into ethanol and carbon dioxide.
- Respiration gives out energy which allows yeast to ferment the sugar to obtain energy for itself and produces carbon dioxide and ethanol as waste products.
- Conditions:
    - Glucose
    - Yeast
    - Range 30°C to 40°C
    - **Note:** Optimum temperature of yeast is 35°C. Since it is a living microorganism, at high temperature the reaction almost stops as the enzyme gets denatured.

$$C_6H_{12}O_6(aq) \xrightarrow{yeast} 2C_2H_5OH(aq) + 2CO_2(g)$$

$$glucose \xrightarrow{yeast} ethanol + carbon\ dioxide$$

- The waste product ethanol is impure with a maximum of 14% alcohol content.
- The aqueous alcohol is further concentrated and purified using fractional distillation method.
- Fractional distillation method is discussed in detail in Topic 2.

Nanoparticles

> 9.35C Compare the size of nanoparticles with the sizes of atoms and molecules
> 9.36C Describe how the properties of nanoparticulate materials are related to their uses including surface area to volume ratio of the particles they contain, including sunscreens
> 9.37C Explain the possible risks associated with some nanoparticulate materials

Key Points: Nanoparticles

- Nanoparticles contain only a few hundred atoms.
- Small number of nanoparticles have larger surface area. This is the reason why catalysts are used as finely divided particles.
- Size of the nanoparticles are measure in nanometers (nm).
- $1nm = 10^{-9}m$
- Nanoparticles are between 1nm and 100nm in diameter.
- The diameter of an atom is around 0.1nm and small molecules have diameters of less than 1nm.

Worked example 3: A silver nanoparticle is 58nm in diameter. Calculate the following:
a) Diameter of silver in metres, m.
b) If the diameter of silver atom is 0.172nm.
Predict how many times larger the silver nanoparticle is compared to its atom?

Solution:

a) $1nm = 10^{-9}m$
$58 nm = 58 \times 10^{-9}m$
    $= \mathbf{5.8 \times 10^{-8}m}$

b) Round off the values to one significant figure.
0.172nm = 0.2nm
58nm = 60nm
Number of times larger $\approx \dfrac{60nm}{0.2nm} = \mathbf{300}$

$\approx$ is to show the answer is an approximate value.

Worked example 4: A nanoparticle in cube shape has sides of 25nm. Calculate the surface area to volume ratio.

Solution:

Total surface area = 6 × 25 × 25
          = 3750nm²

Volume = 25 × 25 × 25 = 15625nm³

Surface area to volume ratio = $\dfrac{3750}{15625}$ = **0.24**

> Total Surface Area = 6 × a × a = $6a^2$
>   (cube has six faces)
> Volume = a × a × a = a^3

Worked example 5: A nanoparticle in cube shape has sides of 5nm. Calculate the surface area to volume ratio.

Total surface area = 6 x 5 x 5 = 150nm²

Volume = 5 x 5 x 5 = 125nm³

Surface area to volume ratio = $\frac{150}{125}$ = **1.2**

From worked example 4 and 5, as '**a**' *decreases* the surface area to volume ratio *increases*.
The smaller the particle the **greater** the surface area to volume ratio.

Key Points: Uses of nanoparticles

- Used as a catalyst which speeds up the rate of reaction.
- Due to its antibacterial properties it is used in wound dressing and deodorants.
- Mixed in sun cream which absorbs the UV rays. Nanoparticles have larger surface area, it absorbs more UV rays and protect us from harmful radicals.
- In cosmetics particularly in moisture cream & lotion to penetrate deep into the skin.
- Nanoparticles are used in medical field – to deliver tiny doses of medicine directly into cells.

Key Points: Risks of nanoparticles

- Nanoparticles are tiny, it may enter into the body and our cells.
- Since it is new in the science field, no one knows the potential long-term effects.
- Therefore, it is necessary that nanoparticles are studied thoroughly.

Materials

> 9.38C Compare, using data, the physical properties of glass and clay ceramics, polymers, composites and metals
>
> 9.39C Explain why the properties of a material make it suitable for a given use and use data to select materials appropriate for specific uses

Key Points: Different materials

- **Glass ceramics**
    - Main component of glass is sand, heated with metal oxides.
    - They are hard and transparent, but it is brittle.

- **Clay ceramics**
    - Made by heating wet clay to a high temperature in a furnace.
    - Clay ceramics are hard, smooth and opaque.

Clay ceramics include bricks and pottery.

- **Metals**
    - Metals can be bent into shape or made into wires as they are malleable and ductile.
    - They are good electrical conductors.

- **Polymers**
    - Properties of polymers are dependent on the number of monomers and types of monomers.
    - They can be tough, hard, brittle and flexible.
    - They are poor conductors of electricity and heat.

- **Composite materials**
    - A composite material consists of two or more materials with different properties.
    - Their different properties enhance the quality of the material.
    - Two components of composite materials are:
        - the reinforcement
        - the matrix, which binds with the reinforcement

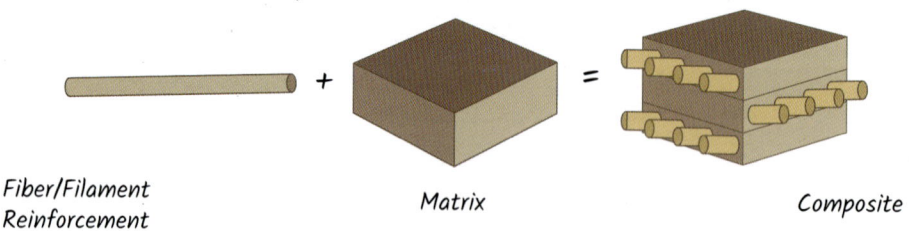

Fiber/Filament Reinforcement + Matrix = Composite

Fig 9.2 - Composition of composites

- Some examples of composite materials:

Composite materials	Reinforcement	Matrix
Concrete	The sand and gravel	Cement
Wood	Cellulose fibres	Lignin
Fibreglass	Glass fibres	Polyester
Bones	Collagen fibres	Minerals

Table 9.9 - Some examples of composite materials

Key Points: Physical properties and its uses of different materials

Properties	Metal (Aluminium)	Polymer (LDPE)	Ceramics (Clay)	Composites (Concrete)
Density	High	Low density	Moderate	High
Thermal (heat) conductivity	Very good	Good insulator	Good insulator	Good insulator
Flexibility	Malleable and ductile	Easily moulded (warm condition)	Cannot be moulded	Cannot be moulded in dry condition
Electrical conductivity	Very good	Good insulator	Good insulator	Good insulator

Fig 9.10 - Composition of composites

Worked example 6: Use the data below to answer the following questions:
a) Which material is the strongest material?
b) Which material is suitable in making reflective tape for life jacket?

Properties	Materials			
	Steel	LDPE Plastics	Clay ceramics	Concrete
Density	7.7g/cm³	< 0.1g/cm³	2g/cm³	2.4g/cm³
Tensile strength	13psi	0.5psi	3psi	8psi

Solution:

a) **Steel** is the strongest material amongst others, as the density and the tensile strength of steel is higher than the other materials.

b) **LDPE** plastics are quite useful, as their density is low which makes the reflective tape light and it can be easily mixed with other materials.

Workbook
Exam style questions

Exam style questions

Q1. This is question about ionic compounds.

a) Complete the table below. (3)

Ion	Number of electrons	Number of protons	Number of neutrons
$^{24}Mg^{2+}$			
$^{16}O^{2-}$			
$^{35.5}Cl^{-}$			

b) Magnesium reacts with oxygen to form the **ionic compound** magnesium oxide.

  I) Define the term **ionic compound**. (1)

  ....

  ....

  II) Draw a 'dot and cross' diagram to show the bonding in magnesium oxide. You only need to draw the outer electrons. (3)

c) Melting point of magnesium oxide is much higher than sodium chloride. Explain why. (2)

  ....

  ....

d) Using the symbol from the table, give the formulae of

  I) Magnesium oxide: ....

  II) Magnesium chloride: .... (2)

Q2. Tungsten is a metal used in light bulbs.

a) Explain in terms of electrical conductivity why tungsten is used in light bulbs. (2)

  ....

  ....

  ....

b) Draw the structure of metal. Your diagram must include **ions** and **electrons**. (2)

c) Suggest any **two** physical properties of tungsten which is suitable for this use. (1)

....

....

d) **Name** the gas which is used along with tungsten in the light bulb. Explain your answer. (2)

....

....

e) Use the periodic table to find the symbol of metal tungsten.
   Symbol of tungsten: .... (1)

Q3. This question is about ammonia reacting with carbon dioxide to form solid urea, CON_2H_4 and water molecule.

a) The dot and cross structure of ammonia is shown below.

I) What **type of bonding** is present in between nitrogen and hydrogen in ammonia molecule? (1)

....

II) Boiling point of ammonia and carbon dioxide is low. Explain why. (1)

....

....

III) Draw the dot and cross structure of carbon dioxide molecule. You only need to draw the outer electrons. (1)

b) Write the balanced chemical equation, including the state symbols, to show the formation of urea from ammonia and carbon dioxide. (2)

....

c) 48dm³ of carbon dioxide is used in the reaction vessel to make urea.

   I) Using the balanced equation from b) calculate the volume of ammonia reacted. (1)

   II) Calculate the amount of urea produced. (2)

Q4. Compound X that is often used for dry cleaning, contains 24.3% carbon, 4.1% hydrogen, and chlorine.

a) Calculate the **empirical formula** of compound X. (3)

   Empirical Formula: ....

b) Compound X has a molar mass of 99g/mol. Calculate its **molecular formula**. (2)

   Molecular Formula: ....

c) Dichlorodifluoromethane, CCl_2F_2 is made by reacting carbon tetrachloride with hydrogen fluoride, HF.

   $$CCl_4 + 2HF \longrightarrow CCl_2F_2 + 2HCl$$

   What is the maximum mass of CCl_2F_2 that can be obtained from 12g of HF? (3)

   Maximum mass: ....g

Q5. A student did an experiment to find out how many water molecules are present in white powdered hydrated sodium carbonate, $Na_2CO_3.xH_2O$.
A student made a solution with 1.58kg of the powder and dissolved it in water. The solution was made up to 250cm³. A pipette is used to transfer 25cm³ of solution into a conical flask which was titrated with 0.10mol/dm³ hydrochloric acid.
At the end of the three trials it was found that 25.6cm³ of hydrochloric acid was required to neutralise the solution.

$$Na_2CO_3 + 2HCl \longrightarrow 2NaCl + H_2O + CO_2$$

a) Calculate the number of moles of hydrochloric acid. (1)

b) Calculate the number of moles of sodium carbonate in the 25cm³ which was titrated with hydrochloric acid.

c) How many moles of sodium carbonate were present in the 250cm³ of solution? (1)

d) Calculate the mass of sodium carbonate in the 250cm³ of solution. (RAM: C = 12, O = 16 and Na = 23) (2)

e) Use your answer from d) to calculate the mass of water present in original powder. (1)

f) How many moles of water were present in the original powder? (RAM: H = 1 and O = 16) (1)

g) Using your answer from c) and d), calculate the value of x. (1)

h) Determine the chemical **formula** of hydrated sodium carbonate? (1)

Hydrated sodium carbonate is ....

Q6. The table shows some information about the atoms of the elements A, B, C and D. You may refer to the periodic table to find the answer.

Element	Atomic number	Mass number	Electronic configuration
A	11		2.8.1
B		12	
C	1	1	1
D		35.5	2.8.7

a) Complete the table. (3)

b) Identify which element is a **metal**. Explain why. (2)

....

....

c) Deduce the electronic configuration of **element D** when it forms an ion. (1)

....

d) Explain why mass number of **D** is not a whole number. (2)

....

....

....

e) Element **B** and **C** combines to form a compound. Using letter B and C from the given table, predict the formula of the compound. (1)

   Formula: ....

Q7. This question is about the fractional distillation of fermented sugar solution. This process is used to make concentrated ethanol by removing water from the mixture.

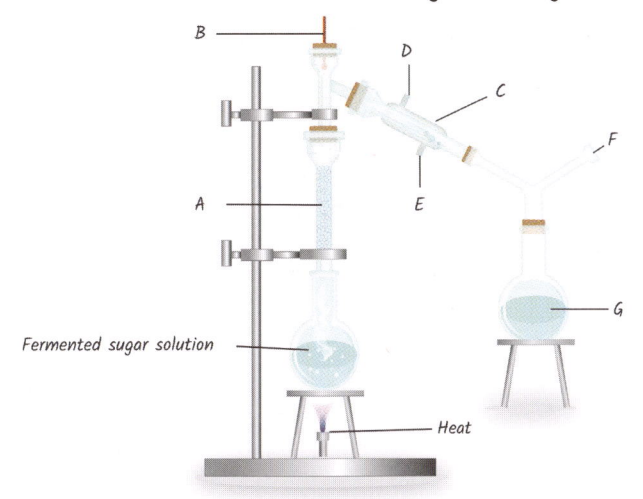

a) Complete the table to name the apparatus and to state its use in the separation technique. (3)

Apparatus	Name	Use
A		
B		
C		

b) Water flows through apparatus **C**. This is indicated with the letters **E** and **D**. State the letter which depicts water in and out. (2)

   Water In: ....

   Water out: ....

c) Suggest the purpose of **F** in the diagram? (1)

   ....

d) Identify the substance **G**. (1)

   ....

Q8. This question is about movement of particles at different conditions.
A student conducted two experiments: Experiment 1 and Experiment 2.

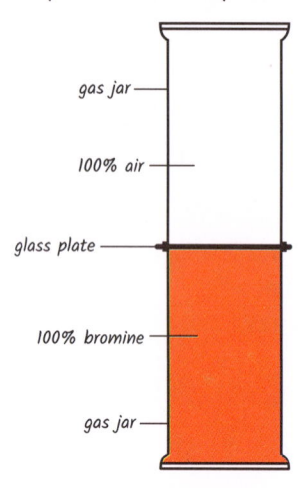

- gas jar
- 100% air
- glass plate
- 100% bromine
- gas jar

a) In experiment 1, setup was made as shown above.

   I) What is the **molecular formula** of bromine molecule? (1)

   ....

   II) Predict what could be **observed** once the glass plate was removed? (1)

   ....

b) Brown gas, nitrogen dioxide, NO_2 is used instead of bromine gas in experiment 2 with same setup. (1)
Rate of experiment 2 is faster than experiment 1. Explain why.

   ....

Q9. Potassium dihydrogen phosphate, KH_2PO_4 is an acidic fertiliser.

a) Fertiliser potassium dihydrogen phosphate can be made by reacting sodium hydroxide with phosphoric acid, H_3PO_4.
   I) Write the balanced chemical equation for the preparation of potassium dihydrogen phosphate, KH_2PO_4. (2)

   ....

   II) Write the ionic equation for the above reaction. (1)

   ....

b) The table shows information about strength of some acidic substances.

Acidic substance	pH
Sulphuric acid	1.8
Ethanoic acid	3.6
Potassium dihydrogen phosphate	4.1

I) Use the pH value from the table and answer the following: (2)

   Strong acid: ....

   Weak acid : ....

II) Explain the term strong acid and weak acid with the relevant ionisation equation. (2)

   Strong acid: ....

   ....

   Weak acid: ....

   ....

Q10. This question is about electrolysis of aqueous and molten substance.

a) Molten lead(II) bromide decomposes to lead and bromine gas.

   I) **Explain** why molten lead(II) bromide conducts electricity but not in solid state. (2)

   ....

   II) Construct the **half equation** at each electrode. (2)

   Cathode: ....

   Anode: ....

b) Aqueous copper(II) sulphate can be electrolysed using different electrodes. Electrolysis of copper(II) sulphate using inert electrodes contains ions, Cu^{2+}, H^+, OH^- and SO_4^{2-}. The electrode reaction at: (1)

$$Cathode:\ Cu^{2+} + 2e^- \rightarrow Cu$$

$$Anode:\ 4OH^- \rightarrow O_2 + 2H_2O + 4e^-$$

I) Explain **why** copper is formed at the cathode and not hydrogen. (2)

....

....

I) Oxygen is the gas formed at the anode. **Describe** how the production of oxygen is tested. (2)

....

....

II) **Identify** the type of reaction which takes place in terms of electrons and **explain** why. (2)

....

....

c) Electrolysis of aqueous copper(II) sulphate using copper electrodes show the gradual change in the magnitude of copper electrodes.

Using half equations, **explain** what changes can be observed in terms of size of electrodes. (4)

I) Anode : ....

....

....

II) Cathode: ....

....

....

QII. This diagram shows an electrolysis tank used industrially to produce aluminium from aluminium oxide.

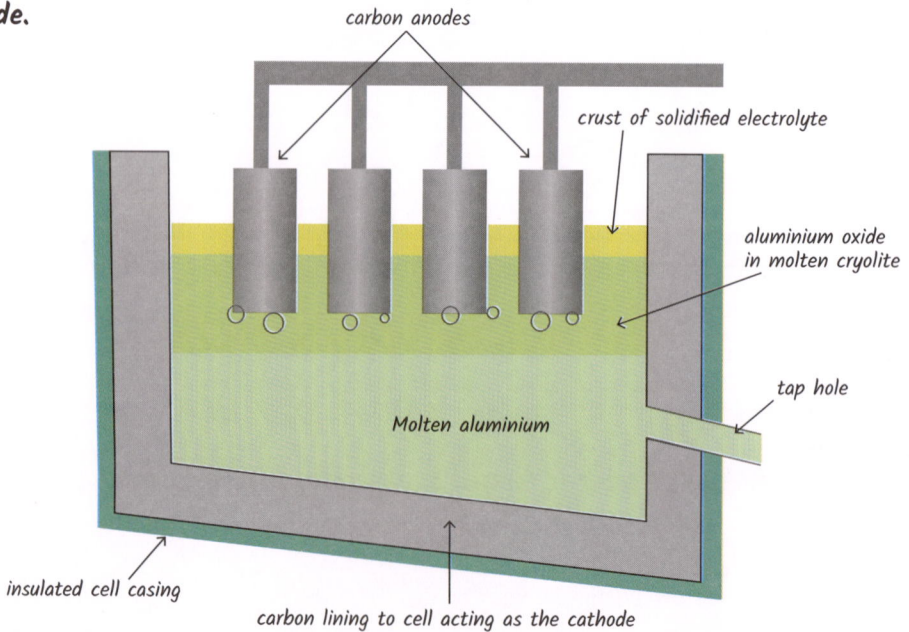

a) Graphite is used as an electrode in both cathode and anode.
   One of the electrodes makes the process expensive.

   I) **Name** the electrode which makes the process expensive. (1)

   ....

   II) With the help of chemical equation, explain why extraction of aluminium proves to be expensive. (2)

   ....

   ....

b) Suggest why adding molten cryolite reduces the cost of the electrolysis process. (1)

....

....

c) State any **two** uses of aluminium with its property. (2)

....

....

Q12. Iron is extracted from haematite, Fe_2O_3 using blast furnace.

a) In the furnace, carbon monoxide is made to reduce haematite to Iron. (1)

$$......Fe_2O_3 + ...CO \longrightarrow ......Fe + ...CO_2$$

   I) Balance the above equation.

   II) **Explain** how carbon monoxide is used to reduce iron from iron(III) oxide. (1)

   ....

   ....

   III) Explain whether iron(III) oxide is undergoing oxidation or reduction. (1)

   ....

   ....

b) Iron is malleable. **Explain** in terms of atom how Iron is malleable. (1)

....

....

c) State and explain **one** property of iron when it is added with carbon. (2)

....

....

e) Suggest why some iron ships have blocks of magnesium attached to them. (1)

....

....

Q13. Ethanol can be manufactured using ethene and steam in the presence of acid catalyst.

$$C_2H_4(g) + H_2O(g) \rightleftharpoons C_2H_5OH(g)$$

a) The reaction reaches a dynamic equilibrium. Explain the term **dynamic equilibrium**. (1)

....

....

b) Once the reaction is allowed to reach the equilibrium, then the pressure was raised. Predict how increasing the pressure will change the amount of ethanol made at equilibrium. (2)

....

....

c) Adding the catalyst increases the rate of reaction. State the change in amount of ethanol made at equilibrium. (2)

....

....

d) Manufacturing ethanol using steam is an exothermic reaction. Draw the energy profile of this reaction and label the diagram **with** and **without** catalyst. (2)

Q14. This question is about making magnesium chloride in stoichiometric terms.

a) Calculate the concentration in **g/dm³** of magnesium chloride solution when 5.0g of magnesium chloride is dissolved in 150cm³ of water. (1)

b) Calculate the concentration in **mol/dm³** of magnesium chloride solution when 2.5g of magnesium chloride is dissolved in 250cm³ of water. (1)

c) Calculate the atom economy for making hydrogen by reacting magnesium with hydrochloric acid, as shown in the equation below: (1)

$$Mg(s) + 2HCl(aq) \longrightarrow MgCl_2(aq) + H_2(g)$$

d) What mass of magnesium chloride would be produced from 6g of magnesium when it is is burned in the presence of chlorine? (3)

$$Mg(s) + Cl_2(g) \longrightarrow MgCl_2(s)$$

e) What volume of chlorine would react with 8g of magnesium in the above reaction? (2)

f) 25.0cm³ of a 0.10moldm⁻³ solution of magnesium hydroxide was titrated against a solution of hydrochloric acid of unknown concentration. 26.3cm³ of the acid was required for neutralisation. Calculate the concentration of hydrochloric acid. (2)

Q15. Group I elements in the periodic table are known as alkali metals. Metals from Group I react with water to form metal hydroxide and hydrogen gas.

a) Write the **balanced** chemical equation for the reaction between potassium and water. *(1)*

....

b) Describe what you would **observe** when a small piece of potassium is dropped on the surface of water. *(2)*

....

....

c) Reaction between potassium and water is more vigorous than lithium and water. **Explain in terms of the atomic structure.** *(2)*

....

....

....

d) Rubidium, Rb is found further down in Group I.
Make a prediction on what you would observe when a small piece of rubidium is dropped on the surface of water. *(2)*

....

....

Q16. This question is about investigating the rate of reaction between marble chips and hydrochloric acid.

- Cotton wool plug
- x
- Dilute hydrochloric acid
- Gas bubbles
- Calcium carbonate chips

a) Marble chips are otherwise known as calcium carbonate, $CaCO_3$.

1) Write the **balanced** chemical equation for the above investigation. *(1)*

....

....

II) Using the choice below: Select the name of the piece of apparatus labelled x by placing a tick in the circle. (1)
   a) ☐ pipette
   b) ☐ burette
   c) ☐ conical flask
   d) ☐ volumetric flask

III) Suggest the purpose of cotton wool in the neck of the apparatus **X**? (1)

....

IV) During the investigation, as the reaction proceeds the mass decreases. **Explain** why in terms of particles. (2)

....

....

b) A student added 100cm³ of 0.5mol/dm³ hydrochloric acid to a conical flask with large marble chips. The total loss in mass of the setup was recorded at different time intervals as shown in the table below.

Time (s)	0	5	10	15	20	25	30	35	40
Mass lost (g)	0	0.25	0.54	0.69	0.79	0.85	0.89	0.90	0.90

I) Plot the above results on a graph and draw a smooth curve. Label the curve as **student 1**. (2)

II) Initially, rate of reaction is fast and it slows down as the reaction proceeds. **Explain in terms of particles** why the initial rate of reaction is fast. (2)

....

....

III) Another student repeated the **same** experiment with **half the concentration** used by the first student.
On the same graph, sketch another curve to show how the mass lost would change over time. Label the curve as **student 2**. (1)

IV) **Explain** why does the mass lost becomes constant. (1)
....

181

c) Other than concentration and catalyst, state **two** other factors which can increase the rate of reaction. (2)

....

....

d) Using a labelled diagram, describe what **other type** of investigation can be carried out to measure the rate of reaction for the same reaction. (2)

Q17. The formation of ozone in the upper atmosphere is an endothermic reaction. The chemical equation is shown below.

a) **Explain in terms of bond breaking and bond making** why this reaction is endothermic. (2)

....

....

b) Using the table below calculate the enthalpy change of the above reaction. (3)

Bond	Average bond enthalpy in kJmol⁻¹
O-O	142
O=O	499

c) Draw the energy profile diagram for the formation of ozone. **Label** on the diagram the activation energy and the enthalpy change. (3)

d) Calculate the energy absorbed to break 10g of oxygen molecules. (2)

e) Draw a 'dot and cross' diagram to show the bonding in oxygen. You only need to draw the outer electrons. (1)

Q18. Ethanol can be prepared using fermentation and hydration process. Ethanol is a member of homologous series.

a) **Name** the homologous series to which ethanol belongs. (1)

....

I) **Explain** the term homologous series. (1)

....

....

II) Using the choice below and by placing a tick in the circle, suggest the correct molecular formula of ethanol. (1)

a) ☐ CH_3OH
b) ☐ C_2H_5OH
c) ☐ C_3H_7OH
d) ☐ C_4H_9OH

b) Write the chemical equation to show the manufacture of ethanol using hydration process. You **must** include the conditions used in this reaction. (1)

....

....

c) Ethanol burns in the presence of oxygen. (1)
I) **Name** the products formed when ethanol burns in excess amount of oxygen.

....

II) **Identify** the toxic gas which forms when ethanol burns in limited amount of oxygen. (1)

....

....

III) **Explain** why the above gas is toxic. (2)

....

....

d) When ethanol is heated with an excess of acidified potassium dichromate(VII), it is converted to ethanoic acid. (2)

   I) State what **type** of reaction is this?

   ....

   II) Write the chemical equation to show the reaction above. (1)

   ....

   ....

Q19. Cracking is an important process in the petrochemical industry. This can be carried out in the laboratory by using the apparatus below.

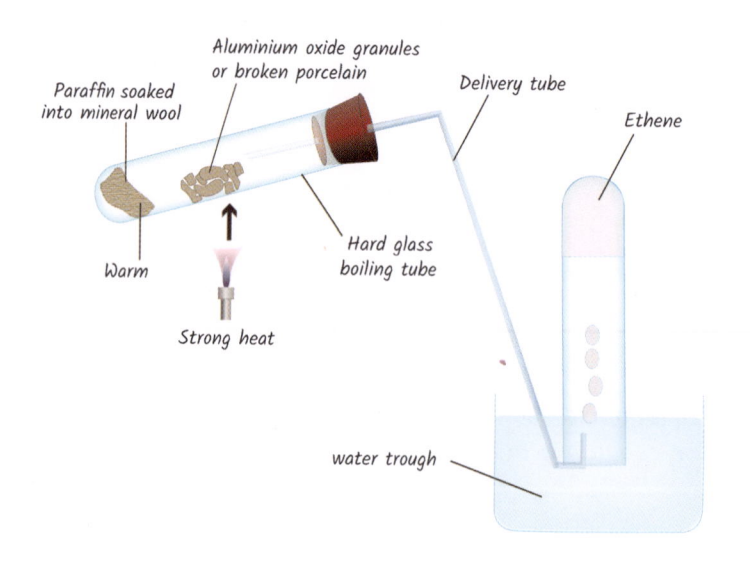

a) Explain the term "**cracking**" (1)

....

b) Suggest the **purpose** of porcelain in this experiment? (1)

....

....

c) The equation below shows the type of reaction which takes places in cracking.

$$C_{10}H_{22} \longrightarrow C_8H_{18} + X$$

I) X is an alkene. Name and draw the structure of X. (2)

Name: ....

Structure:

II) Describe the **test** and **result** to confirm **X** is an alkene. (3)

....

....

....

d) **X** can be used to make polymers **Y** using polymerisation reaction.

I) Name the **type** of polymerisation (1)

....

II) Draw the **structure** of polymer Y. (1)

III) Explain the **use** and **property** of polymer Y. (1)

....

....

185

Q20. A student was given an excess of metal strip zinc, Zn and 100cm³ of aqueous copper(II) sulphate in 250cm³ beaker.

a) State the **appearance** of the following at the beginning of the experiment. (2)

   I) Metal strip zinc : ....

   II) Aqueous copper(II) sulphate: ....

b) When the zinc was placed into the aqueous copper(II) sulphate a chemical reaction takes place. (1)

   I) Name the **type** of reaction which takes place.

   ....

   II) Complete the following equations of the above reaction. (2)

   x) Chemical equation: ....

   y) Ionic equation : ....

c) Presence of copper ions, Cu^{2+} can be confirmed using a simple flame test.

   I) **Describe** the procedure of flame test (2)

   ....
   ....
   ....

   II) What flame colour can be **observed** for copper ions? (1)

   ....

d) Presence of sulphate ions, SO_4^{2-} can be confirmed using anion test. Describe the **test** and **result** of sulphate ions. (3)

....
....
....
....
....
....

Exam Style Questions

Six Mark Questions

> Q.1 Explain why atom of sodium is neutral.
> Your answer must explain in terms of structure.

Key words: ....

....

....

....

....

....

....

....

Student/Teacher Assessment Grid

	Description	🟥	🟨	🟩
Strength	Can **state** the subatomic particles present in sodium atom			
	Can **draw** the atotmic structure of sodium atom			
	Can **identify** the location of sub atomic particles			
	Can **compare** the relative charge of sub atomic particles			
	Can **support** the link between number of protons and electrons			
	Can **develop** the conclusion to prove that sodium atom is neutral			
Action	Circle S, P and G:			

Q.2 Discuss the development of the modern periodic table from Mendeleev's periodic table.

Key words: ....
....
....
....
....
....
....
....
....

Student/Teacher Assessment Grid				
Target	Description	🟥	🟨	🟩
Strength	Can **recall** the discovery of early elements			
	Can **describe** the arrangement of elements in Mendeleev's table			
	Can **apply** the concept of gaps in Mendeleev's table			
	Can **distinguish** the arrangement of elements in both Mendeleev's and the modern periodic table			
	Can **construct** the development of the modern periodic table in terms of metals and non-metals			
	Can **evaluate** the development of the modern periodic table			
Target	Circle S, P and G:			

Q.3 Describe how you would carry out an investigation to show that group 7 element aqueous chlorine is more reactive than aqueous bromine and aqueous iodine is less reactive than aqueous bromine. Given reagents are aqueous solution of sodium chloride, sodium bromide and sodium iodide.

Key words: ....

Student/Teacher Assessment Grid

	Description	🟥	🟨	🟩
Strength	Can **define** displacement reaction			
	Can **describe** the reactions of the halogens, chlorine, bromine and iodine, with sodium chloride, sodium bromide and sodium iodide			
	Can **explain** the relative reactivity of the halogens with colour changes			
	Can **compare** the relative reactivity of halogens with chemical equations			
	Can **support** the explanation with balanced chemical equations			
	Can **develop** the conclusion to prove chlorine is the most reactive halogen			
Target	Circle S, P and G:			

Q.4 Ammonia is manufactured using Haber process. With the balanced chemical equation, explain the conditions which is applied during the process to make reasonable yield of ammonia.

Key words: ....

....

....

....

....

....

....

....

....

Student/Teacher Assessment Grid				
	Description	🟥	🟨	🟩
Strength	Can **state** the conditions for Haber process			
	Can **illustrate** the Haber process with a balanced chemical equation			
	Can **explain** the effect of catalyst on the rate of reaction			
	Can **explain** the effect of pressure on the yield of ammonia			
	Can **describe** the effect of temperature on the rate of reaction			
	Can **develop** the conclusion on the optimum conditions required to obtain a reasonable yield of ammonia			
Target	Circle S, P and G:			

Q.5 From the time the first plants and land animals appeared on earth the percentage of carbon dioxide and oxygen changed. Identify the process involved with balanced chemical equations for this change.

Key words: ....

....

....

....

....

....

....

....

....

	Student/Teacher Assessment Grid			
	Description	🟥	🟨	🟩
Strength	Can **explain** how the amount of carbon dioxide in the atmosphere has decreased			
	Can **describe** the effect of growth of primitive plants on carbon dioxide levels			
	Can **explain** the effect of plants on oxygen levels			
	Can **identify** the main processes for change in oxygen and carbon dioxide levels			
	Can **support** the explanation with balanced chemical equations			
Target	Can **evaluate** the change in percentage of carbon dioxide and oxygen			
	Circle S, P and G:			

Q6. Explain the formation of the products in electrolysis of dilute sodium chloride and water acidified with sulphuric acid using inert electrodes. Identify the products using chemical test.

Key words: ....

....

....

....

....

....

....

....

....

Student/Teacher Assessment Grid

	Description			
Strength	Can **state** the chemical formula for sodium chloride and water			
	Can **list** the ions formed during electrolysis of dilute sodium chloride			
	Can **list** the ions formed during electrolysis of acidified water			
	Can **predict** the products formed at anode and cathode during electrolysis of dilute sodium chloride			
	Can **predict** the products formed at anode and cathode during electrolysis of acidified water			
	Can **determine** the gases formed using a suitable chemical test			
Target	Circle S, P and G:			

Q.7 Using electrolysis process, explain how impure copper can be purified.

Key words: ....

....

....

....

....

....

....

....

....

....

	Student/Teacher Assessment Grid			
	Description	🟥	🟨	🟩
Strength	Can **recall** the electrodes and electrolyte used in purifying copper			
	Can **identify** where oxidation and reduction occur			
	Can **describe** the process taking place at anode			
	Can **describe** the process taking place at cathode			
	Can **explain** any observable change in electrolyte			
	Can **illustrate** the location of precious metals			
Target	Circle S, P and G:			

Q.8 Environment and the supply of valuable raw materials are preserved by recycling. Evaluate the advantages and disadvantages of recycling common metals.

Key words: ....

....

....

....

....

....

....

....

....

	Student/Teacher Assessment Grid			
	Description	🟥	🟨	🟩
Strength	Can **state** the reason for recycling			
	Can **list** the common recycled metals			
	Can **discuss** the economic implications of recycling metals			
	Can **explain** the impact on the environment due to recycling metals			
	Can **discuss** the supply of valuable raw materials due to recycling metals			
	Can **evaluate** the advantages and disadvantages of recycling metals			
Target	Circle S, P and G:			

Q.9 Impact of manufactured products are analysed by LCA. Explain the key stages of LCA.

Key words: ....

Student/Teacher Assessment Grid				
	Description	🟥	🟨	🟩
Strength	Can **sta**te the five stages of LCA			
	Can **explain** the effect of using raw materials to make the product			
	Can **compare** the pros and cons of the process of disposal			
	Can **describe** the utilization and implementation of the products			
	Can **evaluate** effect on pollution due to transportation			
	Can **explain** the key stages of LCA			
Target	Circle S, P and G:			

Q.10 Rusting can be prevented by using different chemical processes. Explain any four ways of prevention you would suggest.

Key words: ....

....

....

....

....

....

....

....

....

	Student/Teacher Assessment Grid			
	Description	🟥	🟨	🟩
Strength	Can **state** any four ways of preventing rusting			
	Can **explain** how rusting can be prevented by electroplating			
	Can **explain** how rusting can be prevented by exclusion of water			
	Can **explain** how rusting can be prevented by exclusion of oxygen			
	Can **describe** the process of sacrificial protection or galvanisation			
	Can **support** the explanations with scientific theory			
Target	Circle S, P and G:			

Q.11 Describe the bonding in aluminium oxide.
Your answer must include the type of bonding, how the bonding takes place and its dot and cross diagram.

Key words: ....

....

....

....

....

....

....

....

....

	Student/Teacher Assessment Grid	🟥	🟨	🟩
	Description			
Strength	Can **state** ionic bonding			
	Can **define** the term 'ionic bonding'			
	Can **draw** dot and cross diagram to show bonding in aluminium oxide			
	Can **discuss** ionic bonding in terms of electron transfer			
	Can **determine** the ions formed with symbol and charge			
	Can **explain** the force of attraction between ions			
Target	Circle S, P and G:			

Workbook – Six Mark Questions

Workbook – Six Mark Questions

Q.12 Describe the pattern in reactivity of the alkali metals, lithium, sodium and potassium, with water; and use this pattern to predict the reactivity of other alkali metals. You must also discuss using electronic configuration.

Key words: ....

....

....

....

....

....

....

....

....

Student/Teacher Assessment Grid

	Description	🔴	🟡	🟢
Strength	Can **predict** the reactivity of group 1 metals			
	Can **list** any two observations when the metals react with water			
	Can **deduce** electronic configuration of lithium, sodium, potassium and discuss the trend in size			
	Can **deduce** balanced chemical reaction			
	Can **discuss** relative reactivity in terms of distance			
	Can **develop** a prediction for the the reactivity of other alkali metals			
Target	Circle S, P and G:			

Q.13 Explain the process of crude oil separation into useful products using the process of fractional distillation. Discuss the physical properties and its uses.

Key words: ....

....

....

....

....

....

....

....

....

....

	Student/Teacher Assessment Grid			
	Description	🟥	🟨	🟩
Strength	Can **recall** what is crude oil			
	Can **discuss** the process of separation of crude oil			
	Can **explain** how the fractions are separated			
	Can **explain** that separation is dependent on boiling point and molecular size			
	Can **discuss** the trend in physical properties of the fractions obtained			
	Can **explain** the uses of the fractions obtained			
Target	Circle S, P and G:			

199

Q.14 Describe how to carry out an acid-alkali titration, using burette, pipette and a suitable indicator, to prepare a pure, dry salt of sodium chloride.

Key words: ....

....

....

....

....

....

....

....

....

Student/Teacher Assessment Grid

	Description	🟥	🟨	🟩
Strength	Can **list** the correct acid and an alkali to carry out the titration			
	Can **recall** the purpose of burette, pipette and indicator in titration			
	Can **deduce** the ionic equation to show the chemical reaction			
	Can **explain** the method of titration			
	Can **state** the colour change of indicator			
	Can **explain** the crystallisation process			
Target	Circle S, P and G:			

Q.15 Discuss the differences between chemical cells and fuel cells.

Key words: ....

....

....

....

....

....

....

....

....

	Student/Teacher Assessment Grid			
	Description	🟥	🟨	🟩
Strength	Can **state** an example of chemical cell			
	Can **state** an example of fuel cell			
	Can **explain** production of voltage in a chemical cell in terms of reactants			
	Can **explain** production of voltage in a chemical cell in terms of products			
	Can **list** the strengths and weaknesses of both cells			
	Can **evaluate** the strengths and weaknesses of both cells			
Target	Circle S, P and G:			

Workbook – Six Mark Questions